1

Jackson, Stanley, 1910-
    Monsieur Butterfly; the story of Gia-
como Puccini. New York, Stein and Day,
c1974.
    267p. illus. 25cm. 10.00

    Bibliography: p.263-264.

1.Puccini, Giacomo, 1858-1924. I.Title.

MONSIEUR BUTTERFLY

By the same author:

Caruso

MONSIEUR BUTTERFLY

The Story of Giacomo Puccini

Stanley Jackson

𝔰𝔇 STEIN AND DAY/*Publishers*/New York

Illustrations

Acknowledgements are due to: the historical archives of G. Ricordi & C. s.p.a., Milan; A. F. Kersting; Radio Times Hulton Picture Library; Mr. Harold Rosenthal; Mrs. Tessa Melen; and Signora Rita Puccini.

Acknowledgements to Publishers

Acknowledgements are also due to the following publishers for the use of quotations from the works mentioned:

Puccini Among Friends by Vincent Seligman, published by Macmillan, London and Basingstoke, 1938.

Puccini by Mosco Carner, published by Gerald Duckworth & Co. Ltd, 1958, and by Alfred A. Knopf, Inc., New York, 1959.

The Lives of Great Composers by Harold C. Schonberg, published by Davis-Poynter Ltd, London, 1971, and by W. W. Norton, Inc., New York 1970.

Letters of Giacomo Puccini edited by G. Adami, translated by E. Makin, published by George G. Harrap & Co. Ltd, London, 1931, and j. B. Lippincott, Philadelphia, 1931.

Immortal Bohemian by D. del Fiorentino, published by Victor Gollancz Ltd, London, 1952, and by Prentice-Hall, Inc., New York, 1952.

Puccini by George Marek, published by Cassell & Co. Ltd., London, 1952, and by Simon & Schuster, Inc., New York, 1951.

First published in the United States of America
by Stein and Day/*Publishers* in 1974
Copyright © 1974 by Stanley Jackson
Library of Congress Catalog Card No. 73-90692
All rights reserved
Printed in the United States of America
Stein and Day/*Publishers*/Scarborough House, Briarcliff Manor, N.Y. 10510
ISBN 0-8128-1651-X

Contents

1

'*I am a mighty hunter of wildfowl, beautiful women and good libretti*'.

GIACOMO PUCCINI

Foreword

While still far from reaching Wagnerian proportions, Puccini literature is already massive. He was not only a voluminous letter-writer, but as artist and man has offered challenging bait to successive generations of biographers. His personality sparks off paradox. He was solitary but restlessly gregarious; a bohemian by instinct, he usually dressed like a banker; his attitude to women was blatantly amoral, yet his most enduring relationship appears to have been platonic; above all, while often accused of cynically pandering to low public taste, he composed in all only a dozen operas (including three one-act pieces) in forty years of almost continuous production.

Half a century after his death, with contemporary impressions and evidence still reasonably fresh and before lichen has settled too thickly on the legend, one can be justified for attempting a redrawn portrait. It is not directed to score-in-hand musicologists but to an audience who, sharing my own middle-brow enjoyment of Puccini's operas, may be more fascinated by his life and times than contrapuntal subtleties or the technicalities of musico-dramatic structure. A vast bibliography is already available for those anxious for a detailed analysis of the operas and the stresses, social and professional, behind their production. In this field the best study by far is Mosco Carner's scholarly and monumental centenary volume.

In the course of my own research I have checked the often conflicting views of Puccini's character, ranging from Freudian analysis in depth by various Austrian or German writers to the composer's countrymen, who have tended to exploit his notorious love-making or have blatantly sentimentalised his dramatic rise to world fame. I have been able to establish the rôle of Sybil Seligman, his closest friend and confidante for twenty years, far more prominently than any previous biographer. In this context I owe a special debt to her grand-daughter, Tessa Melen, who gave me unrestricted access to the composer's letters, supplementing those previously selected and edited by Mrs Seligman's son, Vincent, apart from her photographic albums, scrapbooks and a treasury of family miscellania.

Among others who gave generous help and advice I would mention D. C. Halliday, manager of G. Ricordi & Co. (London) Ltd, by whose courtesy I was enabled to use illustrations from the firm's historical archives in Milan. Finally, my warmest thanks are due to Harold Rosenthal, editor of *Opera*, who read the book in manuscript and offered many valuable suggestions, although he is in no way responsible for any deficiencies either in the selection of my material or its presentation.

PART ONE

Albina

Chapter One

Early in the eighteenth century, a Tuscan villager from the Val di Roggio strapped a few possessions to his mule and rode down to the ancient walled city of Lucca. He failed to prosper, but gained some comfort when one of his sons was appointed organist and choirmaster at the Cathedral of San Martino. Giacomo Puccini's great-great-grandfather and namesake, the first of four successive generations to hold that post, received the same pay as the municipal hangman. After some protest he was given an extra small loaf of bread each month to register his superior status. But the tight-fisted council still insisted that a grant to his son, enabling him to study in Bologna, would be repayable with interest. The composer of *La Bohème* would never lose this native sense of thrift, even when a cascade of royalties from the world's opera houses brought him an income of over £30,000 ($150,000) a year.

At the time of his birth on 22 December 1858, Lucca's thirty thousand inhabitants enjoyed the fruits of a fertile valley on the left bank of the Serchio, yielding excellent wine and the purest olive oil in Italy. They still manufactured silks and high-quality leather goods but seemed far prouder of their piazzas and *palazzi*, recalling an affluent era when their city, as capital of a small but powerful republic, had dictated the commercial, political and cultural destiny of Tuscany. Land-locked, although only a few miles from the once-thriving port of Viareggio, they were dour, insular and tended to self-satisfaction. Strangers would be treated with genteel disdain and sent on their way once they had admired Tintoretto's altar-piece in San Martino and the small chapel housing the Volto Santo, a cedar-wood simulacrum of Christ at Calvary, said to have been carved by Nicodemus at the command of an angel. Pilgrims of every nationality also visited the twelfth-century church of San Frediano, built in honour of a former

3

Bishop of Lucca believed to be Saint Finnian from Galway. Legend credited him with having turned back the swirling waters from the Apennines with a plain garden rake.

Giacomo Puccini's birthplace was the first floor of a three-storeyed house with faded green shutters in narrow Via di Poggio. It led into a piazza erected on the site of an old forum and dominated by the beautiful church of San Michele. The neighbouring streets had formerly been enclosed by the walls of a Roman fortress. In mediaeval times still more walls were put up to encircle Lucca and, by the middle of the seventeenth century, some mellow red brick ramparts which offered a vista of the green Pisan plain with its pine-covered hills and olive groves, threaded by the river. In the hazy distance towered the marble mountains from which Michelangelo had chiselled his *Pietà*.

Dating from their early ancestor's appointment at San Martino, the Puccinis had won distinction as composers of music at church festivals and symphonic works performed by municipal orchestras on State occasions. They had survived every political upheaval, including Napoleon's abolition of the Republic of Tuscany when he installed his sister, Marianne Elise, and her husband, Felice Baciocchi, as rulers of the new principality.

Under their régime Puccini's grandfather, Domenico, was appointed to form a court orchestra. He invited distinguished musicians to direct operatic performances at the imposing Palazzo Provinciale where Paganini was said to have spent most of his nights in the arms of Princess Elise, a nymphomaniac of quite outstanding hideousness. In fact he had extended his visit to pursue a liaison with her more fetching lady-in-waiting, but composed a military sonata for the G string entitled 'Napoleon', which was tactfully dedicated to the princess. Although she soon decided to transfer her court to Florence, Lucca continued to claim her affection. She had been loudly cheered when hoisted by crane over the city walls in 1812 after the Serchio had defied San Frediano's garden rake.

4

Two years later Tuscany was given to the Bourbons by the Congress of Vienna, but Domenico Puccini had rashly involved himself in a liberal anti-Austrian plot. He died painfully in May 1815 after drinking a goblet of poisoned wine at a nobleman's banquet. The clan was not penalised professionally, but his unfortunate excursion into politics may have indirectly influenced Giacomo, who would always support the *status quo*. While still in his infancy a plebiscite had incorporated Lucca into the new kingdom of Italy, which may possibly explain his lifelong veneration for the monarchy.

His father, Michele, had ritually succeeded as cathedral organist and choirmaster after studying in Naples under Donizetti, among others. A quiet, wistful-looking man, he had some minor talent as a composer on formal and strictly academic lines. His gentleness made him a popular director at the local Conservatoire, the Istituto Musicale, and he married a former pupil, Albina Magi, eighteen years his junior. She was then a local beauty with jet black hair, an unusually clear pale skin and dark eyes that still twinkled after almost continuous pregnancies. Six daughters had been born before Giacomo, who was five years old when his father died suddenly at the age of fifty-one and was honoured with a public funeral. Three months later Albina gave birth to another son, Michele.

She had to bring up her young family—the eldest daughter was only thirteen when her father died—on a pension of only 75 lire* a month from the council, supplemented by a grudging allowance from her brother, Fortunato Magi, who had taken over at San Martino and the Istituto until such time as Giacomo came of musical age. The 'regency' did not warm him towards his nephew whom he soon wrote off as without talent and lacking in serious application. One early school report states flatly, 'He comes here only to wear out the seat of his pants. He pays no attention to anything and keeps tapping on his desk as though it were a keyboard. He never reads a book.'

* £1 ($5) was then worth 25 lire.

Quick-tempered and without a father's restraining hand, he was impatient of discipline and often played truant to go bird-watching or gather the ripe olives which the peasants shook down with long bamboo poles. It brought a few soldi but his mother disapproved of such menial work for her adored son and would often remind him of his heritage. She liked to recall that his father had first familiarised him with the cathedral organ by guiding his fingers over coins distributed across the keyboard.

Donna Albina was soon forced to sell her husband's books, paintings and most of the scores inherited from his ancestors, but she would never part with the family piano on which Giacomo reluctantly practised. He was far more eager to climb the city walls or doze in the vineyards on languorous summer days. At night, when it was too hot for sleep and his sisters chattered on while their mother sewed, darned and ironed, he would wander across the moonlit paddies to listen to the croaking frogs and the river's whispered secrets. Although he trapped and killed birds without inhibition, he already showed a streak of sentimentality. He once vanished after playing hide-and-seek with his companions and was found several hours later high up in a tree. He had run off when a cortège passed on its way to the Sant'Anna cemetery where a favourite aunt of his was buried. 'How could I play in the sun while she is in that dark grave all alone?' he sobbed.

But such melancholy interludes were rare. When a heat haze lay over Lucca he would join in and memorise the choruses sung by barefoot peasant girls working in the fields. He also developed a keen ear for bird song and church bells, but otherwise showed little feeling for music. He sang in the choir at San Michele, earning a precious lira or two on feast days until his voice broke and then began studying in the organ loft under his uncle, a sarcastic martinet who used to kick his shins if he missed a note. In later years he would often jerk his leg instinctively whenever anyone sang out of tune.

By the time he entered the Istituto he had a rudimentary knowledge of music, although only an average organist, as

Magi never tired of reminding him. Luckily, another teacher, Carlo Angeloni, proved kindlier and more discerning. Instead of discouraging his excursions, he introduced him to the delights of water-fowling on the marshy Lago di Massacuiccoli where many of Hannibal's warriors had perished during their advance through Tuscany. He would turn a blind eye when the boy puffed hungrily at a cigarette or a cigar butt which he had picked up outside some *caffé* and stuffed into a pipe. Giacomo became a nicotine addict in his early teens and also acquired an abnormally sweet tooth. His teacher soon discovered that he could be tempted to practise harder with some local delicacy like the anis-flavoured *buccellati* or an occasional cigarette.

In time his organ-playing had improved enough for him to assist his uncle at San Martino and sometimes earn a few extra lire at smaller churches in the district. Angeloni, himself an above-average composer, had meantime detected early signs of a talent for composition which, planning ahead for the boy's scheduled future as the Cathedral organist, he directed towards church music. Significantly, however, he also introduced him to Verdi. Before long the rousing scores of *Rigoletto* and *Il Trovatore* had transformed Lucca's ramparts into prison walls.

Brought up in a household of women, he grew undisciplined. His mother, work-worn and despairing of marrying off her daughters without dowries, was more than grateful for the extra money when he began playing the piano at weddings, but less pleased by his engagements at various beach resorts, which seemed to her beneath a Puccini's dignity, apart from being morally dangerous for a handsome youth tall for his age. He could not resist accepting an engagement at the casino in Bagni di Lucca and found these dances a welcome diversion after pedalling the organ for his uncle or trying to master harmony and counterpoint at the Istituto. But he soon became restless and had the piano turned round to face the window, rather than watch the dark-eyed girls in the arms of their fortunate partners. Without Albina's knowledge or approval, he sometimes played the piano at a house of pleasure in Via della Dogana where one of the girls, Lola, was kind to him.

It seems that he had not only lost his virginity but all religious faith by his mid-teens. Albina chided him over his erratic church attendance but had herself become less devout. Soured by early widowhood and resenting the meagre pittance from a hypocritical Commune, she sympathised when Giacomo returned from the musty cathedral loft, still squirming from his uncle's criticism, and found excuses to avoid all but obligatory church services.

While she darned his shirts in the yellow glow of a kerosene lamp or patched the dresses which his sisters inherited from each other, he would often sit beside her and confide brave hopes of future glory and prosperity. To him she would always remain an idealised and beautiful Madonna, doomed to undeserved suffering, but sentimentality did not preclude deceit or petty meanness. He sometimes played the organ at the local Barbantine convent where the Mother Superior used to offer him a cup of sweet hot chocolate plus his fee of a few lire in a sealed envelope. This he would break open, extracting enough for tobacco, until Donna Albina caught him out. Henceforth, the fee was sent to her direct, but she soon forgave him, blaming evil companions for his lapse.

He joined a joke-loving street gang, headed by a disreputable young painter and sculptor, Zizzania, who revelled in shocking the bourgeoisie. He mastermined the plan which soon brought Giacomo into collision with the authorities. He was playing the organ at a small village church, his brother acting as blower, when 'Zizz' suggested that some easy cigarette money might be picked up by disposing of the pipes to a scrap dealer. The thefts remained undetected for a while, due to Puccini's ingenious improvisations on the pillaged organ. When the carabinieri were called in, Albina pleaded for mercy but the charge was only dropped after one of her kinsmen, a cathedral canon, agreed to pay compensation for the missing pipes.

8

Puccini was soon back with his old playmates. Zizz lodged with a widow, Maddalena, a few doors away in Via Poggio, and used to inflame him with obscene accounts of their nights together. Until then his sexual experience had been limited to a skilful induction by Lola, followed by occasional romps with a raven-haired girl who worked in the local cigar factory and used to smuggle out very acceptable rejects. Under Zizz's tutelage he became a more accomplished seducer and rejoiced in raiding neighbouring villages where girls from migrant gipsy families could be stripped like peas. His presence was an asset. Tall, with an attractive oval-shaped face, sensual lips under a prominent nose and a thick mop of dark wavy hair, he had a lazy charm and was less coarse-mannered than his companions.

He continued to play the piano at weddings and would often accompany singers at the Buon Gusto *caffé* where he was paid five lire a night and as many pastries as he could swallow, usually managing to sneak one or two for his mother. He also gave organ tuition to a young tailor's assistant who paid him 60 centesimi a lesson and good-naturedly lengthened his sleeves or trouser-legs for feast days. Puccini became more confident after his pupil had performed a number of his organ pieces at town concerts.

While deputising for the regular organist in small churches he would introduce a few improvised variations which usually went unnoticed or even earned a word of praise from some tolerant priest. This encouraged him to lighten the Recessional at San Michele with excerpts from folk music and operas. Most of the congregation approved except his sister, Iginia, who would soon enter a convent and was horrified by such profanity.

Soon afterwards he took a far more spectacular leap away from church music. Since the first performance of *Aida* in 1871 the world had acclaimed Verdi's masterpiece, but it had taken five years to reach Pisa. Although Puccini could not raise the price of a theatre ticket or even his train fare, he was determined to see this opera. Packing a few *panini* (bread

9

rolls), he persuaded Zizz and a school friend, Carlo Carignani,* to walk the nineteen kilometres over the hills with him. He had never before ventured so far from Lucca but wasted no time admiring the white marble Cathedral and the Leaning Tower, so much smaller and more insignificant than he had imagined. While the others panted to keep up with him, he half-ran to the Teatro Verdi and informed a porter that they had a private letter for the manager, a native of Lucca. He let them in after some argument. They hid in the gallery and calmly took their places in the front row as soon as the doors opened.

Aida was the first opera he had ever seen and proved an unforgettable experience for a youth not yet eighteen and unsure of his future. 'I felt that a window had opened for me', he once recalled. As they walked back through the night, weary but exhilarated, his head seemed to be bursting with the exotic spectacle and ceremonial. By dawn, when Lucca's walls at last rose from the mist, he was still humming half-remembered arias and orchestral rhythms which had fired his blood like some potent new drug.

He now needed no encouragement from Angeloni to analyse the work of either past or contemporary composers, but Verdi remained his exclusive god until he discovered Wagner. Soon he was busily scribbling scores of his own, including a *Preludio Sinfonico* and several choral pieces, until the chance came to make his public début in a local music competition. His cantata failed to win the prize and merely earned him rebuke for an almost illegible script. But some months later a *Motet*, composed in honour of San Paolino, Lucca's patron saint and legendary inventor of church bells, was so well received at a performance by his fellow-pupils that he adapted it for his graduation exercise. The full-scale Mass for singers and orchestra, with an ambitious number of lyrical choruses, plainly derived from Verdi, but many good

* Carignani became a singing teacher in Milan and later arranged several of Puccini's operatic scores for the piano.

judges had nodded approval at a concert to celebrate the saint's day.

Donna Albina's uncle, Niccolo Cerù, a music-loving bachelor physician was among these who congratulated him on gaining his diploma. As a sideline, he wrote regularly for the local paper and very naturally rhapsodised over his great-nephew's Mass. Puccini called to thank him and passionately confided his hopes of continuing his musical studies beyond Lucca, as his father and earlier ancestors had done. Cerù, immensely tall and cadaverous, paced his study on spindly legs while the young man talked of the operas he would surely write once he had acquired the necessary technique. Milan, he stammered excitedly, had Italy's best Conservatoire as well as the Teatro alla Scala. Why should he not emulate one of Lucca's favourite sons, Alfredo Catalani, who had recently graduated from the Conservatoire and was already being spoken of as a talented composer of opera and chamber music?

Dr Cerù stroked his white beard and promised to canvass the City Council for a grant or, failing that, a loan. But the young man's raffish past had not been forgiven; further, his obvious enthusiasm for opera made them doubt his professed intention of following earlier Puccinis into the organ loft at San Martino. Their reluctance to help merely stiffened Donna Albina's backbone, but the outlook was bleak. Her youngest daughter, Romelde, was now married (to an ill-paid clerk in the tax-collector's office) and Iginia had entered a convent. Even so, her paltry pension would not feed and clothe the rest of the family, still less cover the cost of maintaining Giacomo in Milan, even with Dr Cerù's help. The one desperate hope, however faint, was an appeal to Queen Margherita, who awarded a few scholarships at the Conservatoire to needy students of promise. Albina guessed that a formal application stood little chance as her brother's essential letter of reference would either be hostile or, worse, withheld altogether. She therefore decided to make a backstairs approach through one of the Queen's ladies-in-waiting whom she happened to know slightly from earlier days. After an agony of suspense, word finally came that the applicant's tuition fees would be paid for a year, together with a grant of 100 lire a month, subject to his passing a formal preliminary examination. Dr Cerù promised impulsively to make himself responsible for any further fees when the royal bounty expired.

Puccini left for Milan on 14 September 1880. At the railway station he embraced his weeping mother, his sisters and sixteen-year-old Michele. Farther along the platform stood a smaller and noisier group, led by Zizz, with Maddalena hanging brazenly on his arm. Puccini waved from the carriage window and puffed gratefully at a cigarette from the stock which Zizz had hoarded for a parting gift. He had only a few lire to last him until the first month's scholarship money arrived, but his mother had provided a hamper bulging with wine, bread, cheese, sausage and, most welcome of all, an enormous flagon of good Lucca oil.

Chapter Two

He rented a fairly spacious room perched over straggling Vicolo San Carlo and was more charmed with his walnut table than the dismal pattern of Milan's rooftops. He had a serviceable piano but was strictly forbidden to play at night. The monthly rent of 30 lire took a substantial slice from his scholarship grant and left nothing for extravagances like tickets to La Scala. However, the manager, formerly an impresario in Lucca, sometimes gave him a free voucher for the *piccionaia* or 'peanut gallery'. He could not afford to buy operatic scores but a classmate passed on one or two, including Boito's *Mefistofele*, which he studied intently while preparing for his entrance examination.

He gained top marks without perhaps appreciating that this had been the least of his obstacles. Nearing his twenty-second birthday he was well above the average age, but his family name, reinforced by the royal scholarship, provided an almost blameless pedigree. The Conservatoire, founded by Napoleonic decree to encourage gifted students of modest means, had steadily assumed a snobbishness which claimed Verdi, the son of a village innkeeper, among its early victims. His application was ostensibly turned down because of his age (he was then eighteen) and 'lack of talent', but the directors had been more affronted by his pockmarked face and uncouth manners. He never forgave the snub. In later years when the Conservatoire wished to rename itself in his honour he snapped back, 'They wouldn't have me young; they can't have me old.'

Soon after his arrival Puccini had filed into the entrance hall of La Scala where a statue of Verdi was being unveiled to stand beside those of Rossini and Donizetti, but the composer had ignored the ceremony, preferring to work on his farm in Sant' Agata, near Parma. Puccini shared that distaste for Milan

13

which he would always identify with hunger and almost unbearable homesickness. 'It seems to me a thousand years before I will be able to go home', he wrote to his mother. During that wretched first year he lived mainly on thin minestrone with beans, made palatable by an occasional can of olive oil from Lucca, as he could not stomach the linseed and sesame concoction served in most cheap restaurants. Only the appearance of Queen Margherita's hundred-lire note enabled him to indulge in a satisfying meal with three helpings of soup, pasta, half a litre of wine, a square of gorgonzola and a much-missed cheroot. He frequented the Osteria Aida, a haunt of students who relied on credit to stay alive during the latter part of each month. Even so, his healthy appetite and a desperate craving for tobacco left him so often in arrears with the rent that his landlord who, unluckily, was also the local postman, pounced on any letter with a Rome postmark and extracted his thirty lire at source. It seemed to epitomise Milan's greed.

He could never acclimatise to the chilly winters or the oppressive stickiness of the summer months when he panted for clean country air and marshes alive with waterfowl. Most of all he missed his adored mother. 'You cannot believe how much I long to see you', he wrote plaintively. 'If sometimes I have given you cause for anger, it is not because I do not love you dearly, but because I am sometimes a beast and a rogue.' As for that charmless city, where no birds sang, he would gladly have exchanged all the fine carriages and the Duomo itself for a carefree cigarette on Lucca's ramparts or an hour in some village barn with a soft-skinned girl. After several weeks of abstinence he had pawned his overcoat for 17 lire to dine with a dancer from the La Scala chorus. Although rather too scraggy for his liking, she ate like a healthy filly but accompanied him back to his room after a few tots of brandy. For weeks he shivered without his overcoat and, like Rodolfo and his friends, found himself stuffing cardboard boxes and even books into his stove to keep warm.

Milan's great industrial fair had opened within a few

months of his arrival. The streets teemed with loud-mouthed visitors who flourished thick wallets, but he could not help being drawn, night after night, to the dazzling arcades, restaurants and cafés in the Galleria Vittorio Emmanuele. Glancing up like a wide-eyed child before a Christmas tree, he would arrive at dusk to watch the huge glass dome being lit by a small clockwork engine which ran round a track to ignite over two thousand gas jets.

Leading from La Scala to the Cathedral, the Galleria was not only a popular meeting-place for business men but the artistic hub of Milan. Puccini would sometimes take his evening promenade with Catalani, only four years older than himself but with a first opera already launched at La Scala and published by Giulio Ricordi. The latter held court at his regular table attended by Boito, Tamagno, the celebrated tenor, and a retinue of impresarios, agents and critics. Catalani nodded to several acquaintances and genially introduced his fellow-Lucchese, who would usually make off with a mumbled excuse. He felt inhibited by these glib successful people and was never quite comfortable even with Catalani who would generously stand treat but often left him marooned while he rushed away to embrace friends and exchange staccato bursts of gossip. His eyes had the too-bright glitter of the consumptive when he lashed the critics who had sneered at him for deserting Verdi in favour of Wagner's mysticism.

Puccini was made sharply aware of these rival gods from the moment he faced his teachers at the Conservatoire. He learned the technicalities of composition from Antonio Bazzini, whose student years in Germany had addicted him to Wagner. His only opera, *Turanda*, had enjoyed a modest triumph but may have planted the seedling for his pupil's last and infinitely superior work. Amilcare Ponchielli, a former cathedral organist and bandmaster in Cremona, was less academic-minded. He taught Puccini counterpoint and passed on his own enthusiasm for Verdi's vigorous dramas. Italian nationalism had inspired his early compositions, but his solitary operatic triumph, *La Gioconda*, a romantic blood-and-thunder melodrama to a libretto by Boito, won the hearts of audiences with the salon-type music of the Dance of the Hours and a handful of splendid lyrical arias. Puccini, who had quickly succumbed to its crashing finales, later put to effective use in his own *Tosca*, could not help agreeing secretly with Catalani's critics. The truth was that he admired his friend's sensitive musicianship but found his Wagnerian-type opera sickly stuff.

Even without the glamorous aura of *La Gioconda*, Ponchielli had much to commend him to the homesick young man. He was kindly, sympathetic and soon became almost a father-figure. Corpulent, with a forked beard and hair like a spiky picket fence, he had a habit of fingering a wart on his left cheek when about to engage in bland reminiscence. He would sometimes recall his years spent on *La Gioconda*, changing scenes up to the last minute and even during rehearsals, a practice which Puccini inherited to the full. After classes he often trudged through the rain under his teacher's immense black umbrella. Ponchielli's wife, a former singer, would serve coffee and cakes while the gentle maestro aired his operatic views, continually stressing the need for strong arias rather than over-instrumentalism. Puccini was urged to study harder and take more pains over his exercises which he sometimes scribbled on odd envelopes and even menus filched from the Osteria Aida, usually with an apologetic '*scusi*' in the margin for an unsightly rash of blots. But Ponchielli had detected an above-average talent which made him charitable over such lapses. No doubt he also half-guessed that the young man with the abnormal appetite was living on short rations and unable to afford notebooks or costly score paper.

Queen Margherita's subsidy expired at the end of the first year. Donna Albina forced herself to appeal to the Town Council but without success. She turned once more to Dr Cerù who agreed to advance his great-nephew's share of the money he had intended leaving the family in his will. But finances again became strained when Michele, restless in Lucca, moved in with his brother and hopefully began taking singing lessons. Some months later a third tenant arrived to make a timely contribution to the rent. He was Pietro Mascagni, then seventeen but already the composer of several pieces of church music and a symphony, apart from an operatic score which he had carelessly mislaid. It was typical of a happy-go-lucky, slipshod outlook that would damage his career after a phenomenal début.

A baker's son, he owed the chance of studying under Ponchielli to a music-loving nobleman in his native Leghorn, but he had too much faith in his facile talent to spend long hours mastering counterpoint and dramatic theory. There was already something of the actor *manqué* in his make-up. Puccini, doggedly working at the piano on his exercises, could not help laughing when his room-mate picked up a poker or a broomstick and started conducting with mock-fierce bravura. Romantically wan and sickly-looking, Mascagni had a shock of black hair and a long nose over a wispy moustache cultivated to emulate Puccini's bushier growth. It grew absurdly blond and had to be sacrificed, but his bouncy resilience helped him survive far more serious misfortunes. He would brag shamelessly about his fine wardrobe left behind in Leghorn, although in fact he possessed only one good suit which he ironed and brushed until it sparkled. He loved food but would invest in a gaudy new cravat rather than spaghetti. However, on one occasion Puccini persuaded him to share an outlay of 120 lire for an orchestral score of *Parsifal* which both rated equally with Verdi's masterpieces.

It was a bohemian existence with many ups and downs but made tolerable by high spirits and sheer *joie de vivre*. It is said they had a wall-map of the city on which they had inked in red any sections dangerously crowded with creditors. Their single earthenware bowl did duty for serving beans and toilet purposes. As they were forbidden to cook in their room, Puccini used to thump on the piano to blot out the sizzling of fat. For a time Mascagni enjoyed these antics and often hid in the wardrobe when his creditors called, but he was less tolerant of the Conservatoire's tedious discipline. He departed without warning to join a travelling operetta troupe as pianist-conductor but soon came to blows with the manager. Years of misery and semi-starvation followed, only relieved by his attachment to a pretty soubrette in the company.

Puccini missed his merry sense of fun and companionship. In that desperate final year, without his royal grant, he forced himself to write an almost grovelling letter to the councillors in Lucca, reminding them of his excellent progress at the Conservatoire and his family's many years of cathedral service. Not too surprisingly, perhaps, this letter was ignored as he had expressed no intention of taking up his duties at San Martino after gaining his diploma. Once again Dr Cerù issued a life-saving prescription by agreeing to pay his tuition fees and another 150 lire a month towards rent, food, books and clothing. Puccini had no doubt that he could augment this allowance by giving a few piano and organ lessons.

He worried over his prospects but less so than Albina who had begun to suffer recurrent spells of illness. Morbidly preoccupied with thoughts of death, she pleaded with Ponchielli to find her son some academic post after graduation. He promised to explore the ground but hinted that an extra year at the Conservatoire would be valuable before the young man 'plunged himself into composing'. He ended on an encouraging note, 'Giacomo is one of the best pupils in my class and I am well satisfied with him.'

For his graduation exercise he composed a *Capriccio Sinfonica*, written as usual on scraps of paper and even newspaper tail-ends. Bazzini liked the vigorous score enough to have it played by the Conservatoire's orchestra, while Ponchielli, a little disappointed that his pupil had played safe with an orchestral piece instead of chancing his arm operatically, praised its rich lyrical passages.

It was directed on 14 July 1883 by Franco Faccio, who had conducted the première of *Aida* at La Scala. As a former graduate of the Conservatoire, his name attracted a distinguished audience who inspired an exceptional performance from the student musicians. A publisher soon offered to print the score, adapted for two pianos, after the critic of *La Perseverenza* had welcomed 'a decisive and rare musical temperament'.

With several copies of this periodical in his valise, together with his diploma and newly-minted bronze medal, Puccini returned in triumph to Lucca. He was still light-headed from Ponchielli's parting promise to find him a suitable libretto for a national competition sponsored by Edouardo Sonzogno, a wealthy industrialist and newspaper magnate. To attract fresh talent to his new publishing house and perhaps break the Ricordi monopoly, Sonzogno had announced a first prize of 2,000 lire for the best one-act opera. It was such dazzling bait that Puccini recklessly declined a teaching appointment at the Istituto in Lucca and also delayed applying for the post of organist at San Martino which, it was broadly hinted, might now be open to him. He waited in a fever of impatience for word from Ponchielli. As the last date of entry for the competition was 31 December, only six months hence, he could picture the horde of would-be composers already at work on their scores while he twiddled his thumbs.

His mother had kept the family piano tuned but he drifted off on solitary walks by the river, too restless and dispirited even to go wild-fowling with his old teacher, Angeloni, who had welcomed him back with tears of affection. He reminded himself gloomily that, at twenty-five, he still depended on his mother for cigarette money instead of being able to provide her with nourishing food and a few weeks at a spa such as Montecatini, whose doctors might restore her frail body. Sonzogno's 2,000 lire, at first a pipe-dream, had now become a tantalising lifeline, needing only a good libretto to rescue his mother and himself from their misery.

Lucca helped temporarily to prop his morale. Time and again he had to produce copies of *La Perseverenza* and seldom lacked an appreciative audience. He could always be sure of a meal in the house of Alfredo Caselli, a kindly music-loving pharmacist who had for years given Donna Albina all her medicines on credit or at nominal charges. Another good friend was Narciso Gemignani, a former schoolmate, now a prosperous merchant in olive oil, coffee, spices, wines and spirits. He and his wife, Elvira, had a pleasant apartment in the Piazza Bernardino where Puccini would often be invited to dine.

Narciso, good-natured and jolly, could be boisterous in his cups. He liked to air a booming baritone and was absurdly flattered when Puccini, anxious to repay his hospitality, lightly promised to write a romanza for him. Elvira was far more serious, indeed almost prim for a woman in her early twenties. She would frown when her husband dropped a coarse word, but her dark velvety eyes softened while Puccini chattered amusingly about the Galleria and a sophisticated world remote from provincial Lucca. Unconscious of his light mockery, she insisted on precise details of what the Milanese ladies wore, their carriages, the elegant shops and, of course, magical nights at La Scala whose tiered boxes could only have been a blur from his perch in the *piccionaia*.

She considered herself socially superior to her husband and could not help being impressed by the Puccinis' association with courts and cathedrals. Tall, stately and full-bosomed, she had an alluringly tiny waist with as yet no sign of her second pregnancy. Her dark-blonde hair, plaited into a tall helmet, complemented the solemn matronly manner, but Puccini had soon noticed her full indulgent mouth and the hardening of her nipples whenever he kissed her hand. Highly-sexed, she had patiently endured her husband's clumsy demands and might have reconciled herself to a dull marriage and a large family but for the arrival of the handsome young maestro. His frankly sensual admiration had thrown her completely off-balance. With another child unwanted and unloved already stirring in her womb, she was fatally poised for a romance but took care, at least in the early stages, to mask her passion by a show of almost motherly interest in Puccini's career. After an excellent dinner it became routine for them to do piano duets while Narciso belched away or, more often, snored in his armchair. She had no real musical taste, but played the piano competently and had sung for a time in a Florence *caffè* owned by her married sister, Ida Gazzi.

In August the long-awaited letter arrived at Via di Poggio 30. Ponchielli reported that a young poet, Ferdinando Fontana, might be persuaded to write a libretto for the competition. It had not been too easy to interest him. Vain and impecunious, he had at first demanded a fee payable in advance but finally agreed on a share of the prize money. Ponchielli then invited him and his ex-pupil to spend a few days at his summer villa.

Puccini arrived, almost famished, but had to make do with a hurried slice of salami as there was much to discuss and the others had already dined. Fontana pompously outlined a story of witchcraft set in the Black Forest. Based on an essay by Heine, it had rather too much Wagnerian symbolism for Ponchielli's taste but he seemed confident that his protégé's lyrical gift would leaven the dead weight. He also made it clear that it would be folly to sacrifice a free libretto.

That summer Milan was an inferno. Hardly able to afford even a few centesimi for an evening drink or cigarettes after paying for his board and lodging, Puccini suffered in his airless room. Chafing at Fontana's slow progress but without daring to criticise him, he counted the hours until he could return home and start work on the opera which they had decided to call, *Le Willis* (The Witches). By mid-September he had pawned his watch and tiepin to pay the landlord and had to appeal to Albina to send him 20 lire for his railway ticket.

He began working on the score almost before he had unpacked. The tortuous libretto, so lacking in sparkle, gave him no peace but he persevered, covering page after page in a frenzied scrawl which soon grew into a thicket of blots and erasures. Chain-smoking, he worked into the small hours, even refusing invitations to dine with the Gemignanis although, hungry for encouragement, he would sometimes hurry over to their apartment to play excerpts from his score. Narciso was often away in Florence or Turin, calling on suppliers, and tongues began to wag when Puccini occasionally strolled on the ramparts with Elvira, now heavily pregnant, and her two-year-old daughter, Fosca, a merry-eyed child who adored him. But they saw each other less often as the closing date for the competition approached. Predictably, their brief meetings became more painful when so much had to be expressed wordlessly with glances or quick touches of hands. He could find some relief in the day and night toil on his score but her torment was intensified after the birth of her son, Renato, whose wailings seemed to echo her own despair. Although Puccini assured her that she was now far more desirable, she would often weep hysterically at the prospect of losing him. Secretly she half-hoped he would not win the competition and might reconcile himself to Lucca instead of escaping into the gilded world of Milan with its obvious temptations for an attractive bachelor.

Apart from an occasional fit of despondency, he grew buoyantly certain of his success but the manuscript was revised up to the very last second of zero hour and without enough time to make a fair copy. Even so, the envelope had to be retrospectively postmarked, '31 December 1883', by an obliging friend of his in the sorting office at Lucca. He now became absurdly light-hearted, tinkling folk songs on the piano to restore a little colour to his mother's cheeks. Although in constant pain, she laughed at his exuberant plans for spending Signor Sonzogno's 2,000 lire. He already pictured her, dressed like an elegant lady of fashion, walking by his side into the most expensive restaurant in the Galleria.

He had started dining again in the Piazza Bernardini and used to hoist Fosca on his broad shoulders for bedtime games. One night he had casually hinted at filling in time by taking a few pupils. Narciso at once suggested that Elvira might benefit from singing and piano lessons as she had seemed dispirited and off-colour since the birth of their baby. The lovers agreed with beating hearts and a proper show of reluctance.

Their idyll was shattered when news came that the opera had failed to capture the prize or even an honourable mention.

The award was shared by two young composers, one of them a contemporary of Puccini's at the Conservatoire, for entries of quite startling mediocrity. Ponchielli hinted sympathetically that, with the exception of Boito, none of the judges had even troubled to read his ex-pupil's almost illegible score. It transpired that Boito had cast his vote in favour of *Le Willis* but Sonzogno had overruled him.

Puccini was now in the blackest despair and would often burst into tears. Elvira's kisses comforted him but his mother's determination proved far more practical. Although ailing and reluctant to lose him, she saw nothing but disgrace ahead if he continued his liaison with Elvira, now an open secret to all but her blinkered husband. She was hopeful that his departure would end the scandalous affair and also restore his self-confidence. In Milan, she argued sensibly, he still had influential friends like Ponchielli while his collaborator, Fontana, kept urging him to return and start revising their opera in the hope of interesting another publisher. Puccini had too little cash left from his piano lessons to support himself away from home but his mother somehow managed to scrape together another 200 lire which would at least buy his railway ticket and keep him alive for a month or so.

Fontana had meantime been lobbying frenziedly for their rejected 'masterpiece'. He soon whisked his collaborator off to a soirée in the home of Marco Sala, a wealthy part-time critic and composer of dance music. Puccini's friend, Catalani, had also been invited but the star guest was Arrigo Boito, the centre of an admiring circle who sponged up his acid witticisms and listened with awe as he confided with a sardonic grin that Verdi had appealed to him to write a libretto for *Otello*. Everyone laughed except Puccini, unaware that composer and librettist were now reconciled after years of angry feuding. Once a staunch Wagnerian, Boito had dared to poke fun at Verdi by impishly turning 'La donna è mobile' into a polka. He became a fervent admirer after *Aida* but it had still needed skilful diplomacy by their publisher, Ricordi, to extract a free pardon from Verdi.

Boito affected an air of dilettantism and world-weary decadence. He burned aromatic pastilles in his apartment while making love to a succession of beauties, including Eleanora Duse, but nobody produced a more massive output of poetry, criticism and libretti or exerted so much influence on contemporary music and letters. Tongue-tied and fumbling like a peasant with his glass of wine, Puccini found it difficult to identify this effeminate-looking dandy with the composer of *Mefistofele*, still less the fire-eating patriot who had once marched to death or glory with Garibaldi's Red Shirts. But his eyes were kindly behind the glinting pince-nez as he urged him to play over the rejected score which Fontana had astutely slipped into his pocket before they set off for Sala's.

He started nervously but, gaining confidence, ended to sympathetic applause. After much chin-rubbing, Boito praised the fine scoring, notably of the symphonic movements, and announced his intention of recommending Ricordi to publish it and put the upstart Sonzogno firmly in his place. As the obvious first step would be to stage a production, he also offered to approach the lessee of the Teatro dal Verme.

Puccini looked on incredulously when the others began heaping banknotes on the table towards production costs. Boito opened the list of subscribers with a 50-lire note, but they were far short of the 450 needed for minimum overheads like costumes and an orchestra. However, Ricordi had agreed to print free copies of the score; Boito and Fontana continued to canvass music-loving patrons, while Michele passed his begging bowl among his brother's fellow-students who pawned watches and sold books, even their walking-sticks, to help the cause.

During this frantic fund-raising, Puccini returned to Lucca and began revising the opera which had been re-titled *Le Villi*. He could do little more with Fontana's stilted libretto but managed to improve the songs and lighten several of the descriptive passages. He thrust ahead, trying to look cheerful although often saddened by his mother's illness. She had become alarmingly gaunt and struggled to restrain her fits of coughing while he sat at the piano. He would often escape to the Gemignanis and seek relief with Elvira who had duped her husband, still blindly uxorious, into accepting her frigidity as the natural aftermath of a painful childbirth. She yearned to accompany her lover to Milan for the première of *Le Villi* but could not leave the children or so openly betray her passion. Albina saw him off at the railway station early in May 1884, promising hopefully to attend the opening if her health improved.

The piece was staged on the last night of the month before a full house which included Boito, Ponchielli, Sala and many others eager to snub the Sonzogno prizewinners while simultaneously demonstrating their loyalty to the House of Ricordi. Puccini was very nervous, more so because he had been unable to buy or even hire correct dress clothes. He had walked into the theatre with only forty centesimi in the trouser pocket of his shabby maroon-coloured suit, but all this was forgotten when *Le Villi* closed to a storm of applause. Flushed and still dry-mouthed from nerves and cigarettes, he stumbled off to send a telegram to his mother, 'Clamorous success. Hopes surpassed. Eighteen calls. First finale repeated three times. Am happy. Giacomo."

Le Perseverenza once again exploded with praise and accused Sonzogno of 'throwing the opera into a corner like a piece of rag'. It was followed by more plaudits for 'the young Maestro from Lucca', this time in the *Corriere della Sera* whose critic, Giovanni Pozza, declared ecstatically, 'In a word we believe sincerely that in Puccini we may have the composer for whom Italy has long been waiting.' Giulio Ricordi happened to be away in Rome but his wife reported the triumph to him. He wired back cautiously, 'It is all right for you to buy *Le Villi* so long as it is not a work that imitates Wagner.' Aware that the opera was not only derivative of Verdi's *Rigoletto*, Bizet and even Catalani's melancholy in a number of romanzas, quite apart from some very distinct Wagnerian echoes, she hesitated to buy the rights but informed Puccini of the firm's strong interest.

On his return Ricordi read the score and quickly picked out the glowing wild orchids from Fontana's jungle of clichés and artificialities. Himself a composer of some distinction, he recognised its symphonic craftsmanship and was even more impressed by the refreshing spontaneity of several arias. But he would hardly have shown any excitement for a newcomer's one-act piece without so much advance lobbying from his clients, Ponchielli and Boito, now endorsed by a wildly approving Press. Above all, *Le Villi*, with all its imperfections, gave him an opportunity to ridicule Sonzogno who had dared to challenge Italy's leading publishers.

The Ricordis, a family of Spanish descent, had founded their publishing dynasty early in the nineteenth century when Giulio's grandfather, originally a copyist at La Scala, enterprisingly bought up the Milan Conservatoire's stock of sheet music and then turned to printing his own. He soon acquired the copyright in the works of Rossini, Donizetti and Bellini and in 1839 started a lifelong association with Verdi by buying his first opera, *Oberto*, for a modest sum, although timidly delaying publication until it had made its way. Verdi's operas had enriched both firm and composer, who was usually paid an advance sum, plus royalties on performances. He always insisted on receiving interest on any arrears and once accused the firm of accounting irregularities which, after an unpleasant investigation, netted him 50,000 lire in back commissions. The relationship became more cordial under Giulio who put a stop to sloppy productions and showed outstanding skill in handling singers, conductors and local impresarios.

The firm ran branches throughout Europe, the United States and Latin America, apart from holding the leases in several of Italy's houses. It owned copyright in practically every major opera produced in Italy, with a profitable sideline from the sales of sheet music and scores for piano or full orchestra. Over the years Casa Ricordi had become influential enough to dictate the choice of singers, conductors and even scenic designers. Managers had to toe the line or risk losing Verdi and most of the other successes in the standard Italian repertory. Composers like Boito and Ponchielli had naturally followed in the wake of Verdi, while newcomers hastened to enrol with a firm who often suggested promising subjects, commissioned librettists and, above all, could steer their work into La Scala and other leading opera houses. The Ricordis looked after their translation rights, protected them from piracy and generally acted as agents, bankers and trusted confidants in exchange for a substantial share of the proceeds.

When Puccini arrived on the scene Giulio Ricordi had virtually taken control. He was not only fluent in several languages but a perfectionist who made a point of attending rehearsals and took endless pains to ensure high-quality productions at home or abroad. He was by now on excellent personal terms with Verdi, having endeared himself to that cantankerous veteran by his intensely nationalistic feeling for Italian music and a rooted dislike of Wagner. Other clients found him friendlier than his father who had inspired more fear than affection, but he could be equally formidable in extending the firm's monopoly. One contemporary Milan cartoon depicts him slapping a boy's face for whistling in the street and warning him sternly, 'No one may whistle without previously arranging terms with my house which holds the exclusive rights to every musical note.'

He had summoned Puccini to his dark and sombrely luxurious office four days after the opening of *Le Villi*. Across the imposing mahogany desk under a huge portrait of Verdi, the nervous young composer faced a keen-eyed man in his late forties. Ricordi's natural senatorial dignity was enhanced by a faultlessly trimmed beard, a waxed moustache and formal English-cut clothes. He wore a high stiff collar, a black silk cravat and caressed a pearl pin with manicured fingers. After a few pleasantries to put his visitor at ease, he outlined his plans. The firm would buy world rights in *Le Villi* if Puccini would agree to recast it into two acts, a more serviceable length for most opera houses. He advised him to pursue his collaboration with Fontana on a full-length opera for which the firm would guarantee production at La Scala. Having been privately briefed on the young man's wretched finances by Ponchielli, Boito and others, he proposed paying him a monthly allowance of 300 lire for a year, on account of royalties, during the preparation of the second opera. While Puccini was mumbling his thanks, the publisher extracted a 1,000 lire note from his wallet and handed it over as an advance on *Le Villi*. He then pulled his right ear lobe which Puccini came to recognise as a signal that the interview was over.

For all his shrewdness and enterprise, Ricordi had made two serious blunders. By contemptuously underrating the publicity value of the Sonzogno Prize, he would deprive himself of such promising composers as Mascagni and Leoncavallo. He had also been over-hasty in continuing to impose a mediocrity like Fontana on his gifted discovery instead of pairing him off with one of the more accomplished librettists whom the firm had on call. With the best of intentions he had carelessly condemned him to five years' hard labour which all but wrecked his career.

A jubilant Puccini, now guaranteed security, could not be expected to nurse misgivings about Fontana. After sending news of his astonishing good fortune to his mother and Elvira, he was eager to start revising *Le Villi*, but that 1,000-lire note, the first he had ever earned or even handled, burned his pocket. He settled his long-outstanding account of 300 lire at the Osteria Aida and splashed gaily on a celebration dinner with his brother, Mascagni and a few other close friends. He ordered all the delicacies so often tasted in mirage during the hungry years; roast beef with mushrooms and asparagus, sluiced down by vintage wines and ending with Roquefort, a basket of wild strawberries and expensive Havana cigars. He also bought a new suit and winter overcoat for Michele and himself.

For the next few weeks he endured the heat of Milan and

tolerated the irritating presence of Fontana while patiently expanding his opera into two acts. Aching with desire for Elvira, he was often tempted to escape but thought it prudent to stay near Ricordi, who planned to stage *Le Villi* in Turin and meantime introduced him to influential critics. One or two dissenters, however, were soon hinting that he had been over-praised. Ricordi brushed this aside as professional jealousy, but he was more concerned that Verdi did not seem to share his enthusiasm for the new piece and wrote to a friend, 'Opera is opera and symphony, symphony. I don't believe in introducing symphonic passages just to give the orchestra a chance to let fly.'

Puccini had been making steadily uphill progress on *Le Villi* when early in July Romelde wired to inform him that their mother had collapsed. He returned at once to Lucca, babbling of Ricordi's generosity and the golden years ahead, often leaving the dying woman's door ajar while he played excerpts from *Le Villi*. He rarely left her bedside. As Narciso had at last become suspicious, it was only possible to meet Elvira for snatched moments after nightfall in some quiet quarter of the city.

Donna Albina died on 17 July 1884. After receiving the Last Rites she took off her wedding ring which he slipped on his own finger. He wore it all his life. Weeping hysterically, he placed on her grave the gilded laurel wreath a friend had given him after the final performance at the Dal Verme. Soon afterwards he visited Iginia's convent and solemnly vowed to buy an organ for the chapel in their mother's memory.

He needed privacy to revise *Le Villi*, without Fontana's querulous interruptions, but could not remain in Lucca where it would have been unseemly to renew his liaison with Elvira so soon after his mother's death. He departed for Torre del Lago, a small fishing village on shallow Lake Massaciúccoli, a few miles from the city. About a dozen houses accommodated the local fishermen and a small colony of bohemian painters who were attracted by cheap living and the brooding land-scape. One or two hunting lodges were rented by sportsmen

29

who arrived at weekends and in the summer months to shoot wild duck and moorhen.

He soon found a comfortable room. Some mornings he would row out among the reeds with a borrowed gun, but the solitude merely deepened his gloom without stimulating him to work. As autumn mists crept in from the lake he grew more melancholy. 'I am always thinking of Mamma and last night I dreamed of her', he wrote mournfully to Romelde. 'Whatever triumphs art may bring me, I shall never be very happy again without my darling mother.'

PART TWO

Elvira

Chapter Three

By mid–October 1884 he was back in Milan completing his revision of *Le Villi*. Still tortured by guilt over his mother's sacrifices, he became intolerably lonely and introspective. Often he was tempted to accept Elvira's desperate offer to join him, but Ricordi's allowance barely covered his own board and lodging. He found some relief in a widening circle of acquaintances, among them Ponchielli's friend, Paolo Tosti, who had emigrated ten years previously and become singing master to Queen Victoria's children. Apart from arranging Court concerts, he composed sentimental ballads which had made him popular with the British public and the darling of Mayfair's hostesses. Each year he returned to Italy for a month or two with his Belgian wife, Berthe, and used to divert the Galleria with irreverent stories of the London social scene. He urged Puccini to persevere with his compositions and ignore fickle or malicious critics.

His old teacher also introduced him to another gay bohemian, Ghislanzoni, a former operatic baritone and editor of Ricordi's influential house magazine, the *Gazzetta Musicale*. He enjoyed the distinction of having versified the libretto for *Aida* but had now semi-retired from the literary world to play the double bass for his own pleasure and run a lakeside hotel at Caprino Bergamasco, where his friends were rarely presented with a bill. That autumn he invited Puccini and Mascagni to one of his weekend parties and soon enrolled them in exuberant charades with Mascagni contributing the piano accompaniment. One night Puccini wore a bustle and blonde wig as Juliet to the host's hilarious Romeo.

A month later Elvira arrived unexpectedly with little Fosca when he was about to leave for rehearsals of *Le Villi* at the Teatro Regio in Turin, announcing flatly that it was no longer possible to face life without him. She would often be condemned for abandoning her baby son but this apparent act of callousness could have been an unselfish gesture towards her wronged husband. Whatever her motives, she had risked much by joining her lover who was still too overjoyed to lose any sleep over the inevitable scandal and an additional strain on his resources. He settled them into a shabby two-roomed apartment before departing for Turin where he soon gave Ricordi a foretaste of many similar confrontations by objecting testily to the acoustics, the singers and an orchestra who had allegedly mangled his score. But even a first-class production could not have salvaged an opera whose two acts simply stressed the libretto's deficiencies without appreciably lifting the music.

Turin was formally polite but La Scala shrugged off the piece when it opened there some weeks later. Without Boito and other partisans to enthuse them, most of the critics objected to its Wagnerian passages aggravated by a large and heavy-handed orchestra who blotted out the more melodious arias. Nevertheless Ricordi's influence was still strong enough to guarantee a dozen more performances, followed by a production at the San Carlo.

Puccini had dared to brave the scandalised Lucchesi while on his way to attend rehearsals in Naples. He stayed with Romelde, who disapproved of his liaison but still regarded him affectionately as an innocent boy (he was twenty-seven!) snared by an unprincipled Delilah. Apart from Dr Cerù, who angrily showed him the door, he was given a far more sympathetic local reception than he had expected or deserved. In a country partial to *opera buffa*, few took the cuckolded Narciso's bibulous threats too seriously. In any event he cut a far less attractive figure than the young maestro whose first opera had been staged at La Scala itself and would shortly be seen in Naples. Puccini's pharmacist friend, Caselli, even honoured him with a banquet at which his health was boisterously toasted by the disreputable Zizz.

Le Villi misfired resoundingly with the San Carlo audience, always prejudiced against composers from the north and

34

particularly those who had dared to choose the rival La Scala ahead of their own opera house. This dull hotchpotch was so indifferently sung and poorly staged that even the few tuneful arias were booed. Too shaken to go before the curtain, the composer took comfort when a chorus girl, whose beauty he had casually noticed, touched his arm and whispered, 'It is nothing, Maestro. Verdi was also hissed here.' He took her out to supper with the last few lire from his travelling expenses.

He was soothed by Ricordi, who announced that the opera had been booked for Verona and Brescia, with negotiations already pending for Buenos Aires. Urging him to ignore San Carlo and apply himself instead to a new scenario which Fontana had based on a melodramatic verse drama by Alfred de Musset, Ricordi rightly sensed that the Carmen-like theme might suit Puccini's lyrical gifts without, however, fully appreciating the need for a lively libretto. Fontana's unfortunate decision to set *Edgar* in gloomy mediaeval Flanders was matched by his stilted characterisation and an unerring instinct for clichés. Puccini had been overjoyed by the prospect of working on another opera but soon found himself shackled with bad Verdi and worse Bizet. His domestic worries made him even more pessimistic. It was difficult enough to breathe fire and passion into Fontana's wooden effigy without having to live from hand to mouth.

They moved house every few weeks, hounded by landlords who objected to late piano-playing and squeezed them mercilessly for arrears of rent. They searched frantically for cheaper lodgings, always farther and farther out of town, before settling in Monza, ten miles away, where their son Antonio was born on 23 December 1886, a day after Puccini's twenty-eighth birthday. The baby, registered as 'father unknown', made another hole in a pitifully small income, but their harsh economies were sweetened by physical delight in each other.

Elvira wore home-made shoes with stitched felt soles but still walked like a goddess. To Puccini she appeared more beautiful than all the elegant ladies in the Galleria even in her faded blouses converted from his old shirts. Little Fosca, whose chiming laugh and honey-coloured curls enchanted him, possessed only one dress and often had to stay in bed while it was being washed, dried and ironed. To save money he became adept at manufacturing envelopes from sheets of paper, but his clothes were always neatly darned when he called on Ricordi to excuse his slow progress on *Edgar* or, more usually, to plead for yet another advance. His monthly allowance, depleted by the small sums he regularly sent his brother in South America, failed to span their bare needs although Elvira, her eyes ringed after disturbed nights with a teething Tonio, used to shop around for the cheapest scraps. She would willingly miss a meal herself rather than deprive Puccini of cigarettes or his nightly glass of aqua vitae heavily laced with sugar. In return she made almost impossible demands on his attention, resenting being left alone for even a few hours while he went off to confer with Fontana. When he returned late one night she threatened, perhaps not too seriously, to go back to her husband unless he stayed at home more and finished his opera. She took to locking him in with his piano, reminding him tartly that Verdi had written *Il Trovatore* in less than a month while his *Edgar* was still in limbo after two years.

Already nerve-racked, he crumpled under the sudden death of Ponchielli, to whom he had automatically turned for advice and encouragement whenever Fontana became tiresome. Giulio Ricordi quickly proved a more than adequate 'second father', although often irritated by the composer's tendency to approve some change in the libretto and, almost immediately, produce page after page of corrections, blotchy with coffee stains. But once the orchestration took shape, Ricordi liked it well enough, notably the chorus scenes, to renew his subsidy for another year. Ghislanzoni's hospitality was another boon and Puccini enjoyed several tranquil and well-fed weeks at the hotel where he drafted his last act in the autumn of 1887.

* * * *

Verdi's *Otello*, his first work for sixteen years, opened that February at La Scala with Tamagno singing the title rôle and a nineteen-year-old Toscanini playing second cello in the pit. Puccini had joined hundreds of other admirers to serenade the veteran composer below the balcony of his suite at the Grand Hotel, but it was some weeks before he saw the opera with a free pass from Ricordi. He went backstage to congratulate the celebrated tenor who casually promised to sing *Edgar* during his forthcoming season in Madrid, but departed instead for a long American tour. Ricordi's enthusiasm had also diminished but, after several months of feverish revision, *Edgar* was finally produced at La Scala on Easter Sunday 1889, under Faccio's baton.

Although most of the audience sat on their hands, Boito persuaded the composer to take several curtain calls which helped to create some illusion of triumph. Next day the *Corriere della Sera* praised the splendid Requiem music in Act 3, while others noted an advance in technical composition, but the overall critical response remained so downbeat that Ricordi had to defend the score in his *Gazzetta Musicale*, hinting that it had triumphed over a sub-standard libretto. This very naturally angered Fontana who resisted every suggestion to shorten the opera or rewrite some of the scenes. They argued far into the night, with the librettist becoming more and more intractable, while Puccini chain-smoked and chewed his fingernails. At noon Ricordi summoned him to his office and urged him to revise the score, preferably without Fontana's help, cheerfully promising the bonus of a second production at La Scala during the next season.

He began condensing the action into three tauter acts but soon became glum enough to ask his brother about prospects in the Argentine. Michele, then barely subsisting on a handful of pupils, urged him to remain in Italy. His situation was now desperate. After being turned out of his rooms for playing the piano at night, he had rented an apartment in a dismal *piazzale*, just outside the new Porta Monforte. He was even forced to ask Ricordi to reimburse him for his bus fares and supply him with manuscript paper free of charge. Fortunately for his peace of mind, he was unaware, until the crisis had passed, that even his modest subsidy had been in the balance. The financial losses on *Le Villi* and the withdrawal of its successor, after only two more poorly-attended performances, had soured Ricordi's fellow-executives, including his less sentimental son Tito. They saw no future in a composer who had already received 18,000 lire on account of royalties, so far remote. Giulio Ricordi had insisted on continuing the monthly allowance and pledged himself to repay the entire debt from his own pocket if the next opera also failed. 'But we will not fail,' he assured his protégé. 'Stop worrying, get to work, look for a good subject and a good poet.' Both had learned much from the fiasco of *Edgar*, and notably the composer, who would never again set any libretto which he had not personally selected or approved.

In July 1889 he left on his first foreign trip, sponsored by Ricordi, who had sensed that a change of scene might boost his morale. The publisher's almost fanatical distaste for Wagner's operas had not prevented him from shrewdly acquiring the Italian copyrights when they came on the market. Puccini was sent off to Bayreuth with Faccio (soon to die in the Monza lunatic asylum) and von Hohenstein, stage designer at La Scala, to suggest possible cuts for a forthcoming production in Milan.

Back home, refreshed in spirit, he gave Elvira and the children a rare treat by taking them to the Buffalo Bill Circus. He was impressed by the sensational trick shooting but even more by the box-office returns. 'In 11 days they drew 120,000 lire!' he reported to Michele. By now he had shelved all thought of emigrating and was feverishly eager to start work on a new opera based on the Abbé Prévost's novel, *Manon Lescaut*, which he had read for the first time with excitement. Although it had already been triumphantly produced at the Opéra-Comique, a study of Massenet's vocal score convinced him that, instead of 'powder and minuets', the subject deserved true Italian passion and bravura. 'Manon is a heroine I believe in and therefore she cannot fail to win the hearts of the public', he wrote earnestly to Ricordi, who had at first doubted the wisdom of following an established success by a far better-known composer. After some hesitation he decided to call in a young librettist, Ruggiero Leoncavallo, then employed by the firm as a part-time editor and literary adviser. The son of a magistrate, he had studied the piano at the Naples Conservatoire before turning to composition. When barely twenty he had written both the libretto and music of his first opera, but a manager disappeared with the advance bookings before it could be staged in Bologna. He had then roamed Europe with a troupe of singers whom he accompanied on a little harmonium. In Paris he played the piano in cafés and attracted the notice of Victor Maurel, the celebrated actor-baritone who created the rôle of Iago in Verdi's *Otello* and had brought him to Ricordi's notice.

Leoncavallo drafted a treatment for *Manon Lescaut* which completely failed to please Puccini whose misfortunes had multiplied throughout that gloomy winter. He had expected a welcome sum of royalties from the promised revival of *Edgar* during the new season at La Scala, but the management pleaded, none too convincingly, that as the leading tenor had fallen ill and could not easily be replaced, the production would have to be 'postponed'. The news from Lucca was almost as depressing. He grieved at being unable to assist his sister, Nitteti, who had recently been widowed and left almost destitute. Furthermore, Dr Cerù was plaguing him to repay, with interest, what he now chose to call his 'loans', arguing that his dissolute great-nephew could apparently afford to maintain a mistress from his reported royalties of 40,000 lire from *Le Villi*. In fact he had earned less than 6,000 from that source over a period of six years and still owed Ricordi a vast sum.

By April 1890 he was again almost ready to emigrate to South America but made no mention of taking Elvira and the children with him. 'I'm weary of this eternal struggle against poverty', he wrote in despair to Michele, 'I would leave everything behind and go . . . Last night I worked until three in the morning and then had a bundle of onions for my supper . . .' His brother urged him to stay put, explaining that he was himself living in penury and seriously planning to return to Lucca.

Things began to look more hopeful after Ricordi had recruited two new librettists for *Manon Lescaut*; Marco Praga, a young playwright fresh to opera, and Domenico Oliva, a music critic and poet. Grateful for the opportunity, they soon produced a scenario and, by the early summer, joined the composer at Ricordi's villa on Lake Como for an exhaustive discussion. Among the house guests was Paolo Tosti, who generously praised their verses and promised to send a few practical suggestions from London. His approval finally decided Ricordi to commission the libretto and opera.

Puccini had returned to Milan eager to start work on the manuscript, but soon found the city too hot for comfort. Out of the blue came a letter from Leoncavallo, who did not seem to resent having had his draft turned down. He had taken a small chalet at Vacallo, a quiet resort on the Italo-Swiss border near Chiasso, and genially offered to find Puccini and his family something similar at a very modest rent. Elvira and the children, exhilarated by the prospect of a holiday, pleaded breathlessly for the chance of escaping from their stuffy rooms. Bags were packed in a matter of hours.

They arrived early in August and were amused to see a canvas sheet bearing the effigy of a clown (*pagliaccio*) hanging from Leoncavallo's window. He explained that it was the subject of his next opera. Puccini took the cue and soon flew a towel on which he had crudely daubed an immense hand (*la mano*), signalling his own work in progress. In this relaxed atmosphere the summer days drifted by. Elvira's bronchial cough, induced by over-smoking, benefited from the clean mountain air which also lifted her spirits. She laughed as she cooked tasty meals while the men drank wine in her kitchen and cracked rough jokes. The children adored Leoncavallo's fiercely upturned, waxed moustaches and loved prodding his paunch. Always perspiring, he used to peel off coat, collar and tie by turns while little Fosca fanned him with his floppy panama and tried to tip him out of the hammock.

For a time Puccini worked cheerfully on a rickety piano in the bedroom-studio, but he soon became disenchanted with the libretto. The writers had not only misinterpreted his *opéra-comique* view of Manon's character but had clearly copied Massenet's over-romantic style. He rewrote several scenes, angrily scrapping the entire dialogue of one act. His temper grew so uncertain that Elvira, now homesick for Milan, packed her things and left thankfully with the children. He stayed on alone in Vacallo throughout the autumn, only returning to Milan for a series of testy conferences with his unfortunate librettists. Praga lost all patience and indignantly withdrew. Oliva struggled on for a time until he too decided to cut his losses.

Ricordi sympathised with them but also saw the logic of his composer's objections. Throughout those stormy weeks, with revisions shuttling back and forth, he had himself made tactful suggestions for pruning a number of unnecessary episodes and had improved the narrative line by eliminating several minor characters. Puccini would later pay emotional tribute to this 'best of poets, mender of other men's faults', but Ricordi's contribution went far beyond that of helpful editor and banker. He listened patiently to an almost routine catalogue of grievances, sleepless nights and ailments which he suspected to be imaginary. Like others, he was partly deceived by Puccini's robust appearance. He had put on weight due to his excessive thirst, a symptom of long-undetected diabetes, and seemed blessed with a digestion which withstood starchy meals, endless cups of coffee and an addiction to cigarettes.

Ricordi handled him with gentle good-humour. 'Give me news in four lines of that model calligraphy which is one of your specialities', he wrote teasingly, 'but don't think of working if you don't feel entirely well.' Puccini had impulsively promised to deliver his score within a year, but almost eighteen months would pass before any real progress was made, with the assistance of yet another team of librettists.

Ricordi had switched to Giuseppe Giocosa, who lectured on drama at the Conservatoire and was an established playwright, poet and magazine editor. He seemed well-disposed towards Puccini but, knowing his reputation for prickliness, declined at first to take more than an advisory interest in the new opera. Instead he recommended Luigi Illica, the young author of several light comedies based on French sources. This alone would have made him an automatic choice for *Manon Lescaut*, but against this was his vicious temper and notorious drinking habits. One of his many duels had cost him an ear. On the credit side he fizzed with witty and original ideas and had so much creative energy that the Galleria wags called him 'Signor Perpetuum Mobile'. Tall, angular and exquisitely aristocratic, he prided himself on being a gastronomic virtuoso. He had owned a chateau where he gave lavish banquets during his flush periods, but he was hiding from his creditors when Ricordi commissioned him to prepare a new draft for *Manon Lescaut*.

Puccini was delighted with his first batch of manuscript. It sparkled with ingenious stage effects, but could not altogether conceal an absence of poetic insight and psychological subtlety. Above all, Illica lacked Giocosa's superb sense of construction. The squat, paunchy and egg-bald dramatist finally agreed to collaborate, but he would soon be clawing his Mosaic beard and bitterly regretting ever having shelved his own plays to please Ricordi. The arguments between the librettists, so complementary in talent but temperamentally opposed, often threatened disaster. 'Signor Perpetuum Mobile', eager to pocket his fee and resume half a dozen other projects, objected to Giacosa's quirky perfectionism, while both combined to oppose Puccini's policy of disputing almost every line. He would change verses, sometimes expunging entire scenes, even after agreement had been reached at night-long conferences. Somehow, Ricordi's tact and firmness kept this unruly troika running in more or less the same direction.

Puccini's difficulties with the libretto were aggravated by Elvira's attitude. She had developed an unfortunate tendency to compare him adversely with other composers, notably Mascagni, who was now tasting the sweet fruits of world success with *Cavalleria rusticana* after years of hardship. He had married his soubrette a week before the birth of their second son (the first had died in infancy) and had been living precariously by giving music lessons in the provinces, travelling about in a rickety farm-cart, when he decided to write his one-act opera, based on a violent peasant tale by the Sicilian writer, Giovanni Verga, and already dramatised with Duse as Santuzza.

He first sent the score to Puccini and asked whether it might be worth submitting for the second Sonzogno Prize, revived after its disastrous start six years earlier. Puccini was staggered by the crude Grand Guignol melodrama but reacted to its catchy beat and, most of all, Mascagni's skilful handling of crowd scenes. Recalling his own experience of Sonzogno, he urged 'Pietrino' to keep well clear of him and volunteered instead to show it to his own publisher, confident that he would welcome such a spectacular break with Wagnerian mysticism. Ricordi, however, dismissed the score as inferior, pointing out contemptuously that the orchestral Intermezzo, linking the two scenes, obviously derived from Puccini's *Le Villi*. His immediate reaction was an off hand, *Non ci tengo* ('I don't care for it'), a monumental misjudgment. Puccini reluctantly advised his friend to enter the opera for the Premio, meantime helping him to find private pupils in Milan. He also secured him a place in the orchestra at the Dal Verme where he played the double bass for a miserable three lire a night. After eight months of stress and misery, Mascagni won the Sonzogno award from seventy-three entries.

On 17 May 1890 *Cavalleria rusticana* was acclaimed at the Teatro Costanzi in Rome. Mascagni, almost buried in a suit too baggy for him, accepted congratulations from Queen Margherita and soon afterwards received the title of Cavaliere. 'Mascagnitis' became an operatic rage. His work was performed throughout Italy and he could soon take his pick from invitations to conduct in several foreign capitals. In

43

Belgrade a hysterical audience had refused to leave the theatre until the whole piece was repeated from start to finish.

Puccini showed no trace of envy and invited the new Cavaliere to a celebration dinner which Elvira cooked appetisingly at little cost, but she then skulked off, chagrined by Mascagni's elegant clothes and unbearable jauntiness. She could never bring herself to forgive him his easy success while Puccini was still struggling. Ricordi showed more realism, although with a similar lack of charity. Discovering that Sonzogno had omitted to acquire formal copyright in the prize-winning opera, he cynically waved a bulky chequebook but Mascagni refused to defect.

Ricordi was also snubbed by Leoncavallo, whose previous scores had gathered dust in the firm's files while he worked on *I Pagliacci*, a piece inspired by a murder trial over which his father had once presided. He had intended entering it for the prize won by Mascagni but the two-act structure made it ineligible. Sonzogno, stimulated by the furore over Mascagni's opera, shrewdly decided that *I Pagliacci* might well attract similar audiences. He hesitated no longer when Victor Maurel, the composer's patron, offered to play Tonio. Toscanini, by now establishing a reputation for inspired conducting (he had even uncovered hidden excellencies in *Le Villi* during a season in Brescia), was engaged to direct the first performance of *I Pagliacci* at the Dal Verme in May 1892. Its full-blooded libretto, gusty choruses and intoxicating arias like 'Vesti la giubba' created a pandemonium which was soon being echoed in dozens of opera houses outside Italy.

This overwhelming triumph, so quickly following Mascagni's, led to a two-pronged assault on Puccini. Racked by envy and weary of living in squalor, Elvira now taunted him with his snail's progress on *Manon Lescaut*, while Ricordi became rather less tolerant of his over-punctilious revisions. But he refused to be stampeded and continued to spend agonising weeks on the complicated Act III which he had deferred until the end.

The opera would undoubtedly have been completed earlier

but for his habit of breaking off to attend productions of his earlier works. Ricordi would sigh but he saw the practical benefit of a break for the harassed composer when Manon or Elvira became intolerable. He also recognised his valuable contribution at rehearsals when his sensitive ear seemed to raise singers and orchestras alike to higher standards.

His musicianship impressed the management of the Teatro Communale in Ferrara where a production of *Edgar* in 1891 started a lifelong friendship with the director's son, Giulio Gatti-Casazza. Then on leave from military service, he looked dapper in his officer's uniform and grey cloak compared with Puccini's shabby brown ulster as they strolled round the town, exchanging hopes and fears. Giulio had set his heart on becoming a concert virtuoso until warned that his hands were too small and delicate for the piano. He had studied mathematics instead and graduated as a marine engineer, but already spoke wistfully of one day taking over from his father. Puccini enjoyed his extravagant praise for *Edgar* but still brooded on his unfinished opera which had reached yet another impasse. 'If it doesn't succeed', he confided glumly, 'I too shall be forced to change my profession.'

His relationship with Elvira was now coming under severe pressure. She loved Milan and had almost reconciled herself to their shabby lodgings and the cheeseparing, for the occasional chance of window-shopping in the Galleria or rubbing shoulders with the well-dressed crowds. Puccini, however, had never felt healthy or at ease in the noisy city which he tolerated only to maintain an almost daily contact with his publisher and writers. Once satisfied, more or less, with the libretto, he made his escape.

In May 1891 they had spent a week or two in San Martino, some miles outside Lucca, while he persevered with his score and Elvira paid brief visits to her mother when Narciso was away on one of his business trips. But with Lucca practically barred to her, and San Martino only a poor exchange for the anonymity and bustle of Milan, she decided to stay with her

45

sister in Florence, taking Fosca with her. Within a day or two Puccini had words with the landlady who had somehow learned of Elvira's adultery. He left angrily for Lucca and lodged with Romelde, who made much of Tonio, looking like a midget cardinal in his little red plush cap. Elvira's mother also doted on the chubby-cheeked lad and used to bake him cakes and other delicacies, while Puccini made excursions into the countryside seeking a quiet place to work and bring up his family.

The weeks of separation were punctuated by reproachful letters from Elvira. She missed her lover and began torturing herself with nightmare visions of being abandoned. He objected to settling in Viareggio, which he thought pretentious and unattractive, and had discouraged her from joining him in Lucca, explaining that her presence at the opening of *Edgar* might stimulate her husband to have it hissed by a claque or even banned altogether. But after thirteen performances had played to full houses at the Giglio (later renamed the Teatro Puccini) and he still seemed in no hurry to send for her, she had every reason to be suspicious.

He was obviously enjoying the company of Caselli and other old friends who shared his taste for the unbuttoned laugh. When in drink he tended to boast about women and make bawdy remarks which would be reported back to Elvira by her family who had never ceased to denigrate him. His sisters retaliated by intercepting or destroying her letters. 'These pure women are capable of anything', he commented cynically to Elvira, while assuring her of his undying and exclusive love. In letter after letter to his adored 'Topizia' (little mouse) or 'Porchizia' (piglet) he urged her to ignore malicious gossip. 'I miss you, my poor angel, who are my all, my only hope in the world . . . You will see what little orgies we will have . . . The evenings are the worst, and the poor little bed without my Topizia: . . .'

He left in June for a progress conference with Ricordi, who now greeted him affectionately as 'Doge', a nickname which apparently originated in Puccini's habit of standing apart in drawing-rooms. He looked so out of place, carrying his large frame as if it needed more space, that one easily mistook his manner for aloofness instead of the mask of a shy man lost in a world of small-talk. When a word escaped him he would snap his fingers impatiently and puff at a cigarette. His trimmed smile also suggested arrogance but really camouflaged the gaps in his teeth caused by an addiction to sweetmeats and sugary foods.

During this visit he had been ceaselessly bombarded with pleas and recriminations from his 'Elviretta'. 'My only desire is to be able to finish *Manon* in peace', he wrote back. 'In November, if we can wait that long, I'll come and fetch you . . . Have faith in me; good God, what more can I tell you? You know I am your love and you are my only and true, holy love.' But with all his passionate longing for her he could not resist a characteristic touch of sadism. He had stayed in their apartment and, guessing how easily she could be inflamed, wrote of 'the adored bed, the sheets with certain suspicious spots . . .'

He kept his promise to send for her, although she did not approve his decision to settle in a dull backwater like Torre del Lago where he had spent the lonely weeks after his mother's death. In September he rented part of a house overlooking the lake. It belonged to the Marchese Carlo Ginori's head keeper and was adjacent to the watch tower once used as an outpost by a Bourbon nobleman who had presided over a small court near Viareggio. It offered a magnificent view of green valleys, ringed by deep pine forests, with an occasional glimpse of the aquaduct which ran out to the sea at Viareggio. Here he could at least breathe crystalline air and awake to the chimes of distant bells. The autumn months were wetter but far milder than in Milan, and there was promise of almost limitless duck and waterfowl on marshy Lake Massaciúccoli. After an undisturbed week or two on his opera, he went off to collect Tonio, who had been staying with his aunt and soon struck up friendships with the fishermen's children.

47

Elvira acclimatised far more slowly. A city-dweller by instinct, she had little in common with the village women. For a time, however, she was pleasantly anaesthetised by her reunion with Puccini and the excitement of setting up house after the cramped misery of lodgings. Puccini was soon composing into the small hours without fear of persecution from unmusical neighbours. The villagers liked him for his geniality and zest for shooting. Before long he was invited to join their card games at the tavern run by Stinchi de Merlo, a former cobbler. Instead of gloomily tramping the streets of Milan, sensitive to his darned suit and leaking boots, he could now lounge at Stinchi's in canvas trousers and rope-soled shoes, drinking the heady rough wine and playing *scopa* until the time came to leave for his evening meal. The food at Torre was both cheap and fresh. He relished lake fish baked and sprinkled with herbs, the regional cheeses and excellent water melons which flourished in the sandy soil, and there were local oysters to be swallowed by the dozen. Elvira had soon proved herself a resourceful cook, capable of producing dishes like *Quaglia alla cacciatora* (quail served with garlic, onions, spices and red wine) at surprisingly low cost for Ricordi or other distinguished guests.

She kept the house and her children scrupulously tidy, although Tonio had quickly fallen in with the village boys and usually returned from play with mud-caked hair and clothes. She tried to shield Puccini from being disturbed at work but could not always keep out the fishermen and bohemian painters who would burst in for card games and a bottle of wine when the weather was too inhospitable for fishing or shooting. Their slovenly dress and coarseness of speech affronted her sense of propriety, but she was partly consoled by Puccini's obvious contentment with village life. In Milan she had often resented his frequent visits to Ricordi and the librettists, dreading the possible presence of attractive wives and daughters. Now he seemed to welcome excuses not to leave Torre and even took to refusing invitations to attend productions of his operas.

Her domestic idyll came under unexpected threat when Tamagno, ceaselessly canvassed by Ricordi and the composer, agreed at last to sing the name-part in *Edgar* during his next season in Madrid. Overjoyed, Puccini at once put his score aside and began work on the earlier opera which he reduced to three acts. He also wrote a special Prelude of 108 bars in honour of the Queen of Spain, who had promised to attend the opening performance. In late February 1892 he departed for Spain with a healthy sum in expenses from Ricordi and an evening dress-suit loaned by a friend in Milan. He had soon wired Ricordi to send him studio portraits 'for the newspapers', but the publisher was not deceived. 'Take care of yourself because the climate of Madrid is specially treacherous at night, *without mentioning other things*! ! ! . . .' he wrote in friendly warning. 'Are the photographs for the newspapers or for some *señora?*'

He often took members of the company out to supper but found Tamagno far less congenial. The tenor would never pick up a bill and had a notorious reputation for smuggling chocolates, flowers and even candles from dinner parties for later use at his own table. Puccini was appalled by his stinginess but already showed symptoms of the same failing. In a letter to Elvira reporting a bad toothache which had led to two painful extractions and the expense of various pain-killing drugs, he complained angrily of being fleeced of 'a sack of money' by an American dentist who had charged him ten lire 'for two little pieces of roots'. He wrote almost every day to assure her of his passionate longing, but could not, as usual, resist touching a sensitive nerve; 'Yesterday I appeared as a prince in full-dress suit and high hat . . . Beautiful women in the boxes, but on the stage horrors (chorus girls and dancers horrible) . . . Nonetheless, there are certain types capable of raising one's trousers. But I am Topizio, the true Topizio. Do not worry . . .'

His opera was superbly sung and conducted but the audience received it coolly. Most of the critics offered only a brief and casual notice, one of them poking fun at the absurdities of the libretto without a word of praise for either the score or Puccini's melodious Prelude. He returned crestfallen to Torre del Lago but Ricordi encouraged him to resume work, mentioning that Verdi had enquired about *Manon Lescaut* and sent his good wishes. He tactfully kept silent about others who were busily disparaging the opera in advance.

Catalani's *La Wally* had been produced at La Scala with indifferent success. Although Toscanini conducted impeccably and would always consider Catalani a far more sensitive and accomplished composer than Puccini, the critics had deplored its strong Wagnerian bent and lack of true Italian fire. Poor Catalani, riddled with venom and tuberculosis, now accused his formerly enthusiastic publisher of betraying him for a flashy newcomer. He became almost paranoic when Ricordi announced in October 1892 that *Manon Lescaut* was now completed and would, in his view, soar above all contemporary works except those of the incomparable Verdi himself. He planned to stage it early in the new year at the Teatro Regio in Turin.

Puccini was already groping for fresh subjects, including a musical biography of Buddha. He fretted at Torre and began paying numerous visits to Milan, making panicky and often trivial corrections on the proof sheets of his new opera. Ricordi, then busily engaged on the imminent production of Verdi's *Falstaff* at La Scala, hit on the expedient of despatching his troublesome 'Doge' to Hamburg for a production of *Le Villi* under Gustav Mahler's baton, followed by another in Vienna, but Puccini hurried back, anxious to supervise preparations for *Manon Lescaut* and, above all, to rejoin Elvira.

It was a pattern which would become familiar over the years. Theirs was the almost classic dilemma of an abnormally sensual and egocentric couple who could not live in harmony for long periods but found it even more intolerable to stay apart. Boredom, melancholia and a morbid anxiety over his work often made him restless for a change of scene or another woman, while Elvira would vent her jealousy and insecurity in bitter reproaches. Yet within hours of parting they would be exchanging telegrams, postcards and letters affirming their love and longing for each other.

This feeling was sincere and mutual, but with one fundamental reservation on Puccini's part. He had no respect for Elvira's musical taste or judgment and found her presence irritating anywhere near the theatre while he was absorbed in rehearsals. At such times he could not tolerate her jealous tantrums or concern himself with details of hotel accommodation, domestic smalltalk and day-to-day trivia. As one of her closest friends, the soprano Gilda Dalla Rizza, wrote after Elvira's death, 'she was always around and always absent'. This exclusion, which she bitterly resented, had already started during their early years together in Milan. It became an established fact from the time he departed for Turin in January 1893. Elvira would receive almost daily bulletins on his health, the progress of rehearsals and even the ticket sales, but he did not ask her to join him.

Ricordi wisely decided not to stage *Manon Lescaut* at La Scala where Puccini's previous opera had been so savagely mauled. Moreover, Verdi's *Falstaff* was already being hailed as the operatic event of the decade. It could not fail to steal all the limelight, with the beloved veteran greeted like an emperor when he attended rehearsals. His hotel was besieged by journalists who buttonholed him for up-to-date news of every possible or impossible topic, including the state of his digestion. With enormous box-office queues already forming, it would have been suicidal to distract Milanese operagoers with claims for an almost unknown composer.

But Ricordi did not neglect his 'dear Doge' whom he joined in Turin for a day or two during the anxious weeks of preparation. Puccini was critical of the acoustics, the lighting, the singers and particularly the veteran conductor, Alessandro Pomé, whom he rated far inferior to Toscanini, now making a considerable reputation in Genoa and other cities. Above all, he would have preferred Leopoldo Mugnone, who had directed the first performance of *Cavalleria rusticana* and was to conduct *Falstaff* at Verdi's own request.

Ricordi assured him soothingly that all Milan's leading critics would cover the Turin première. Excellent publicity, reinforced by favourable reports on the rehearsals, had also guaranteed a complete sell-out. It was rumoured, quite without foundation, that Verdi himself would honour the opening, but Puccini was cheered by a loyal contingent from Lucca, headed by the pharmacist Caselli, and the last-minute arrival of Giulio Gatti-Casazza, who had recently succeeded his father as director of the municipal theatre in Ferrara. Catalani declined an invitation to attend and even wrote to Depanis, a prominent local critic, 'The truth I shall find, as usual, in your notice', plainly urging him not to be deafened by Ricordi's drums.

Manon Lescaut opened on 1 February 1893 in almost a gala atmosphere, with Princess Letizia of Piedmont in the Royal Box. Puccini sat at the back of a lower box chewing his fingernails while Elvira, with Fosca by her side, whispered comfort. Early in Act One the audience had already begun to applaud Manon's arias gracefully sung by Cesira Ferrani, a native of Turin and a local favourite, but few suspected that the madrigal in the next act had been salvaged and transformed by the composer from his *Agnus Dei* in the Mass written for the Lucca Istituto in 1880! Giuseppe Cremonini's 'Donna non vidi mai' was so wildly encored that Puccini had to join him before the curtain. Again and again he left his box to take bows between scenes, notably after Manon's gavotte and the poignant love duets in Act Four.

His melodic impulse clearly proclaimed an exciting new talent. Moreover, he had proved himself a born man of the theatre who could skilfully balance action with lyrical music. In this, the first of his operas for which he had chosen the subject and actively shaped the script, he had demonstrated his sense of construction, despite a certain unevenness inseparable from a libretto so mongrel that its various authors were not even credited in the programme. There were other and more obvious flaws. His eagerness for fast-moving action had made him jerk too abruptly from the shy Manon of Act One to the flashy courtesan. He was also guilty of a cheap theatricality absent from Massenet, who had also developed Manon's personality far more convincingly, but none could doubt the new opera's sheer tunefulness and vitality.

The whole audience stood up to cheer the composer who shared thirty curtain calls with the company and afterwards hugged Ferrani. Next day the critics unanimously applauded him for contributing to the best native tradition of 'lyric drama' by not sacrificing strong vocalism to over-orchestration. The influential *Corriere della Sera* opened its review with an ecstatic paean.; 'Puccini's genius is truly Italian. His song is the song of our paganism, of our artistic sensualism.' Significantly, Depanis had ignored Catalani's warning and also ended his eulogy on a note of high emotion, 'Last night was a good night for art and for Italy.'

It was also good for Puccini whose name registered abroad for the first time, thanks to extensive quotes from the reviews in numerous foreign newspapers and periodicals. Ricordi's son Tito swiftly negotiated lucrative contracts with impresarios in several European capitals and South America. Most Italian audiences greeted *Manon Lescaut* with an almost hysterical enthusiasm which Catalani vainly sneered at as 'Puccinianismo'. His own *La Wally* had been shelved by Ricordi who now seemed to have no time for anything but the works of Verdi and 'the little Maestro from Lucca', as his former friend contemptuously called him.

Soon after the triumphant première he was fêted at a banquet given in his honour by the local critics. The Mayor of Turin congratulated him on maintaining the tradition of Verdi whose *Falstaff* would open in Milan the following night. Puccini scribbled some reminders on his shirt-cuff and was about to make his speech of thanks when a clumsily spilt glass of wine made his notes indecipherable. Hoarse from chain-smoking, he could only stammer, 'Thanks to you all', before subsiding red-faced in his chair.

Like Mascagni he was soon decorated with the cross of

Cavaliere but would rarely wear the ribbon or use the title. He hurried away to shoot wild duck on Lake Massaciúccoli and took his ease at Stinchi's tavern, only returning to Milan for the Italian première of Massenet's *Manon*. It had a splendid reception, thanks to superb acting and singing by the principals, but without dimming Puccini's own triumph. Almost every post now brought him cheques and announcements of new productions of *Manon Lescaut*, including one in Cairo where an unknown young Neapolitan, Enrico Caruso, sang des Grieux for the first time. Ferrani was booked for a season in Buenos Aires which prompted Puccini to invite his brother to return and share his new prosperity. But poor Michele had contracted yellow fever and died before he could book a passage. As a sentimental gesture Puccini bought the old house in Via Poggio where he installed his widowed sister, Nitteti, and also kept his pledge to provide an organ for Iginia's convent in memory of their mother.

Nevertheless, he found some difficulty in feeling financially secure after so many years of poverty. With his first royalty cheque he acquired a cheap second-hand camera but Elvira had difficulty in persuading him to buy a new bicycle to help him lose weight. Although it cost only 220 lire, he made a small down payment and cautiously arranged for his publishers to pay the balance by monthly instalments.

If anything, he grew even more niggardly and would torture himself with visions of bankruptcy. He had soon repaid all the advances from Casa Ricordi but still demanded free supplies of score paper and his favourite Stephen's blue-black ink. He would spend hours bottling strawberries and cherries and arguing with Elvira over food bills, always claiming he could shop more economically. This was true, as he would often be deliberately undercharged for his fish, meat, oil and fruit! The villagers doffed their hats to the Marchese Ginori, but he failed to command anything like the same affection as 'Sor Giacomo', whose operas and amours had brought new colour to drab Torre del Lago. It was a lasting love affair on both sides which would never include Elvira.

Chapter Four

One of Puccini's first cycling expeditions took him into Lucca to lay flowers on Catalani's grave. That summer the doomed composer had left for a cure in a Swiss sanatorium but suffered a haemorrhage on the train. He was brought back to Milan and died in Toscanini's arms. Even on his death-bed he could not help rebuking him for having admired *Manon Lescaut*. 'Believe me, Arturo', he gasped, 'it is not sincere. And that man is not sincere.' Puccini nursed no resentment and paid tribute on each anniversary of his death. Toscanini later named his daughter 'Wally' after Catalani's opera, but would not allow sentimental regard for his friend's memory to alter his judgment of Puccini's work. In March 1894 he directed *Manon Lescaut* in Pisa where, only a few days before, a bomb had been thrown at him during a performance of *Otello*, apparently by some musician dismissed for incompetence.

Puccini had thanked him emotionally for his inspired conducting but could establish little rapport with the peppery Maestro whose manner matched the croaky voice and tight undertaker's suit. On the rostrum, however, he became a master swordsman, probing every weakness in his orchestra. Used to deference from provincial conductors, Puccini found himself barely tolerated at rehearsals, but he had left Pisa impressed by a subtle beat and a memory that enabled Toscanini, like Hans von Bülow, to conduct without a score.

Catalani's death had left vacant his Chair at the Milan Conservatoire. Puccini's old teacher, Bazzini, now Director, at once offered him the appointment but he courteously declined, having little taste for the academic world and even less for city life. He was impatient to return to Torre del Lago and smiled into his moustache at Ricordi's parting admonition to 'keep one eye at the gun sight but your thought on *Bohème*!'

The plan to adapt Murger's autobiographical sketches of the Latin Quarter had first taken root in Illica's nimble brain while he was still occupied with *Manon Lescaut*. Puccini had borrowed a translation of the novel which looked operatically promising, but he showed only mild interest until Giacosa agreed to collaborate on the libretto. Although now prepared to put Buddha aside, he was still unconvinced about *La Bohème* and had begun tinkering with a story by Giovanni Verga, who had provided such a rich vein for Mascagni. The current vogue for 'veristic' melodrama like *Cavalleria rusticana* and *I Pagliacci* now tempted him to study the Sicilian's work more closely. Soon he was pestering Ricordi to buy the musical rights in *La Lupa*, a violent tale of incestuous love culminating in murder during a religious procession. Ricordi privately thought the Murger subject a more appropriate successor to *Manon Lescaut*, but he had his own reasons at this time for cultivating the Sicilian writer, whom he knew personally and liked.

For some years Verga had shuttled between his native Catania and Milan where he was lionised in literary circles and enjoyed the close friendship of Giocosa and Boito. But his numerous affairs with aristocratic women had dissipated both talent and income. He was heavily in debt when Mascagni had adapted *Cavalleria rusticana* to reap a fortune for himself and Sonzogno. The latter, however, had behaved shabbily towards Verga, not only refusing to pay his rightful share of the royalties but even denying him a credit on the score, except in minute print and sometimes not at all. Verga at last won satisfaction but the acrimonious lawsuits left him so embittered that he returned home to melancholy semi-retirement attended by his 'Boswell', the young critic and novelist, Federico de Roberto.

Ricordi's flattering interest in *La Lupa* helped to restore his morale, severely shaken by a fickle public who had turned to the rising star, d'Annunzio, of whom he had grown pathologically envious. Eager to pursue his own vendetta with Sonzogno, Ricordi quickly commissioned de Roberto to write a libretto of the Sicilian story for a fee of 1,000 lire. This move came at exactly the right moment for Puccini, then smarting from his disappointing first visit to England.

He had felt disorientated almost from the moment he arrived in London in May 1894 for the première of *Manon Lescaut*. Although Paolo Tosti made him welcome and gave a dinner in his honour at Pagani's, nobody else had shown the slightest interest in the newcomer. Knowing hardly a word of the language, he was soon adrift at the Covent Garden rehearsals and found the management unsympathetic when he criticised singers or orchestra. He was unaware at the time that Sir Augustus Harris had been coerced by Tito Ricordi into accepting his opera as the price of presenting Verdi's *Falstaff* that same season.

He took several calls with the company after each act but could not deceive himself that his piece was more than moderately successful. The audience had applauded politely enough but almost all the critics showed such apathy that Harris felt justified in declining to repeat the production.* The composer returned home before seeing a notice in *The World* which might have comforted him although the name of the lone critic in his favour was then quite unknown to him. George Bernard Shaw thought Mascagni and Leoncavallo overrated and declared sagely that the author of *Manon Lescaut* looked to him 'more like the heir of Verdi than any of his rivals'. He also approved 'a genuine symphonic modification and development . . . of the thematic material, all in a dramatic way . . .'

That frustrating trip was more than a pinprick to Puccini's ego. It not only stimulated him to resume work on a new opera but may have tipped the balance in favour of *La Lupa* as

* The opera was not seen again at Covent Garden for a decade, while the Metropolitan, taking a cue from London, only decided to stage it after *Bohème* and *Tosca* had established themselves in New York, with Caruso's des Grieux as cast-iron insurance.

57

his next subject. While in London he had learned from Tosti that Leoncavallo's *I Pagliacci* had been last season's outstanding triumph at Covent Garden. Moreover, Queen Victoria had received Mascagni in her box to assure him that she felt 'moved to tears' by his opera. Such approval for violent melodrama could well have switched Puccini's attention towards the Sicilian story despite the many weary months Giacosa and Illica had spent on draft after draft of their libretto. They became even more vexed when Ricordi announced publicly that *La Bohème* had now been shelved and that the composer was about to leave for Sicily with his camera to absorb 'local colour'.

Early that summer he set out for Catania to confer with de Roberto on the draft script. He thought it promising enough, although rather over-stuffed with dialogue and, more seriously, lacking a sympathetic central character. But he was confident of making the necessary adjustments and was further cheered by Ricordi's agreement to pay all his expenses with *carte blanche* to buy native costumes which might be useful for a future production.

He at once took to Verga, whose lavish dinners were followed by salacious accounts of past bedroom acrobatics with some of Italy's most celebrated beauties. And de Roberto's willingness to listen to criticism was a refreshing change from his two prickly librettists back in Milan. The savage landscape also excited him and he spent fascinated hours listening to folk music, but time slipped by without sign of the first Act which he had promised Ricordi. After several weeks he was still dissatisfied with the plot and began to despair of ever visualising his heroine or disengaging her from a gallery of almost uniformly coarse characters.

At this point an unknown British soldier entered the scene and indirectly made operatic history.

For a diversion Puccini had booked himself an excursion passage to Malta. He took various innocent snapshots but, mischievously ignoring the warning of a military policeman, pointed his camera at the fortifications. He was promptly arrested and searched. His wallet disclosed a letter in which Ricordi, obviously referring to the dangers of giving unguarded newspaper interviews about his next opera, wrote 'Remember, please, that it is imperative you keep your mouth shut, and that you do not talk to anyone about your plans.' The soldier interpreted this as plain evidence of espionage and locked him up on suspicion. Further enquiries cleared him but this unpleasant experience had brought all his disenchantment with the libretto to breaking point. He returned angrily to Catania, took hasty leave of Verga and sailed for Leghorn. On the steamer he met Cosima Wagner's daughter, the Countess Gravina, who enjoyed his impressions of Verga but seemed horrified that he could even contemplate such a brutal subject as *La Lupa* after his exquisite Manon. 'It will surely bring you bad luck', she commented, an alarming prophecy for such a superstitious man.

It has often been implied that her views settled the issue, but Puccini had almost certainly made up his own mind during those gloomy hours in the police cell. Within a few days he was assuring Ricordi that he would 'plunge head over heels' into *La Bohème*, a decision no doubt reinforced by the rumour that Leoncavallo contemplated an opera on the same subject. The truth has never been precisely established; it seems that Leoncavallo had unwisely confided his plan to Ricordi, but there is no proof that he had also shown Puccini his preliminary notes.

Whatever the facts, his resentment burst like a boil when they met by chance in the Galleria later that summer. They had been chatting of old times when, to Ricordi's consternation, Puccini mentioned casually that he was currently engaged on a superb libretto derived from Murger's Latin Quarter romance. Leoncavallo became apoplectic, his Kaiser Wilhelm moustaches almost sparking as he accused Puccini of stealing the idea and even daring to make use of his libretto. Next morning Sonzogno's newspaper, *Il Secolo*, proclaimed that Leoncavallo was working on the Murger subject. Within hours Ricordi had countered in the *Corriere della Sera* with the news that Maestro Puccini's next opera would be entitled *La Bohème*, based on a libretto from the distinguished playwrights Giuseppe Giacosa and Luigi Illica.

Whether or not Leoncavallo's accusation had any validity, he had no legal title to Murger's novel which was now out of copyright. It is extremely unlikely that he had already written a libretto, even in rought draft, before that stormy Galleria meeting. As his own librettist and a fast composer, his opera would surely have preceded Puccini's if he had indeed advanced much beyond the stage of 'thinking aloud' or making notes. To forestall 'Kaiser Leoncavallo', as he now called him, Puccini began exerting more pressure on his unfortunate collaborators who, already angered by his own dilatoriness and vacillations, had no taste for panicky deadlines. Moreover, they were now at odds with each other. Illica disliked Giacosa's hair-splitting, while the veteran playwright objected to his partner's erratic 'Illicasyllables' and a long-winded first draft running to twenty acts. He also complained to Ricordi that, in attempting to please the over-fussy composer, he had used up more paper on a couple of scenes than would normally be required for the whole of one of his own plays.

During this exasperating period, with Giacosa regularly threatening to resign after re-writing some scenes four or five times, Puccini stayed away from Milan as much as possible. In the summer it was insufferably hot and the first autumn nip chilled him. Even on spring days when the light had almost a Swiss brilliance and a balmy breeze lifted the women's skirts or rustled the tablecloths of the Galleria cafés, an occasional chirrup of birdsong would make him homesick for Torre. Mainly to please Elvira, who found it convenient for shopping expeditions, he had taken an apartment in Via Verdi, near La Scala, but kept it barely furnished, with only a piano, a double divan, and a wardrobe for several dark suits of thick woollen cloth and Elvira's clothes. As soon as the first royalties from *Manon Lescaut* began to arrive, he had moved out of the cramped maisonette in Torre del Lago and rented a nearby villa with a large studio for his piano, books and manuscripts. The three comfortable bedrooms were more than adequate when nine-year-old Tonio entered a fashionable boarding-school at Varese.

The first act of his new opera may have been coloured by his own student days in Milan, but Torre also provided ready-made inspiration. After Stinchi the cobbler had emigrated to Brazil, Puccini put up some of the cash to buy his shack. It became the headquarters of the Club La Bohème whose members met most evenings to play cards and exchange ribald stories over tumblers of local-grown wine. As President he helped to formulate a constitution which Rodolfo and his friends would surely have endorsed. 'The members swear to drink well and eat better . . . Grumblers, pedants, weak stomachs, fools and puritans shall not be admitted . . . The Treasurer is empowered to abscond with the cash . . . The President must hinder the Treasurer in the collection of the monthly dues . . . It is prohibited to play cards honestly, silence is strictly prohibited and cleverness allowed only in exceptional cases . . . The lighting of the clubroom shall be by means of an oil lamp. Should there be a shortage of oil, it will be replaced by the brilliant wit of the members . . .'

Several of them volunteered as carpenters, handymen and gardeners to form a cheap labour force for the Puccinis. Gnicche was a sly and soft-voiced jack-of-all-trades whom Elvira dared not dismiss for rudeness because Puccini valued him too highly as a companion on his waterfowling trips. Arnaldo Gragnani had a small house opposite their villa and appointed himself unpaid major domo. He possessed a good musical ear and enjoyed the privilege, denied to Elvira, of having the maestro's compositions played over for his approval. A local woodsman, Manfredi, nicknamed 'Lappore' because of his white eyelashes, also did odd jobs about the house but was even more appreciated for his poaching talents. The rest of the members were bohemian painters like Marotti and Pagni, who together decorated the club walls with gaudy

61

and obscene frescoes, one of which significantly portrayed their president as the King of Hearts.

His escapades delighted them. Not suspecting his diabetic condition, they joked about his frequent urination which was gaily ascribed to exhibitionist pride in his organ. They took turns to row him across the lake to assignations in the pine forests from which he would often return exhausted, late at night, assuring Elvira that he had been trying to reach the open sea from the canal. He once spent many days in a forest shack entertaining an attractive young woman from Viareggio who, fortunately for him, also happened to be unusually muscular. One evening, when their rowboat capsized, he stunned himself against the side and she had to help him ashore.

Elvira must have observed that he clipped his moustache with unusual care for these frequent boating trips but his guile, aided and abetted by friends who often carried love notes, helped to cover his tracks. It was less easy to deceive Fosca, who worshipped him but without blinding herself to his faults. One drowsy afternoon while Elvira bustled about in the kitchen, they sat together lazily flicking through an illustrated book on butterflies. Fosca stared at him from long-lashed dark eyes and remarked suddenly, 'If I were in Mamma's place, I'd pay you back the same way.' He hung his head so contritely that she let out a peal of laughter and gave him a forgiving kiss.

He saw nothing unusual or immoral in dalliance, needing the catharsis of sex as other artists and writers crave alcohol. 'It is possible to write a march after drinking a pail of wine', he once wrote in self-justification, 'but for a love duet you must have a warm heart and a cool head.' Years later, nettled by Elvira's jealousy, he attempted to explain to her that his casual amours had no relevance to their own far deeper and more solid relationship, 'All artists cultivate these little gardens in order to delude themselves into thinking that they are not finished and old and torn by strife. You imagine immense affairs; in reality, it is nothing but a sport to which all men

62

more or less dedicate a fleeting thought without, however, giving up that which is serious and sacred; that is the family . . .'

But during those early days in Torre del Lago, before suspicion became painful certainty, Elvira rarely made scenes in public. He remained an enthusiastic bedmate and often repeated his promise of marriage if and when her husband departed this world. So far, despite Narciso's obesity and reported heart spasms, that seemed a distant prospect. Elvira shed private tears over Tonio's illegitimacy but he appeared insensitive to his bar sinister. A big-boned lad with a winning smile, he enjoyed his school holidays, fishing and bird-nesting with the village boys or endlessly cleaning his father's guns. In Lucca, Puccini's sisters spoiled him quite as much as his mother's family.

Suspecting that the villagers snickered behind her back, Elvira grew even less outgoing and would address tradesmen and servants with more than a hint of superiority. Although now wider of hip, she was still conspicuously erect and always looked the picture of city elegance in the high-waisted gowns made for her in Viareggio or by her sister's dressmaker in Florence. But she rarely ventured out without Fosca or Puccini, preferring to spend hours in her kitchen. Ricordi and other discriminating eaters would return to Milan with mouth-watering tales of freshly-killed birds roasted over a charcoal fire, and Giacosa's boot-button eyes misted over for weeks afterwards when recalling her *Cinghiale alla maremmana* (wild boar cooked with tomatoes and herbs, served with cheese).

Without such rare visitors—Ricordi was a particularly welcome guest—she found the village claustrophobic and would often invite her relatives to stay for long periods, despite Puccini's protests. They seemed to muffle the house in whispered secrets, but their presence at least gave him an excuse for renewed excursions 'to reach the open sea from the canal'. During their visits Elvira scoured each room with almost neurotic frenzy and smothered them with kindness.

She had no patience with Puccini's coarse companions, who often staggered back with him after an evening at the Club La Bohème. Scratching their groins and filling the house with the smell of tobacco and sweat-soaked clothes, they drank more wine and resumed their card games, keeping to one end of the study while Puccini sat at his upright Förster piano or made notes on the adjacent writing-table. He seemed to find their presence a stimulating background so long as they did not interrupt him. After they had departed he would settle down to serious composition, often continuing until dawn. Night work became a ritual once he was satisfied enough with a libretto to start on the actual score. He used to say that 'the weariness which comes with sunset stirs the imagination and the mind'.

Smoking almost incessantly and stimulated by coffee, he chewed his pencils while he wrote and rewrote scenes of *La Bohème* in the silent house. According to local legend his superb dramatic instinct was activated by a small model stage on which he moved his characters back and forth. This was pure fantasy, but undoubtedly he had a strong visual sense and often scribbled little sketches on a score to memorise a point. The habit even invaded his letters. When, as often, he used the phrase, 'touch wood', it would invariably be accompanied by the sign of two fingers touching to keep off the evil eye.

He would recite parts of the libretto out loud while marching back and forth, stopping only to make a hurried note when the words failed to match his rhythms. Wearing a scarf, cardigan and mittens, even on summer nights, he sweated profusely but kept the huge log fire blazing. He was ultra-sensitive to cold and draughts and wore his big stetson hat indoors, although his friends suspected that it was worn less for warmth than for a quick exit with his gun.

Mendelssohn used to find relief from the agonies of composition by counting the tiles on his neighbour's roof. Marshy Lake Massaciúccoli beckoned Puccini as soon as dawn streaked his window. He could rarely resist Manfredi's pebble signalling the appearance of duck or wildfowl, but had to outwit

Elvira, who often complained that he was neglecting *La Bohème* for his worthless playmates. Sometimes, when he had arranged to go shooting, he would smuggle in a friend to tinkle the piano for an hour or two while Elvira was stirring. By the time she had brought in his breakfast he would have sneaked back and yanked off his corduroy breeches, fisherman's jersey and heavy boots.

This hunting fever soon led to trouble. Accompanied by Manfredi, he went duck-shooting in the close season on the Marchese Ginori's estate across the lake. It was foolhardy as they had often only narrowly escaped being shot by the gamekeepers. This time they were caught because Puccini, standing tall in the rowboat, was spotted from the shore, although the watchman did not recognise him. By then the carabinieri had been summoned and it was too late to hush up the affair. Both were taken into custody and charged with trespassing and carrying firearms without a permit.

The case was heard at nearby Bagni San Giuliano and provided a merry outing for the Club La Bohème. Puccini's attorney pleaded ingeniously that his client was not out shooting but only looking for a suitable cabin to rent for the season. He argued that the defendants had carried guns to poke the reedy banks and ensure passage for their boat. According to him, their bags would certainly have been full instead of empty if they had been poaching. Puccini took this as a cue to jump to his feet and shout, 'I never miss a bird, do I, my friends?' His clubmates roared assent, although perfectly aware that he was anything but a first-class shot. The magistrate seemed too intimidated by the spectators and Puccini's name to make difficulties. He declared a verdict of 'Not Guilty' which encouraged the culprits to continue their poaching until Puccini was issued with an unrestricted shooting permit. He reciprocated handsomely by dedicating *La Bohème* to the Marchese, who became a lifelong friend.

Ricordi taunted his 'Sharpshooter and Doge' over the poaching affair, expressing mock regret that he had not been sent to prison, which might have expedited his work on the new opera. With valuable time already lost on *La Lupa*, it was not until the early months of 1895 that he began seriously to orchestrate *Bohème*, although continuously shredding the libretto. Ricordi acted as a buffer between writers and composer but found it equally difficult to keep Puccini from grieving over unflattering criticisms of *Edgar* and *Manon Lescaut*. He reminded him sharply that Verdi had always ignored such 'gnat bites', and in the autumn of 1894 reported from Paris where *Otello* was having its first production, that the Maestro was still clear-eyed and bursting with energy at eighty-one. According to Ricordi, who was not above flattering half-truths, Verdi had interrupted his almost non-stop drilling of singers, dancers, chorus and orchestra to enquire graciously about the progress of *La Bohème*.

Illica also chanced to be in Paris at this time, juggling with a libretto based on Sardou's melodrama, *Tosca*, in which Puccini had previously shown some interest. Ricordi agreed that it had operatic possibilities, but Sardou had shown no eagerness to hand his very successful play over to the then fledgling composer of *Edgar*. Puccini, soon preoccupied with *Manon Lescaut* and *La Bohème*, had almost forgotten the piece, but not Ricordi. He engaged Illica to sketch out a libretto which Alberto Franchetti would put to music with Sardou's blessing.

Baron Franchetti was the scion of a distinguished Turin family long connected socially with the Ricordis. By the whimsy of chance he had studied for a time with Puccini at the Istituto in Lucca before furthering his musical education in Germany. A devotee of Meyerbeer, his sound craftsmanship was backed by considerable wealth (his mother was a Rothschild) which helped him to finance and stage elaborate productions of his work. His *Cristoforo Colombo*, with a libretto by Illica, had been successfully produced in Genoa and La Scala while Puccini was still putting the finishing touches to *Manon Lescaut*. Although not outstanding for melodiousness, it had brilliant ensembles and demonstrated a skilful handling of big crowd scenes which had obviously attracted Franchetti to the potentialities of *Tosca*. He was delighted by Sardou's approval of Illica's story draft and became even more enthusiastic when Verdi, who happened to be present at the first reading, declared that but for his advanced years he would himself have made an opera out of it. Ricordi slyly relayed this scrap of gossip to Puccini who was too involved with *Bohème* during that busy autumn of 1894 to feel more than a passing spasm of irritation at the loss of such a promising subject.

Other possibilities were opening. In December he attended a banquet in Milan held in Zola's honour by the Society of Italian Authors, under Giacosa's chairmanship. Soon afterwards he started reading some of Zola's works in translation, among them *La Faute de l'Abbé Mouret*, the story of a young priest's doomed love affair. He was simultaneously turning over in his mind the possibilities of a score based on the life of Marie Antoinette which the indefatigable Illica had already sketched out in scenario form.

Throughout 1895 he worked almost continuously on *La Bohème*, even declining to join a shooting-party on Ginori's estate, but he broke off briefly in February to visit Milan for the opening of *Ratcliff*, the romantic tragedy which Mascagni had begun during their student days at the Conservatoire. At the celebration supper afterwards, Mascagni took him aside and promised to conduct a forthcoming production of *Manon Lescaut* in Leghorn, hinting that his baton might entice the crowds in his native town. After Leoncavallo's surliness the gesture was so welcome that Puccini kissed him on both cheeks.

His unfortunate librettists received far more slaps than kisses. Having had his dialogue curtly dismissed as 'too poetic', Giacosa declared haughtily that he wanted no payment at all for his months of toil and threatened to withdraw. Illica was too short of money to make such a gesture but defended himself by playing a double game. He used to prod Puccini to work faster by over-praising Franchetti's *Tosca* score, while simultaneously baiting the baron with the excellence of *La Bohème*. Franchetti could be difficult over revisions but nothing

67

like as tiresome as Puccini, whose rash of almost indecipherable criticisms ruined Illica's eyesight and his digestion. He had often to be placated with soft words or a hamper of gastronomic delicacies. This became standard practice whenever Puccini had gone too far and driven even the patient Ricordi to the very edge. On one occasion, to excuse himself for quibbling over certain scenes, he sent the publisher two boxes of grapes as a peace offering and 'some very special beans' for which he enclosed a detailed recipe. Without Ricordi the opera might never have been completed. He managed to keep a truce between Puccini and the librettists with a quite remarkable blend of guile and applied psychology. He would nurse Puccini through frequent spells of melancholia while judiciously dosing the testy couple with flattery. In dozens of private but valuable acts of kindness he eased Puccini's burden. Fosca recuperated from an illness at his holiday villa in the Dolomites and was warmly invited to return the following summer with her mother.

The libretto had at last surfaced with a crisp and clear story line from two years of agonising preparation during which the last act had been re-written four times. The score itself was composed in little over eight months. Before the last act had been orchestrated, Ricordi had already begun to enthuse over the composer' subtlety in ringing the changes between feverish gaiety and sadness with superb vignettes like Musetta's Waltz, which Puccini had originally composed as a piano piece. Ricordi could already visualise enormous sheet sales for both Rodolfo's dreamy 'Che gelida manina' and the passionate moonlit duet 'O soave fanciulla'. The final scene, with the lovely phrases from previous acts forming an effective background for Mimì's last song, confirmed Puccini's originality and his astonishing advance in orchestration.

In view of what followed it was obviously no sudden whim of Ricordi's to urge his 'Doge', during the final frenzied days of composition, to go and see Sarah Bernhardt's performance in Sardou's *Tosca*, then hypnotising Italian audiences. Accompanied by Elvira, he duly visited Florence on 9 October 1895.

Although understanding only a few words of French, he could easily follow the whole action. Not for nothing had Sardou proclaimed his credo, 'A well-contrived play, like a good novel, can be told about in three minutes. One minute for the subject, one for action and plot, and one for the dénouement.' It was a maxim which Puccini translated into operatic terms by removing any sub-plots and historical details that threatened to clog the action.

As Ricordi had foreseen, he again became excited over *Tosca* without, however, sharing the audience's acclaim for Bernhardt's acting which he thought lifeless. (She was ill and had forced herself to go on stage rather than disappoint the public.)

Ricordi promptly organised a Machiavellian plan of almost breathtaking unscrupulousness. With Illica's approval he had decided to pass his *Tosca* libretto over to Puccini, who was naturally overjoyed but took no active part in the 'conspiracy'. Illica suddenly refused to tolerate Franchetti's finicky revisions while Ricordi further undermined his confidence by insisting that the sordid theme was ill-suited to his talents and almost certain to alienate his public. As anticipated, Frenchetti hurriedly abandoned all work on the score and agreed instead to attempt a comic subject. Within hours Illica and Puccini had formally arranged to take over the opera, with the distinct possibility of Giacosa once again being conscripted. Thus assured of another subject, Puccini could now work on *La Bohème* with far more peace of mind.

It was completed at Torre just before midnight on 10 December 1895. As he wrote the last notes of Mimì's death scene, Puccini later recalled, 'I had to get up and, standing in the middle of the study, alone in the silence of the night, I wept like a child. It was like seeing my own child die.' Characteristically, this sentimentality soon gave way to an outburst of animal spirits. Early next morning he wired his pharmacist friend, 'Opera finished. Come!' Caselli arranged for a party of friends, all dressed in outlandish costume, to travel from Lucca. At the little railway station in Torre they were joined by members of the Club La Bohème who jigged, with fife and drum, all the way to Puccini's villa where he received them wearing an imperial toga and a brass helmet. For once Elvira lost her severity and kissed each of the guests, even Pagni, while the pharmacist dispensed tumblers of bubbly Asti. Puccini did not forget to send Illica a hamper, followed by a gigantic Christmas cake, flatteringly inscribed, for Giacosa.

He departed with Illica for Turin early in January to supervise three weeks of rehearsal, leaving Elvira behind with the familiar excuse that he could not submit her to lonely hours in a hotel room while he was at the theatre. She was spared a disagreeable experience. He criticised all the arrangements and grew morbidly certain that Ricordi had blundered in staging the production in Turin. He would have preferred Rome or Naples, which promised better lighting and acoustics, but Ricordi reminded him of the *Manon Lescaut* triumph in that very theatre. He was also persuaded to accept Toscanini, who had opened that season in Turin with a superb *Götterdämmerung*, its first Italian performance. Puccini still sighed for Leopoldo Mugnone, but soon reported to Elvira that Toscanini was 'highly intelligent and a very sweet nice man'. The company had rather different views after being rehearsed daily for six hours at a stretch and often past midnight! However, he had endeared himself to the composer with a perfectionism that forced stage crews to work in stockinged feet during each scene change. More important, it soon became clear that he was distilling every subtle nuance from the music.

Toscanini apart, Puccini objected to almost everything else even after the lighting and costumes had been improved. His suggested cast would have bankrupted any impresario, as Ricordi wearily informed him, but he had good reason to criticise the mediocre Gorga (Rodolfo), and Wilmant, 'a terrible actor', in the rôle of Marcello. He was reassured only by the selection of Cesira Ferrani, his first Manon, who would

70

sing Mimì. He continued to write grumbling notes to Elvira but could not help teasing her; 'I have a bunch of letters to answer including the thousand bores who want first-night tickets, and women who want to make an appointment with me. Ah, I seem to hear you! But be easy in your mind. I won't answer'.

With zero hour approaching he grew sensitive to every adverse whisper. Tito Ricordi had mounted a lavish publicity campaign for the opera, including the display of huge posters which some critics condemned as vulgar and too garish for their municipal theatre. Sonzogno was also spreading false reports that he had seen Puccini's score and judged it far inferior to his client's *La Bohème*, now nearing completion. Moreover, Leoncavallo was said to have booked a block of seats for himself and several of his admirers to form a hostile claque.

Puccini took comfort from two favourable omens; the opera would open on the third anniversary of his triumphant *Manon Lescaut*, and Princess Letizia of Piedmont would again occupy the royal box. Her presence, he prayed, might help to nullify Leoncavallo's 'evil eye'.

Chapter Five

Leoncavallo could not bring himself to witness his rival's probable triumph, and his friends had to bite their lips among an audience plainly moved by the opera's sentimental passages, particularly the driving pathos of Mimì's death scene. There was generous applause for 'Che gelida manina' and the Musetta Waltz, although many resented Toscanini's stern ban on encores. He conducted flawlessly but failed to camouflage the deficiencies of the leading tenor and baritone who fell short of Ferrani's quality. Summoned to join Princess Letizia for the third act, Puccini had cowered at the back of her box, discomfited by a reception that was anything but ecstatic except for the showpiece arias and duets. He took five curtains but left the Regio to spend a sleepless night worrying about the reviews.

The Press was chilly. Several critics expressed disappointment after *Manon Lescaut*, while the local Wagnerians, still intoxicated by *Götterdämmerung*, sharpened their pencils on what seemed a syrupy confection by comparison. The few who noticed and approved its harmonious blending of music with dialogue were far outnumbered by others who dismissed the piece as 'empty and puerile'. One hinted darkly that it would not survive until the end of the season, and Sonzogno's newspaper sneered that 'Puccini reminds one of himself too insistently'. A scribe from the *Gazzetta del Popolo*, who had previously failed to interest him in one of his own libretti, asked, 'What has pushed Puccini on this deplorable road of *Bohème*?'

Deflated and melancholy, he would have returned at once to Torre del Lago but for his anxiety to make a few changes in the rhythmic pattern of the opera and some adjustments to the action in Act Two. By the time he had delivered the corrected autographed score to Casa Ricordi at the end of February, *La*

Bohème was already confounding the local critics by playing to full houses. Rome, however, had received it so coolly that he became anxious about the forthcoming production in Naples, particularly over the choice of conductor.

At this stage of his career he was far less concerned with vocalists and often repeated the Berlioz dictum: 'A bad singer only damages his own part; the incapable or malevolent conductor ruins everything.' Fortunately, Ricordi did not take him too seriously when he insisted that Arthur Nikisch should be engaged for San Carlo. Puccini had met the picturesque little Hungarian and succumbed to his lock of hair, foppish lace cuffs and exquisite tailcoat. Ricordi had some difficulty in convincing him that Nikisch's histrionics in the pit might make the ladies swoon but would certainly infuriate the Neapolitan claque with its implacable hatred of all foreign artists.

While they wrangled over Naples, the whole future of *La Bohème* was about to be decided in, of all places, remote Sicily which still held painful memories for Puccini. He had half-heartedly agreed to supervise a production that April by a second-rate company in Palermo. Leopoldo Mugnone would conduct, although horrified to learn that the piece would open on Friday the thirteenth. He shook his head gloomily when the impatient Sicilians started hissing a delayed curtain-rise due to the late arrival of an oboist, but before the end of the first act they were clamouring for encores. They refused to leave the theatre even after some of the orchestra had departed with their instruments and Ada Giachetti (Musetta) had already changed. She and the other singers were recalled again and again until Mugnone had to repeat the whole of the last scene with his depleted orchestra. It was a night of such delirium that every Italian newspaper carried reports, swiftly reprinted in many other countries. The publicity was invaluable to Ricordi's salesman son Tito, who soon arranged productions for England and Latin America.

Palermo gave Puccini a most welcome fillip after some weeks of acute irritation over *Tosca* which Illica had shelved

73

while concentrating on a new opera by Giordano. Ricordi had hopefully passed his draft libretto to Giacosa, who at first declined to collaborate on 'a drama of gross emotional situations, without poetry'. He thought the Sardou play no more than a vehicle for some showy actress like Bernhardt; by contrast, the lyrical qualities of *Bohème* had more than compensated for a weak plot.

While Ricordi continued to woo the poet, Puccini was unprofitably exploring several alternative subjects. Zola informed him that he had more or less promised *La Faute de l'Abbé Mouret* to his countryman, Massenet. His hope of adapting *Pelléas et Mélisande* was also dashed by a visit to Ghent where Maeterlinck wearied him with accounts of the prize bulldogs he bred, and finally announced that Claude Debussy would set his poem to music.

Puccini's nail-biting weeks of frustration ended with Giacosa's reluctant surrender. By August 1896 the first act of *Tosca* was already in draft and, within three months, most of the remainder. Giacosa, anxious to return to a play of his own, had produced his verses with unprecedented speed and was soon gently chiding the composer for spending too much time on frivolities like his new yacht, *Mimì I*, instead of replying promptly to letters. Puccini would counter-attack with a mass of ink-blotted revisions which always led to an angry conference, with Ricordi again trying to keep the peace.

Nevertheless, they co-operated far more harmoniously than in the past. The librettists were now familiar with each other's quirks while Puccini had obviously gained in confidence from the success of his last two operas. This time, moreover, they had the benefit of Sardou's well-constructed play with its crisper story line. The delays were not due to writing difficulties or Puccini's sporting excursions at Torre del Lago, which he willingly abandoned to receive or visit Ricordi and Illica, but his frequent trips to supervise productions of *La Bohème*. In February 1897 he broke off a series of story conferences to prepare the La Scala company for a first performance under Mugnone. Two months later, accompanied by Tito Ricordi, he left sunlit Milan for the cold, rain and choking soot of Manchester where the Carl Rosa would stage an English version, entitled *The Bohemians*.

Rehearsals tried his patience as he could not follow the translation and thought the singers almost grotesquely un-Latin. But he became more sociable, thanks to a friendly management, and one afternoon he frivolously shaved off half his moustache, so that Tito had to implore him to remove the rest before going down to dinner. Although rehearsals had been unpromising and he disliked the circus-like arrangement of the orchestra, with the bass and drums sited at each end of the stage, the piece was so warmly received that the company promised to repeat it at Covent Garden that autumn. In the train back to Euston he was in uproarious mood and amused the London critics with his broken English and some mimed impressions of the Mancunian Rodolfo.

A fortnight later he was relieved to hear that Leoncavallo's *Bohème* had signally failed to win the expected laurels at its opening in Venice. It had dramatic power but audiences missed the tenderness, sparkling humour and sheer enchanting lyricism of Puccini's version which Toscanini, while on honeymoon, conducted to capacity houses at a neighbouring theatre.

Italian babies by the thousand were now being christened 'Mimì'; municipal bands never tired of playing excerpts from Puccini's opera; scores of sopranos trilled Musetta's Waltz, and every other tenor in the land seemed eager to sing Rodolfo. One of these hopefuls travelled specially to Torre del Lago from Leghorn where Ada Giachetti was preparing to repeat her previous success in Sicily, but this time as Mimì. The company included her lover, who was so enthusiastic to take the leading rôle that he had offered to sing without fee and for only his living expenses of 15 lire a day. His voice and style seemed ideal, but as he happened to be under contract to Sonzogno, the local manager naturally hesitated to risk offending the powerful Ricordis. Giachetti, a woman of much determination, persuaded the young tenor to dare all by demanding an audition from the composer himself.

In June 1897 while Puccini was busy on *Tosca*, his handy-man announced that someone had arrived unexpectedly to plead for an interview. 'He speaks like a Neapolitan and calls himself a singer,' growled Manfredi. 'A runt of a fellow with a bit of a moustache. Wears a hat to one side and calls himself Caruso.'

'That street singer from Naples!' snorted Puccini. 'Tell him I'm busy.'

Manfredi shook his head. 'I've told him but he still refuses to leave.'

Puccini, wearing his soft wide-brimmed stetson, linen trousers and slippers, got up from the piano and shambled irritably to the door. '*Chi è lei?*' ('Who are you?'), he shouted. Caruso laughed nervously and entered, singing Rudolfo's answer, '*Chi son? Son o un poeta*', ('Who am I? I am a poet').

Puccini roared with laughter and admitted him to a studio so hot with its blazing log fire that Caruso, already sweating nervously, wanted to remove his jacket but dared not risk offending his host. He attempted 'Che gelida manina', explaining modestly that the high C at the end sometimes gave him trouble. Puccini assured him that it was not compulsory. 'Too many sing the whole aria badly just to hold themselves for the C', he observed. Nevertheless, Caruso accepted the challenge and sang so blamelessly that the composer swivelled round in his chair and murmured in astonishment, 'Who has sent you to me? God?' He promptly wrote a note to the manager in Leghorn, commanding him to engage the little Neapolitan.

Caruso sang the opera twenty-eight times that season to wildly approving audiences, including Puccini, who brought Elvira and Fosca with him and often stayed overnight to supervise rehearsals. 'I have been in Puccini's house and have sat down to eat with him at his table . . . He treats me like a brother,' he reported warmly to his teacher and agent. 'I have been pushed two years ahead in my career through having been chosen by him for Rodolfo.' It would prove a mutually profitable association, with the advantage tilted in favour of

Puccini, who had gained an always superlative interpreter, even for his lesser operas.

He coached Melba painstakingly for the London première of *Bohème* in Italian, hopeful that Covent Garden would improve on a scratch production at Wallack's Theatre in New York, which the *Tribune* had dismissed as 'summer operatic flotsam and jetsam'. Melba stayed six weeks in Lucca where he often visited her hotel and went through the score with her, bar by bar. She recalled that he talked in staccato bursts and would perch shyly on the edge of his chair, only becoming animated when he sat down at the piano to play a medley from *Manon* and *Bohème* for her pleasure. He annotated her score, dedicating it to 'the Mimi of my dreams' in what she afterwards described, quite incredibly, as 'his neat little hand-writing'.

With an increasing number of house guests and the extra space needed for his guns, music scores and accumulating para-phernalia, he welcomed the Marchese Ginori's generous gift of a site formerly occupied by his first home in Torre, now a ruin. He started to build a new and larger villa, leaving room for a garden fronting the lake. It was at first amusing to approve plans but before long he protested that his work on *Tosca* kept being interrupted by architects and builders, quite apart from Elvira's chattering relatives whose visits had become tiresomely regular and prolonged.

He was already suffering from the Lucchese weakness for moving house, the *mal della pietra*, which could be indulged by a man of means and rationalised as essential to an artist needing to retreat from time to time. Early in 1898 he had bought a small estate at Monsagrati near the village of Chiatri, some miles north of Torre and about 1,300 feet above sea level. Ringed by pine woods and with spectacular views of the Tuscan mountains, it gave some relief from the fierce summer heat of the valley, but he was soon forced to smoke cigars almost continuously to repel the mosquitoes. There were other disadvantages. Once a piano had been hauled up from Lucca, almost all other human contact ceased. The postman took his time delivering letters and grumbled at having to climb the rough country roads even with telegrams. The dozen or so peasant families kept to themselves and Puccini, sleeping most of the day, would rarely meet a soul when he took his evening donkey ride before starting work on the piano sketches for *Tosca*.

Elvira had briefly enjoyed the novelty of driving about in a farm wagon but the cart tracks rattled her bones and she could seldom coax a smile from the villagers. She also complained that the thin mountain air affected her breathing. Backed by Fosca, even more depressed by this forbidding eyrie, she begged Puccini to cut his losses and sell the place. He refused and stayed on alone to continue scoring his first act, but by early May he was more than thankful to leave for the first production of *La Bohème* at the Opéra-Comique.

He arrived during a spell of abnormally cold and rainy weather and was soon writing to his friend, Caselli: 'I am sick of Paris and panting for the fragrant woods, for the free movement of my belly in wide trousers and no waiscoat . . . I hate the steamer, the top-hat and the dress-coat!' He forced himself to be polite to reporters but found excuses not to accompany Tito Ricordi to receptions. 'Money disappears in Paris with nothing to show for it,' he groused to his publisher who had to send him a money-order for 2,000 lire, quickly followed by another. He was flattered at being asked by Boldini to sit for a pastel portrait but less so when a textile manufacturer marketed a new foulard in a depressing colour he called 'Caca de Puccini'.

At the Comique he was irked by jobs left half-finished and repeated postponements of the première. He complained bitterly to Ricordi of his failure to 'infuse a little Italian vitality into these passive workmen'. Albert Carré, the handsome autocratic manager, seemed to regard any criticism of his singers, musicians or stagehands as almost a national insult. *La Bohème*, staged a month later than the scheduled opening date, pleased the public, although the critics, Massenet admirers to a man, aired their dislike of an impertinent foreigner who had made himself unpopular at rehearsals and could not be cornered for small talk at *soirées*.

The one positive benefit from this wretched visit was an opportunity to see Sardou who had invited him to dinner but kept putting him off through illness. They met at last when Illica arrived in Paris and insisted on discussing his libretto with 'The Magician', as Puccini nicknamed him. Sardou shared his own terror of draughts and received them in an overheated room, wearing a voluminous muffler and a beret.★ Throughout dinner he poured out such a torrent of amusing anecdotes, punctuated by his pet expletive, '*Saperlipopette!*' that Illica for once had to play prompter while Puccini, giggling helplessly, tried to memorise some of the stories. He was adroit enough not to be drawn into a wrangle over the composing rights for which Sardou demanded 50,000 francs. (He later accepted fifteen per cent of the gross takings—a far more profitable arrangement.)

Over coffee, liqueurs and *millefeuilles*, Sardou's great weakness, he cross-examined Illica shrewdly and agreed, after some argument, that the second Act of his play might be excised and the prison cell scene merged into the execution. Without warning he abruptly asked to hear the score. Puccini had so far completed little more than part of Act One, but he managed to rattle off a pot-pourri on the piano, skilfully interspersing the *Tosca* music with snatches from earlier operas. Sardou, now mellow with food and drink, applauded generously and proposed a future meeting when the score and libretto were more advanced, hinting that he might have some thoughts for the final scene.

Puccini quickly left Paris, eager to resume work on *Tosca* and assure himself of his family's safety. There had been two attempts on the life of King Umberto, with alarming

★ His death was accelerated by contracting a severe cold, followed by pneumonia, while presiding in a chilly wind at the unveiling of Rodin's statue to Henri Becque. Ironically, his own memorial statue was first erected at the draughtiest corner in Paris, the *carrefour* of the Madeleine.

newspaper reports from Milan of eighty people killed in street riots and Rome in almost a state of siege. Once satisfied that Elvira and Fosca had come to no harm in sleepy Torre, he went up to Monsagrati, too hot that June for anything but night work. Living mainly on his usual pernicious diet of cigarettes and coffee, he made steady progress but missed Elvira in his bed and the cheerful card games at the Club La Bohème. At two o'clock one morning he wrote to Caselli, enclosing some butterflies; 'Let them remind you that when evening comes we must all die. While I am racking my brain in the silence of the night to give colour to my Roman heroine, I am executioner to these poor frail creatures.' But by dawn he had recovered and ended his letter facetiously, suggesting that the druggist might distil some new drug from the corpses to benefit sufferers from toothache and elephantiasis! 'In the eighteenth century they were used as a snuff excellent for scouring the noses of parish priests,' he solemnly assured Caselli, who appreciated the joke.

Puccini had written several times to various clerical friends in Lucca, imploring them to send him the exact Latin words of a prayer for the solemn *Te Deum* in his first act. Nothing arrived, due either to their laziness in replying or, more likely, the erratic village postman. In despair he turned to Father Pietro Panichelli, whom he had met in Rome some months earlier. The priest was helpful and would later confirm the correct order of the Cardinal's procession together with minute details of the uniform worn by the Swiss Guard.

That autumn he visted Rome to thank Panichelli and attend the première of Mascagni's new opera, *Iris*. Based on a libretto from Illica's busy pen, it had been published by Ricordi who discovered sadly that Mascagni had little gold dust in his pan after *Cavalleria rusticana*. But the evening was not entirely without dividends for Puccini. He had been intrigued by Mascagni's choice of a Japanese heroine and also greatly taken with the Rumanian prima donna, Ericlea Darclée, whose voice and beauty had already captivated La Scala audiences. Still a far sounder judge of orchestras than acting, he over-charitably ascribed her coldness to Mascagni's deficiencies and convinced himself that she would make an ideal Tosca.

After leaving her dressing-room, he went off to supper and listened with only half an ear to his neighbour, Giovanni Pozza of the *Corriere della Sera*, who mentioned casually that a promising libretto might be made from *Two Little Wooden Shoes*, a novel by the expatriate English writer, Ouida. Puccini, then preoccupied with *Tosca* and still uneasy about his next meeting with Sardou, thanked him politely and dismissed it from his mind.*

He had a useful meeting with Father Panichelli whom he questioned closely about the Matin bells at St Peter's with which his Act Three would open. The good-natured little priest introduced him to a friendly cathedral organist, but Puccini took the additional precaution of mounting the ramparts of Castel Sant' Angelo at dawn to listen to the exact pitch of the *campanone*.

On the way back to Torre del Lago he stopped off in Milan for talks with his librettists. Illica, spinning like a tornado between half a dozen other projects, objected peevishly to every correction, but the more benign Giacosa seemed delighted at their almost miraculous progress by comparison with past experiences. He assured Puccini that Sardou could not fail to approve the libretto, backed by his fine score.

In genial humour for the first time in months, he also enjoyed an emotional reunion with Giulio Gatti-Casazza, the newly-appointed business manager of La Scala. His old friend from Ferrara had now cultivated the Assyrian beard which, with his hooded bloodhound eyes, made him easy prey for generations of caricaturists, but he was not yet the solemnly forbidding figure who would intimidate even the most temperamental prima donnas. He embraced Puccini and excitedly confided his plans for the celebrated opera house which had been closed for months, due to such a disastrous sequence of sloppy productions, with half-empty houses even for Verdi,

* The Ouida project would be revived many years later with serio-comic consequences for both Puccini and Mascagni (Chapter Twelve).

that the municipality had finally withdrawn its subsidy. It would re-open under the joint administration of the Duke Visconti and Boito, who had been energetically lobbied by Puccini, Mascagni and others to engage Gatti-Casazza, with Toscanini as his conductor and artistic director. They had pledged themselves to weed out inferior artists and attract back audiences with a traditional but well-produced national repertoire, while still making room, at Toscanini's strong insistence, for Wagner, Debussy and other 'foreigners'.

The new régime had been welcomed so warmly in musical circles that Puccini was quite taken aback by Ricordi's tight-lipped hostility when he chanced to mention Toscanini's name. He was unaware that, during his last season in Turin, Toscanini had bluntly rejected a composition submitted by Ricordi under a pseudonym. Later, hearing the story behind the vendetta, Puccini was careful to stay neutral. Like Verdi he still considered Mugnone superior to Toscanini, but he respected the younger man's artistic integrity and almost fanatical dedication. Moreover, although loyal to Ricordi at all times, he was not blind to the practical advantages of having two good friends in charge of La Scala.

He often joined them for supper at the Ristorante Cova, a pleasant refuge from the more fashionable Galleria where too many unemployed singers would stop hopefully at his table, although sometimes a pretty soprano or chorus girl could be persuaded to 'audition' privately at his apartment in via Verdi. The Cova was also the haunt of a tall and elegantly tailored baritone, Antonio Scotti, whom Gatti intended to engage for *Falstaff* in his first season. He was an easygoing, open-handed bachelor who did not appear to mind being teased about his large nose or a recent love affair which had gone sour.

Isidore de Lara was another habitué with a reputation as a ladies' man. Puccini had met him once or twice in the Ricordi offices or at Boito's receptions and occasionally saw him cycling furiously through the city, a fantastic figure with his cavalry officer's moustache, deerstalker and spruce knicker-bocker suit from Savile Row. A Londoner by birth, he was of

The composer's parents. Michele gave him his first organ
lessons. Puccini was devoted to his mother, Albina, and
wore her wedding ring all his life.

The Cathedral of San Martino, Lucca, where Puccini's ancestors all officiated as choirmasters and organists. He was the first to break the tradition.

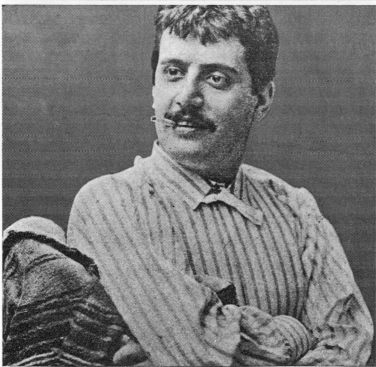

(top) Puccini in his student days at the Istituto Musicale, Lucca. (below) Before the opening of his first opera, *Le Villi*, in Milan, 1884.

Elvira in Rome for the disastrous première of *Tosca*, January 1900.

The composer with librettists, Giacosa and Illica. Their brilliant collaboration, starting with *Manon Lescaut*, ended after a decade with *Madama Butterfly*.

Enrico Caruso. Still unknown when first auditioned by Puccini, his superb interpretations of Rodolfo, Des Grieux, Cavaradossi and Pinkerton won world acclaim.

Sybil Seligman, Puccini's devoted friend and confidante for twenty years.
They were first introduced by Paolo Tosti, Mrs Seligman's singing
teacher.

With the London merchant banker, David Seligman, and his wife, Sybil, during a visit to Puccini's villa at Abetone in the Appenines.

aristocratic Sephardic origin with a gentle manner which often misled incautious anti-Semites or anglophobes. He happened to be an excellent amateur boxer who sparred daily with his valet, an American ex-pugilist, and as a leading light of Milan's Fencing Club, he was the last man to challenge to a duel although many a wronged husband had been tempted. Among his numerous loves was a beautiful French princess whose Riviera hotel he used to visit in the small hours to avoid scandal. Their secret liaison was exposed by a punning rival who followed him one night and nailed a card to the bedroom door, announcing 'Ici dort de Lara'.

He needed little persuasion to recall his amours but always turned serious whenever music was discussed. He listened attentively to Toscanini and praised Puccini's scores with obvious sincerity. So far his own operas, based in style on Saint-Saëns and Massenet, had enjoyed little success outside France. He seemed confident that La Scala's less chauvinistic new policy might favour his latest work, *Messalina*, which would shortly be staged at Monte Carlo with Calvé as the voluptuous empress and Tamagno in the gladiator's rôle.

It had been a stimulating interlude but Puccini seldom regretted leaving Milan. At Torre he celebrated his fortieth birthday and Tonio's twelfth with a family party on 23 December 1898,* but was soon afflicted with melancholia. With both his opera and the new villa unfinished, life had become a vacuum. He haggled over the substantial advances demanded by the contractors and resented every day lost through bad weather or the indolence of workmen. He vented his ill-humour on Tonio who almost welcomed returning to boarding school after a dismal vacation. He had cheerfully lent a hand on the building site when he was not fishing or sailing, but Puccini sternly ordered him back to his violin scales. Unfortunately, he had inherited his father's physique without

* Puccini was born on 22 December, his son on the 23rd, but for years he would insist that the latter was his correct birthday. It may have pleased his idiosyncratic fancy to claim the same birthday as his son. A combined celebration would certainly have appealed to his thrifty nature!

a trace of musical talent. After hearing him scrape away on his violin, Puccini had cracked it over his knee and tossed the pieces into the lake. Fosca, on whom he had always doted, was also treated roughly. Now a pretty and flirtatious twenty-year-old, she had no shortage of admirers, but each would be ridiculed in turn by her over-possessive 'stepfather'.

He was plainly suffering from the early signs of 'middle-age syndrome', aggravated by his poor physical condition. His throat was constantly inflamed by cigarettes and he drank far too much coffee while working at night. Although he went out shooting and sailed his boat when Lake Massaciúccoli was mist-free, his outdoor sport involved little muscular effort. His bicycle now rusted in the shed. He had grown heavy, slept badly and often walked with lagging steps which reminded him unpleasantly of his years. For reassurance he sought more and more sexual diversion. Still unaware that his headaches and listlessness were diabetic symptoms, he continued to gorge sugary dishes. He ate too fast and disliked using a fork, preferring to extract the full flavour of oil and sauces with a large spoon. The heavy meals, washed down by rough wines, affected his digestion and temper. Caselli now supplied him with an armoury of lozenges, powders, tablets, hair dyes and lotions, apart from 'elixirs' to improve his extra-marital performances and also disarm Elvira's suspicions.

His inner tension, manifested in nail-biting and a morbid sensitivity to weather changes, could be soothed by lovemaking, but the more normal outlets for relaxation were closed to him, both intellectually and temperamentally. He escaped eagerly enough to the sea, woods and mountains but his appreciation was sensual rather than aesthetic and gave only temporary relief. His music rarely exhibits any instinct for Nature. He remained insensitive to scenery, except as a backcloth to his moods and valued the countryside purely for its solitude, during his most painful working crises, or as an arena for killing birds and animals ('Ah! to be out shooting where there is really some prey!... It is the supreme moment when the spirit is at rest', he once wrote to gentle Father Panichelli.)

Literature meant little or nothing to him, although he enjoyed dipping into a pocket copy of Dante's *Divine Comedy* on railway journeys. Unlike Verdi, who had a library of several thousand volumes at Sant' Agata and a bookcase four feet high by his bed, he would only pick his way hungrily through novels or biographies recommended to him as possible libretti. Blinkered by introspection and almost completely immune to the glories of art and architecture, he relied on a romantic dream world rather than the fruits of personal observation.

In his last two operas these defects had been more than balanced by stagecraft and a sure instinct for translating sentimental drama into lyrical or forceful musical terms, but during the bleak winter of 1898 he felt far less confident of sustaining his new tale of cruelty and horror despite a close-knit libretto. His melodies could soften its brutalities but, whereas Manon and particularly Mimì had touched his heart, Tosca's anguish moved him far less.

With the whole of Act One scored and the rest of the opera already sketched out, he left gloomily for Paris in January. Sardou, in sprightly mood, soon shrugged off his misgivings. 'It's all the same thing,' he laughed. 'Women in love all belong to the same family.' When Puccini hinted that a French composer might feel more at home with the play, he disagreed bluntly, '*Tosca* is a Roman work which needs your Italian song.' He also scoffed at his suggestion that even Verdi had found the subject too intimidating, reminding him that the Maestro was nearly eighty when he wrote *Falstaff* and had never intended to compose anything but a few short sacred works in his last frail years. He smiled even more cynically on being reminded that Franchetti had also 'abandoned' *Tosca*. Both were perfectly aware of the shabby manoeuvre which had given Puccini his chance.

'The Magician' would boast later that he alone had saved the opera from being abandoned. The truth was that Puccini had only needed reassurance midway through a challenging score. Nevertheless, Sardou contributed a number of shrewd ideas for lightening the libretto and seemed impressed by

Puccini's dramatic flair. They disagreed only over the finale. Sardou had made a sketch of the panorama and jabbed his finger at a huge map of Rome on the wall of his study, declaring that Tosca should leap into the Tiber from the ramparts of Sant' Angelo. He made light of Puccini's objection that the river flowed some fifty feet away on the other side of the Castello, but yielded with an airy, 'Oh, that's nothing!'

Puccini had benefited in morale from this brief visit. Paris was enjoying an unseasonably warm spell and he could promenade on the boulevards without Tito Ricordi bustling at his side or rushing him off to tiresome receptions. Albert Carré invited him to see Bernhardt in a revival of Sardou's play at the Opéra-Comique, and he dined once or twice with Marcel Prévost, who complimented him in excellent Italian on his *Manon Lescaut*.

He returned to Torre with gifts for Elvira, Fosca and his 'dear and beloved Don Giulio', who was even more delighted when the score of Act Two arrived ahead of time in mid-July. He rhapsodised over Tosca's emotional prayer 'Vissi d'arte, vissi d'amore' and was already making provisional plans for Mugnone to conduct the première. However, the shortish final act led to a bitter argument with Illica who had written a Hymn to Life and Art for Cavaradossi to sing before the execution. Puccini preferred a more poignant and less philosophical lament appropriate to the aria 'E lucevan le stelle'. Giacosa smiled pacifically and lumbered off to his villa to write new verses.

The scoring went, in Puccini's words, *'piu che benone'* (at top speed). He worked almost every night but most days managed two or three hours of water-fowling with Manfredi. He resisted all invitations to attend productions of his earlier operas and even refused to meet any of the women who often sent photographs signed, 'Your Mimì'. His business correspondence, normally answered without delay, went unattended, but he congratulated Isidore de Lara whose *Messalina* had survived a last-minute crisis brought about by Tamagno's meanness. During his American tour, he had insisted on being supplied with wax candles in his dressing-room although electric light was available at the Metropolitan and other opera houses. He returned to Europe with a huge trunkful of candles on which the Italian Customs demanded full duty. Tamagno refused to go on to Monte Carlo until the impresario, Raoul Gunsbourg, who was already paying him 10,000 francs a performance, had settled up for the duty and released his candles!

With his own opera at last moving to its climax, Puccini grew altogether more relaxed, only flying into a rage when Fosca threatened to marry a feckless young cellist whom he detested. He had some support from Elvira, who was enjoying a welcome spell of serenity and had considerately spared him visits from her relatives. He rewarded her, quite exceptionally, by singing and playing excerpts from his opera for her approval. When Mugnone arrived for a run-through of Act Three, he was surprised to find their ménage so easy-going and good-natured, contrary to all the Galleria rumours of violent quarrels.

By the end of September the opera was completed but for a short Prelude to the last act for which Puccini still needed a quatrain in dialect to suit the shepherd boy's wistful offstage song. After Mugnone's enthusiasm, he was less prepared for a most disagreeable letter from Ricordi, who now appeared to dislike the whole structure of the final act and fully endorsed Illica's original conception of the Hymn. He also condemned the use of 'fragmentary' music from the long-discarded Act Four of *Edgar* for the doomed lovers' final duet. Puccini did not yield, although tactfully offering to 'run over to Milan and discuss it together, just *we two alone*, with a piano and with the music in front of us'.

'Papa Giulio', racked by rheumatism and feeling his years, side-stepped the invitation but he stood his ground in refusing to stage the première in Milan, reminding Puccini that his operas had never been treated too gently in that city. Although Rome still seethed with discontent after parliament had been closed by royal decree, a general political amnesty was expected on 31 December, a clear fortnight before the opening of *Tosca*. Since the opera was set in the capital, it seemed to him the logical venue.

Puccini agreed, but he remained very nervous of the ultrasnobbish, conservative Roman public. For this reason he withheld the leading tenor rôle from Caruso, who was enjoying a successful season at the Teatro Costanzi. Puccini embraced him with genuine affection and passed him over for an established local favourite, Emilio de Marchi, who had a far more romantic stage personality than the tubby little Neopolitan but lacked his exceptional beauty of voice. It was a mistake of judgment paralleled by his choice of the stiffish Rumanian soprano whose Tosca needed Caruso's dramatic intensity.

The company also missed Giulio Ricordi's urbane diplomacy. His son, Tito, was so determined to triumph in his first major production that he bullied the chorus while tending to pamper the principals who had more need of discipline. He had soon antagonised the local critics by excluding them from all rehearsals. They sniped back at him through a German-born scenic artist whom he had dared recruit from La Scala in place of the resident designer. Morale slumped even more when an almost daily batch of unpleasant anonymous letters began to arrive at the theatre for Puccini. Most of them seemed to be inspired by Franchetti's partisans, who claimed that he had been 'robbed' of *Tosca*.

Tense and unhappy without Giulio Ricordi's soothing presence, Puccini had broken all precedent by asking Elvira to join him during the last anxious weeks of rehearsal. She calmed his nerves and was careful to avoid irritating him with trivial family gossip or any recriminations when he had late suppers with Darclée. She steeled herself to keep away from the theatre and sympathised when he reported his backstage troubles. Slowly he grew more optimistic as Tito began to demonstrate his undoubted genius for publicity. He had arranged lavish hospitality for all the leading Italian and foreign critics, including a number from the United States and Canada, even installing a telegraph service in his office for their convenience. The Prime Minister, General Luigi Pelloux, and the whole of his Cabinet had accepted invitations to the première which had attracted the most glittering names in Roman society. Gossip writers had been bribed or cajoled to predict such a brilliant operatic event that all the reserved seats were snapped up for the first three performances.

At midnight on the last day of the year Puccini stood with Elvira on the balcony of their hotel suite to hear the bells of St Peter's and other city churches booming a majestic welcome to the new century. He had shed all his previous nervousness about *Tosca* which would open in a fortnight. 'This time I am in good hands; management, orchestra, artists and conductor', he wrote cheerfully to Father Panichelli. 'We shall see if my instinct is right.'

It seemed appropriate, indeed almost symbolic, that the Royal Box would be occupied on the opening night by Queen Margherita, whose modest bounty had first liberated him from an organ loft in provincial Lucca.

Chapter Six

Lengthy queues had already formed for unreserved seats by noon on Sunday, 14 January 1900. The company had been drilled to near exhaustion by Tito Ricordi, yet a quite abnormal air of tension hung over this particular première. Although the government had kept its pledge to pardon political offenders, disquieting rumours persisted that some kind of demonstration was being planned against General Pelloux, who had not been forgiven for ordering his troops to open fire on street rioters. Just before the curtain went up, a police officer bustled into Mugnone's dressing-room and advised him to play the National Anthem if anarchists attempted to assault the Prime Minister or, as was feared, tossed a bomb into the Royal Box. He intimated that Queen Margherita and her retinue would enter the theatre by a side-door during the first interval. Mugnone became very agitated but, fortunately, could not warn Puccini, who was still holding court in a *caffé* opposite the Costanzi. His well-wishers included some bohemian friends from Torre del Lago, all in boisterous spirits and brandishing heavy sticks which they swore to use on any hostile claque.

The theatre was buzzing as he slipped quietly into the back of his box with Elvira. Some of the audience had jeered the Prime Minister but gave no hint of violence. Franchetti was cheered and a roar of recognition went up for Mascagni who, ostentatiously sporting his Cavaliere's ribbon, made an actor's entrance, bowing left and right to acknowledge the applause.

The curtain rose as the chattering audience finally subsided, but others were still milling about in the foyer. The opening bars could scarcely be heard for angry shouts which Mugnone mistook for the first signs of an affray. He dropped his baton in panic and locked himself in his dressing-room until Tito assured him that some late-comers were merely trying to locate their seats in the dark. He went back but his nervousness inevitably rattled the principals. In the circumstances they gave sound performances, Darclée winning several encores, although de Marchi was ineffective except in their duets and his aria 'E lucevan le stelle'.

Puccini, pale-faced, took a few calls but none at the end of Act Two. The audience seemed numbed by the torture scene which had played to shocked silence. The final curtain fell to some applause, but with nothing remotely like the first night enthusiasm for *Cavalleria rusticana* in that theatre. Puccini was congratulated by the Queen and perhaps a shade too effusively by Mascagni, but only Tito Ricordi seemed ebulliently confident of success. At supper he kept reminding the gloomy composer that his last opera had captured world acclaim after an even more uncomfortable baptism.

Most of the critics praised his skilful orchestration but plainly disliked the harsh melodrama. Some conveniently forgot their own strictures on *La Bohème* and now sighed for its lyrical tenderness. A minority noted that only the brilliant score had salvaged a story top-heavy with violent action. Mascagni echoed that view in a newspaper interview; 'I have been victimised by poor libretti. Puccini is the victim of a libretto that is too good.'

His sympathy, if sincere, proved misplaced. Darclée and de Marchi would never succeed in characterising their rôles as effectively as successors of superior calibre, but after the tense first night they raised their performances and played to capacity for the rest of that season. While Tito Ricordi was arranging productions for other Italian opera houses, apart from Buenos Aires, Covent Garden and the Metropolitan New York, Puccini returned to Torre del Lago. The new villa was almost ready. His studio, designed as a combined second dining-room and study, had a ceiling attractively criss-crossed with heavy beams. During his absence one of his bohemian friends had completed the gay wall panels which portrayed a sequence of changing hours, from dawn to dusk. Once the piano had been installed, with a side-table and racks for his scores, he filled the alcoves with a profusion of shrubs and potted palms. The studio led to a small gunroom where he spent hours of delight with his rifles, trophies and stuffed birds. Almost every day pieces of furniture, comfortable but not luxurious, arrived from Florence, Pisa or Milan. Manfredi and others worked in shifts to clear the garden after fitting zinc screens on all the windows to keep out the mosquitoes which had plagued Puccini in his former villa.

His exhilaration at moving house soon faded. He shot, sailed and wrote letters but brooded dismally on Fosca's infatuation with her 'downtrodden fiddler' whom he had reluctantly steered into a Milan orchestra. To keep his mind off 'the sweet and beloved thing who must one day fly the nest', he immersed himself in Debussy scores which only made him more anxious to start work on another libretto. 'I am sick to death of being *inoperatic*', he wrote gloomily to Elvira from Brussels where he was attending rehearsals of *La Bohème*. He then darted off to Paris to see Charpentier's *Louise* at the Opéra-Comique. He sat inconspicuously well back in the stalls and applauded the piece with distinctly mixed feelings. It had been rapturously received by every French critic who praised the charming blend of atmospheric realism and lyrical day-dreaming. Several had indirectly complimented Puccini by noting and approving certain echoes from *La Bohème*, thereby confirming his own instinct to return to a more romantic genre. Rome's initial response to *Tosca* still rankled, and La Scala's opening performance on 17 March gave no comfort. The production was technically admirable and Toscanini had thawed the Rumanian soprano, but the critics remained half-hearted about the score and almost unanimously condemned the subject as distasteful.

Puccini arrived back in Torre, feverish for a gayer libretto. He urged Illica to re-read Daudet's *Tartarin de Tarascon* and draft him a scenario, but could not convince Giacosa of its operatic potential. The genial poet received him most hospitably at his home near Parella, and set all his chins chuckling at Tartarin's adventures, but nothing could persuade him that Puccini had a comic bent. While Illica was still preparing an abortive draft (for which Ricordi would yet again have to foot the bill), Puccini had already had second thoughts. He was briefly attracted to both Hugo's *Les Misérables* and Rostand's *Cyrano de Bergerac*, but Ricordi had doubts about his ability to handle such predominantly masculine themes. None of his previous heroes, even with strong arias, had possessed anything like the emotional appeal of Manon, Mimì and Tosca. The life of Marie Antoinette seemed to him a far better prospect than Tartarin, but Puccini refused to make a final choice until Illica's draft was ready.

Early in May, while visiting Milan, he poured out his troubles to Paolo Tosti, who had returned home with his wife for their summer vacation. He sympathised with the composer's desperate need of a suitable libretto and introduced him to Gabriele d'Annunzio, whose latest novel *Il Fuoco* had wagged almost as many tongues as his flamboyant politics. He had been elected as a right-wing deputy but crossed the floor of the Chamber to declaim 'On one side there are men half dead, and on the other a few who are alive, so as a man of intellect I shall move towards life.' He predicted the government's imminent downfall, but Puccini steered him gently back to his own immediate dilemma. D'Annunzio adjusted a monocle, combed his scented, faun-like goatee and languidly promised an early visit to Torre del Lago with half-a-dozen ideas. A month later, still without a word from him, Puccini went off to London for rehearsals of *Tosca*.

He was warmly greeted at the Savoy Hotel by Scotti, who would be singing the first of many memorable Scarpias. Tosti often entertained them at Pagani's where they met several sociable countrymen including Denza, the composer of 'Funiculì, Funiculà', and the convivial Carlo Pellegrini who had made a reputation in England with his biting caricatures for *Vanity Fair*. Puccini was flattered at being invited to autograph the wall of an upstairs room already adorned by signatures such as that of Tschaikovsky, who had written his name across a bar or two of music.

Pagani's became a regular rendezvous but he was made almost as welcome at the Savoy where the Italian waiters would sometimes neglect other guests to encircle his table. The maître-chef offered to 'create' a special Tuscan dish for him, obviously to emulate Escoffier's 'Pêche Melba', but Puccini declined the honour. He also refused to follow Mascagni's precedent in demanding celebrity treatment by the hotel staff. Recalling their seedy days in a Milan attic, he was amused to learn that during a recent visit to London his fellow-composer had lost a trunk containing dozens of shirts and no fewer than 176 collars in transit from his laundry in Leghorn.

He overcame his dislike of wearing full evening-dress—*de rigueur* in the mahogany-panelled Savoy Restaurant—and supped there two or three times a week. He looked embarrassed, although secretly gratified, whenever the orchestra signalled his arrival with selections from *La Bohème*. He was often the guest of Melba or her close friend, Lady de Grey, one of London's most brilliant hostesses and a powerful influence in the backstage politics of the Royal Opera House where her husband, a prominent member of the governing syndicate, dutifully echoed her views. An elongated Renaissance-type beauty with an imperial manner possibly inherited from her Czarist forbears, she disliked symphony concerts but had a fanatical devotion to grand opera. She had endorsed Covent Garden's policy of engaging top-ranking stars like Jean de Reszke, and approved its recent face-lift, with new electrical equipment and safety curtain, a larger stage and the whole auditorium refurbished in red plush.

Puccini had won her favour in advance thanks to Melba's triumph in *La Bohème* during the previous season. She asked him to one of her musical soirées, followed by an invitation to share her box with the Tostis for a Verdi production. He was dazzled by the liveried attendants and the tiers of elegant gowns, tiaras and boiled shirts, but disapproved of the almost continuous hum of chatter which would not have been tolerated at La Scala. (He could almost believe the story of a talkative dowager who had cancelled her box when she lost her voice!) But he was agreeably surprised—and relieved—at the absence of any claque.

In the first interval Tosti had pointed out all the duchesses and wealthy box-holders like Alfred de Rothschild, a bachelor aesthete and art connoisseur who complimented Puccini on his music and soon gave a reception for him, with Patti among the guests, at his mansion off Park Lane. Next day he visited Rothschild's château-like Halton House in Buckinghamshire and inspected his miniature circus from a zebra four-in-hand driven by the eccentric host in full ringmaster's regalia. Regrettably, he had no opportunity to hear the private symphony orchestra which de Rothschild used to conduct with a diamond-studded ivory baton, but had to listen instead to his hypochondriacal litany of symptoms.

He was lionised by the Italian colony whose hospitality helped to console him for the chilly weather. At the Embassy he attended a banquet in his honour after a splendid performance of *La Bohème* so ecstatically received that he became more and more optimistic about *Tosca*. 'The theatre is completely sold out,' he reported gleefully to Elvira. 'I hope to have a great success because the artists are very good ... better than at La Scala. I am most always invited out, tonight also. I went to dine with some friends at Maxime's, where there were plenty of *cocottes*. What elegance and what beauties! But afterwards we went home quietly, quietly like good boys. A hundred thousand kisses. Topizio, who is going to bed.'

The rehearsals were somewhat rushed. He missed Tito Ricordi's punctilious attention to detail but could rarely fault the principals, who made their predecessors seem quite second-rate by comparison. Fernando de Lucia had the voice and presence for Cavaradossi, Scotti's interpretation of Scarpia was superbly in character, while the Croatian soprano, Milka Ternina, hitherto excelling in Wagnerian rôles, gave Tosca's tragic moments almost unbearable pathos. Puccini considered her 'Vissi d'arte' a little too Germanic in emphasis, but she would remain his ideal Tosca until Jeritza's spectacular advent.

The opening night on 12 July 1900 attracted a fashionable audience who greeted the opera almost as frenziedly as the excitable Italians in the cheaper seats. Puccini was beckoned from his box by the conductor, Mancinelli, and went forward with him, hand in hand, to acknowledge roars of applause. Some critics remained cautiously non-committal about the score, but all praised the quality of the performances, singling out Ternina and Scotti for special bouquets. Next day a flood of advance bookings confirmed that the opera would surely take its place in the repertory with *La Bohème*.

Puccini's nagging sense of being 'inoperatic' returned almost as soon as *Tosca* had been successfully launched. He had seen a few plays but nothing of potential interest until he was recommended to look at a one-act piece, *Madam Butterfly*, currently thrilling audiences in a double bill at the Duke of York's Theatre. Based on a magazine story adapted and produced by David Belasco, it was nearing the end of a capacity run. Londoners had reacted almost as tearfully as New York to the love-doomed geisha. With his limited vocabulary Puccini could absorb little of the stilted dialogue in pidgin English, but he had no difficulty in following the simple plot. He was enchanted by the picturesque settings and moved by pathetic Cio-Cio-San, although one questions whether he had 'rushed backstage, with tears in his eyes', as Belasco recalled, to beg for a chance of buying the operatic rights. If so, it was astonishingly out of character. He rarely wept except at funerals, and was far too diffident to behave so emotionally with a complete stranger. Nor had he previously conducted business without consulting Ricordi, who had burned his fingers on Mascagni's *Iris* and might have hesitated before embarking on another Japanese subject. But *Madam Butterfly* had undoubtedly excited Puccini enough to congratulate its author and hint at a possible operatic adaptation. He may have been hypnotized by the ebullient Belasco, whose cloud of silvery hair and semi-clerical collar gave him the air of a fallen bishop hastily reincarnated on Broadway. Years later, backed by hindsight, he claimed almost total recall, if not clairvoyance, about that first meeting with Puccini, 'I never believe he did see *Madam Butterfly* that night. He only heard the music he was *going* to write.'

Such rapture does not square with Puccini's unhurried return to Italy. Instead of hastening back with news of his discovery, he spent a few days in Paris checking on a newspaper report that Leoncavallo had been given exclusive rights to adapt Zola's *La Faute de l'Abbé Mouret*. A mutual friend sounded out Zola, who at once scotched the rumour and again confirmed that Massenet had first refusal. The Daudet project was another cul-de-sac. A third-rate French composer, who had already adapted Tartarin's adventures for a mediocre operetta, would not part with the rights which he claimed (wrongly, it turned out) as his exclusive property. One disappointment followed another. It soon became clear that little could be expected from d'Annunzio, now absorbed in politics after the hated government's collapse in June, followed a month later by King Umberto's assassination.

These irritations had sharpened Puccini's appetite for the adaptation rights in *Madam Butterfly* which Ricordi, although not enamoured of the subject, instructed his New York office to negotiate. But Belasco seemed in no hurry to proceed beyond the preliminaries. Puccini spent restless summer weeks at Torre either on shooting parties or speeding in his motor boat with an attractive shipmate smuggled on board at Viareggio. He also amused himself in Ginori's new car, the very first imported into Italy. He was soon able to take the wheel himself but drove far too recklessly for the Marchese's comfort.

Meanwhile, he flitted between new productions of his operas, usually enjoying sexual diversions in transit. He hurried from a performance in Lucca to supervise another in Genoa, stopping off at Pisa to await the night express on which he had reserved a double sleeper. While pacing the platform with a young woman, he was recognised by a neighbour of one of his sisters, who soon wrote to reproach him for not calling on her. Unfortunately for him, she also mentioned his 'beautiful companion', whom she had been unable to identify from her friend's description. As he planned to be away for several weeks, Elvira had opened the letter and at once taxed him with cruel infidelity. He replied contritely but accused her of being in part to blame; 'You are no longer the same, your nerves dominate you, no longer a smile, no longer an open mien . . . You are unhappy? I am doubly so . . . In my own house I feel myself more of a stranger than you do . . .' As expected, this thrust at her relatives quickly put her on the defensive, and she had almost forgiven him by the time he returned to Torre. A spell of passionate lovemaking, followed by the gift of a pair of diamond earrings, brought reconciliation. Although never a generous man, he knew exactly when to make judicious peace offerings.

Elvira wore the earrings on their very next visit to Milan. While he was in conference one morning with his publisher, she sat in the waiting-room flipping the pages of a magazine. One of the directors stopped to kiss her hand and ventured a heavy-handed joke. 'I see some beautiful diamonds paid for by Ricordi,' he laughed. 'And I see some luxurious offices paid for by *Bohème*,' she retorted stiffly.

By now *Tosca* was filling opera houses. Audiences, no longer shocked by the sombre melodrama, responded almost frantically to its music. During the winter months of 1900 Puccini was constantly gratified by the applause for his duets and arias even when given by average singers. He had missed the performance of Caruso and Ada Giachetti at Treviso, near the Austrian border, but caught up with them soon afterwards at the Communale in Bologna where Mugnone was directing *Tosca* and Mascagni's *Iris*. The company included tenors like Giuseppe Borgatti who alternated with Caruso in the leading rôles. Once again Mascagni's opera failed to gain anything like the acclaim for Puccini, due largely to Caruso's sensational Cavaradossi.

Puccini rehearsed the company for the first performance and disliked both the staging and *ensemble*. He was equally doubtful of Giachetti's ability, either as actress or singer, to

98

handle Tosca. On the opening night, perhaps unnerved by his irritability at rehearsals, she almost froze, but the audience was too overwhelmed by Caruso to notice anyone else. His passionate outbursts of 'Vittoria! Vittoria!' electrified them, and many wept unashamedly when he sobbed 'E lucevan le stelle'. It stimulated so many encores that Mugnone collapsed at his desk and needed several minutes to recover. After the dispiriting rehearsals Puccini had been in two minds about staying for the performance, but when the curtain fell to thunderous cheers he was persuaded to go on stage and afterwards assured Caruso that his Cavaradossi was the best he had ever heard. Within a few days the Neapolitan tenor was summoned to Gatti-Casazza's office and engaged for his first season at La Scala. He would make his début in *La Bohème* as Milan still remained apathetic about *Tosca*, loftily ignoring its enthusiastic reception in lesser houses.

This engagement almost ended in disaster even before the first night. *Tristan* was scheduled to open the season but had to be postponed through Borgatti's indisposition. Gatti-Casazza's decision to replace it with *La Bohème* gave Caruso an acute attack of nerves. Puccini encouraged him, but Toscanini had already begun his reign of terror in the cause of perfectionism. During the previous season he had cancelled the entire production of *Norma* because the leading soprano failed to satisfy him at the dress rehearsal. He had also overruled Tamagno himself for attempting to sing a passage of Verdi's *Otello* in his own way.

He was even less disposed to consider the feelings of a newcomer like Caruso whom he ordered to sing full voice at rehearsals which often dragged on past midnight. Toscanini walked out angrily when he persisted with his high C falsetto. While Gatti-Casazza pleaded with him to return, Puccini was trying to calm the tenor who threatened to tear up his contract. These pre-opening storms had their effect. Caruso's Rodolfo was far below his best and the whole performance suffered. That very night, however, Melba had triumphed in the first production of the opera at the Metropolitan New

York, although the *Tribune* critic, Henry E. Krehbiel, dismissed it as 'foul in subject and fulminant but futile in its music; quite unworthy of comparison with Verdi's *Traviata*'.

Puccini was so dispirited by the La Scala audience that he cut short his stay and escaped to Torre for a few days' hunting. But he soon returned to argue with Illica, who had spent fruitless months on *The Austrian Woman* (Marie Antoinette) which he was now asked to abandon in favour of vague discussions about some Japanese opera. He was even more put out by reports that Puccini, while scouting for new subjects, had made a tentative approach to Arturo Colautti, who had written the libretto for Giordano's successful *Fedora*. That misunderstanding was cleared up but the whole atmosphere of Milan, and La Scala in particular, seemed edgy and disaster-laden. This time, however, the fates had spared Puccini and selected Mascagni as their victim.

His new opera, *Le Maschere*, had not only been publicised as La Scala's star attraction of the season but would open simultaneously in half a dozen other cities. This extraordinary decision by Mascagni, unprecedented in operatic history, was plainly symptomatic of a megalomaniac urge to assert his superiority over all contemporaries, notably Puccini, whose triumphs had spotlit his own modest record since *Cavalleria rusticana*. Although that opera continued to earn him vast royalties, neither wealth nor his popularity as a composer-conductor could compensate for the lack of a second world success.

Puccini had many faults but he was himself too sensitive to unkind criticism to disparage any fellow-composer, least of all an old friend with whom he had shared so many youthful escapades. Without suspecting Mascagni's envy, he had occasionally visited him at Pescaro on the Adriatic coast and admired his fine collection of china and old watches. He loved putting on some of his host's wildly eccentric ties and always made himself agreeable to his wife, who was a good enough actress to conceal her almost pathological dislike.

On the night of 17 January 1901 he occupied the directors' box at La Scala and stood up to applaud when Mascagni arrived, like an emperor, with his retinue. The laurels soon wilted. Caruso sang with enormous verve but was defeated by a mediocre score and Illica's unusually sub-standard libretto. Mascagni had rashly ventured into *commedia dell' arte*, a field quite unsuited to his more robust style. He was shown no mercy by the disappointed audience who interrupted scene after scene with shouts of 'Bohème!' and 'Viva Puccini!' It was a night of almost universal disaster for the composer. Rome had been fairly tolerant, but Genoa howled the piece off the stage, while the San Carlo management offered devout thanks to a singer whose illness had opportunely cancelled their own première. Gatti-Casazza and Toscanini, who still hoped desperately to win back patrons, had to give up after two more performances had played to thin houses.

Within a few days, however, the fiasco was obliterated by the shock announcement of Verdi's death. The façade of La Scala was draped in black and flags flew at half mast throughout Italy and in many cities throughout the world. D'Annunzio expressed the feelings of millions in his memorial ode; 'He wept and loved for all'. The poet, together with Boito, Ricordi, Puccini, Mascagni, Leoncavallo and a few weeping servants, followed the plain hearse to the city cemetery. After a short service, 'very modest and without music and singing', as Verdi had requested, the coffin was laid beside that of his wife. On the night of 1 February 1901 Puccini and Elvira sat among the vast audience at La Scala for a memorial concert conducted by Toscanini, with the first Otello, Tamagno, as the leading soloist. Caruso sang the Duke in the Quartet from *Rigoletto*.

A month later, a hundred thousand mourners lined the city streets when the two coffins were re-buried in the cemetery of the Casa di Riposo, the convalescent home for musicians which Verdi had endowed with half his enormous fortune and future royalties. Outside the chapel a choir of eight hundred, under Toscanini, sang the stirring lament from *Nabucco*, 'Va, pensiero sull' ali dorate'. Puccini was again present but this time, officially, as Lucca's municipal representative.

La Scala had reopened in an atmosphere of gloom which affected artists and audiences alike. De Lara's *Messalina* had the misfortune to be staged while Milan was still grieving over its beloved Maestro. The critics did not welcome 'the lascivious and mediocre work of an upstart foreigner' and condemned it in advance as a gross affront to Verdi's memory. The volatile French prima donna, Emma Calvé, became so upset that she abandoned rehearsals, leaving a note to explain that Verdi's ghost had appeared in her dreams to predict sudden death if she sang in the opera! Her understudy also grew nervously sick and could do little with the title-rôle.

On the first—and last—night Puccini did what he could to comfort the unhappy composer who stood in the wings throughout the performance, guarded by detectives. Toscanini imperturbably ignored the claque who only stopped hissing when Tamagno was on stage. De Lara, unwisely joining him for a curtain call, narrowly escaped physical assault. Puccini thought the opera tasteless and mediocre, but he stopped for a sympathetic word with de Lara, who sat with bowed head in the Ristorante Cova waiting for Toscanini. Puccini shook his hand and urged him to disregard the claque. 'Do not forget, my dear friend,' he said warmly, 'that only a few months ago the savages of Rome tried to butcher my *Tosca*, and now everyone wants to see it, even the Americans.' He did not exaggerate; Milka Ternina and Scotti had repeated their Covent Garden success at the Metropolitan where it would become almost as consistently popular, season after season, as *La Bohème*.

Before returning to Torre del Lago he begged Ricordi to expedite negotiations with Belasco and also arrange to have the play translated. In the interim he relied on a crude translation of Long's original short story in which the geisha wounds herself, but not fatally, the story ending with Pinkerton's return to a deserted house. To avoid delay he sent Illica this version but reminded him that the Belasco play had a far more dramatic ending and many excellent bits of stage business. By the time the copy arrived in June, Illica had already sketched out a treatment for three acts and Ricordi had wired his New York agent to finalise arrangements. Even Giacosa, rarely given to snap judgments, confessed that he adored delicious Cio-Cio-San and could visualise many poetic touches. But unlike his impetuous co-librettist, he would not pick up his pen until the adaptation rights were fully cleared.

During these delays Puccini became increasingly exasperated with critics who reproached him for his limited output and pointed bleakly to the sad state of Italian opera, with only Verdi revivals to remind audiences of his immortal legacy. They scoffed at Mascagni's recent disaster and saw no comfort in Leoncavallo's latest piece, *Zaza*, a tuneful and entertaining study of a café-concert singer but sadly disappointing after *I Pagliacci*.

Tito Ricordi continued to report gratifying news of more *Tosca* productions abroad. Caruso had sailed for Buenos Aires with a company under Toscanini and sung Cavaradossi ten times to delirious audiences. Such a golden torrent of royalties poured into Torre del Lago that, by June 1901, Puccini felt confident enough to buy himself an expensive new toy. It was an evil-smelling powerful Clement in which he roared through Torre and scattered the populace in the narrow flagged streets of his boyhood. Wearing a chauffeur's overalls, cap and goggles, he took corners at breakneck speed on the road to Viareggio and made impulsive dashes 'to see if the Tower of Pisa is still leaning'. Tonio, now a big raw-boned youth, often joined him during his school vacations and never tired of polishing and tinkering with the car. Fosca sometimes risked life and limb in driving to Milan to meet her fiancé, Leonardi, a young tenor of limited prospects but still vastly preferable, in Puccini's estimation, to her seedy cellist.

Elvira, far too shy of making herself conspicuous, did not share these excursions except to visit her sister in Florence. Quite apart from her terror of accidents, she acquired an almost neurotic loathing for the Clement which, she rightly guessed, would give Puccini more mobility for his casual flirtations. While fretting for the Belasco agreement and with Illica's detailed draft still in preparation, he started an affair with a pretty schoolteacher from Turin and persuaded her to spend a number of weekends with him. He would take out his boat ostensibly for a day's waterfowling and drive over to Viareggio where he used to leave the car and cycle off to a hunting lodge in the pine woods. He covered his tracks with the help of the painter, Ferruccio Pagni, who acted as post-man and intermediary, but his portrait now appeared in too many newspapers and magazines to guarantee anonymity. The big car was also too much of a novelty to avoid notice and inevitable gossip.

Word of these assignments soon reached Elvira who finally decided to raid the love nest. Puccini had been delayed, but his unfortunate partner took several hard blows from Elvira's umbrella before making her escape. That night, during a violent scene, she scratched him so viciously that he carried the scars on his nose for days. He fled to Milan, more hurt perhaps by Fosca's coldness and her refusal to kiss him goodbye, than Elvira's frenzy which, he guessed, would quickly subside. He wrote to protest his deep love but begged her to be 'less nervous and less of a policeman; thus our former peace will return.' When this went unanswered he played his trump card by complaining of a fever, probably malaria, which had kept him awake for three nights, without anyone to nurse him.

He soon returned, suitably shamefaced and humble, but instead of an enraptured welcome followed by their ritual lovemaking, he found Elvira pitifully sad and withdrawn. It was not, of course, their first quarrel. Almost from their early days together in Torre, her over-possessiveness and dread of being abandoned had caused tension, but she had never before spied openly on him or given way to such hysteria.

There were several reasons, other than routine jealousy, for her outburst. She had developed a chronic bronchial cough and now rarely left the house except for shopping. Inevitably she put on flesh which added to her gloomy dissatisfaction.

Puccini had become sprucer with affluence, while she already looked dowdy at forty-two and took to wearing black. Moreover, she had denied herself the social stimulus to dress more becomingly. In all their years at Torre she never accepted an invitation to the Ginoris' handsome villa, La Piagetta, across the lake. Apart from infrequent visits to La Scala or the Ricordi offices, she saw nobody in Milan and spent her days shopping or endlessly tidying the apartment. Acute middle-aged depression had accentuated the anomalies of her unmarried status, while Puccini's growing celebrity simply magnified her fears instead of bringing reassurance. She now found it difficult to face receptions where he might look twice at a younger and more attractive woman or make some remark to signal a new liaison. Instead she took refuge behind the walls of the villa, entertaining her relatives or occasional guests like Giulio Ricordi, who had always shown her respect and gentle sympathy.

She could not be faulted as a devoted and much-loved mother, but even that consolation was now threatened. Fosca would soon marry and leave for Milan, while Tonio seemed to be growing away from her. She continued to torture herself with guilt for his illegitimacy, misinterpreting adolescent changes of mood as clear evidence of his contempt, if not hatred. On the contrary, he was surprisingly extrovert for a fourteen-year-old and had grown more attached to his father, who took him hunting, sailing or on exhilarating drives in the Clement. As Fosca had stopped adoring Puccini and now warmed to men of her own generation, Tonio had automatically benefited, but this shift in relationships left his mother feeling even more loveless and isolated.

After so many months of being 'inoperatic', Puccini was too concerned over *Butterfly* to brood on Elvira's prolonged malaise which he dismissed perfunctorily as post-bronchial depression. Ignoring his own addiction, the source of constant throat trouble, he solemnly advised her to abandon cigarette-smoking! Since a change of scene was his usual panacea for most ills, physical or mental, he prescribed a holiday away from sticky and mosquito-infested Torre. He would have enjoyed Chiatri, but Elvira had never overcome her dislike of the place and preferred a more accessible hill resort. They drove up to Cutigliano in the Clement towards the end of July 1901 and spent six peaceful weeks which improved Elvira's spirits, although her rasping cough often kept them both awake. After a month of sunning himself, with long walks and a daily swim, he felt healthier but still far from relaxed. He would sit down at a piano, night after night, and twiddle his thumbs for want of a libretto.

Giacosa had at last decided to start work, but he would not be hurried until the Belasco agreement was signed and sealed. However, soon after their return Ricordi wrote to announce that it had at last arrived from New York. Puccini promptly hurried off to Milan for several talks with the librettists who, for once, seemed to be in complete harmony. Illica was already familiar with the Japanese setting, a useful legacy from his libretto for Mascagni's *Iris*, while Giacosa, enchanted with the geisha heroine, promised to work on nothing else that winter at his villa in Parella.

They made good progress but still not fast enough for Puccini, who spent irritable nights in the studio scribbling piano sketches while his three gun dogs, Lea, Schaunard and Nello, dozed before the huge log fire. He worked in breeches and riding boots, with a loaded gun beside him and at the ready for a whistle from Manfredi. He studied the Belasco play minutely and reassured Ricordi that the plot would stretch to a full-length opera. He also began making notes on the American characters, whom he still found difficult to focus with conviction, particularly the unattractive lover ('Sir Pinkerton' in the early version!).

To authenticate the oriental details he visited Milan for a meeting with the celebrated Japanese actress, Sada Jacco, whose intonation he carefully memorised. Madame Ohyama, wife of the Japanese Ambassador, then vacationing at Viareggio, also sang native songs for his benefit and promised to write to Tokyo for some folk music. She became interested

106

enough to visit him several times at Torre. 'Very intelligent and, although plain, attractive,' he reported to Ricordi. Acting on her advice he started collecting drawings and books on Japanese art, customs and décor.

With scripts spinning back and forth he now had no time to attend rehearsals of his earlier operas, but kept himself informed of productions. *Tosca* had made a stir in Montevideo, with arrangements also in hand for Paris, Geneva and Dresden, but the most exciting reports came from Monte Carlo where Caruso had made such a splendid début in *La Bohème* with Melba, that Covent Garden soon booked him for his English début. Before leaving for London he amused Puccini, Gatti-Casazza and other friends at the Ristorante Cova with his gay account of an afternoon's recording in the Grand Hotel, just above the suite in which Verdi had died. Standing on a packing case he had sung ten songs, including 'E lucevan le stelle', into a bell-shaped tin horn dangling from the ceiling. He still chuckled in disbelief at being paid the stupendous sum of a hundred sovereigns by the London impresario for a two-hour 'recital'. Puccini congratulated him but had no suspicion that anyone save the singer and his gramophone company might possibly benefit from the sales of these scratchy waxed discs. Leoncavallo, however, was quick to appreciate their publicity value; within a few months he offered to play the piano for Caruso's first recording of 'Vesti la giubba' and soon afterwards composed 'Mattinata' for the tenor's next session, again playing the accompaniment.

Puccini was sufficiently intrigued to buy a phonograph on which he played the records over and over for his family and guests. Quite apart from the novelty of hearing his arias sung by Caruso, it was impossible to resist such a fascinating mechanical toy. He already possessed two of the latest cameras and also devoured catalogues advertising gadgets for cars and motorboats. He would rarely visit a foreign city without calling on gunsmiths to examine new weapons. In his studio at Torre he now had a separate shelf for periodicals describing the wonders of ballooning and aeronautical experiments by pioneers like Wilbur and Orville Wright. He had also been wildly excited by the achievements of the Bolognese inventor, Guglielmo Marconi, and filed every newspaper account of the historic wireless message transmitted between Cornwall and Newfoundland.

Throughout 1902 he urged his librettists to work faster, although most of the delays were due to his own insistence on scrapping entire scenes, like that set in the American Consulate, which he had dismissed as irrelevant. Having emphatically approved the three-act structure, he suddenly insisted on two, overruling Giacosa's strong plea for a curtain between Cio-Cio-San's futile night vigil and Pinkerton's appearance. Ricordi was not convinced and sympathised with the poet who objected vigorously to 'unstitching' months of careful writing. He threatened to withdraw altogether and publish his scenes separately so that the world might judge his own contribution.

Puccini was unrepentant. He seemed intoxicated by this opera and had absolutely no doubt that audiences would share his own fascination. None of his earlier heroines had moved him as deeply as the pathetic geisha, so vulnerable in her innocence. Years later, when his opera had captured world audiences, he wrote, 'There is no comparison between my love for Mimì, Musetta, Manon and Tosca and that love which I have in my heart for her for whom I wrote music in the night.'

He often visited Albina's grave while composing *Madama Butterfly*, but it would be unwise to draw extravagant psychological inferences from his behaviour during a period of melancholy domestic stress. Nevertheless, he has been the subject of so much posthumous psycho-analysis, in an attempt to interpret him as man and artist, that his mother's influence cannot be altogether ignored. One of the more interesting theories, fascinatingly deployed at some length by Mosco Carner, centres on Puccini's 'unresolved bondage to the mother-image', which might have motivated not only his sexual promiscuity but his choice of doom-laden women as central characters in his operas. 'In order to pacify the godlike Mother . . . the "degraded" heroine had to be offered up as a sacrificial animal,' argues Dr Carner.

In this Freudian context a number of facts deserve passing consideration. Orphaned at the age of five, Puccini had naturally gravitated towards such 'substitute fathers' as Ponchielli and Giulio Ricordi. He also leaned heavily on maternal figures like Elvira and, later, Sybil Seligman, but it should not be forgotten that he was rising twenty-six and already far from innocent at the time of Donna Albina's death. There seems to be nothing darkly sinister or neurotic in either his characteristically Latin devotion to his 'Mamma' or his lusty pursuit of attractive playmates. His handsome looks alone, quite apart from his celebrity, made him a magnet for many women. Any sub-conscious desire on his part to avoid competition with the so-called mother-figure can only be considered hypothetical, if not fanciful.

Although his standard heroine is frail and dies for love, whether in crinoline or kimono, one must beware of dismissing them as 'rivals of the exalted mother-image, who therefore have to be punished,' as Dr Carner suggests. This hypothesis tends to ignore Puccini's obvious creative limitations, subject-wise, as an operatic composer. From Manon onwards he had discovered a rich box-office vein in these flawed young women, but he was far from obsessively drawn to them. As already noted, he would no doubt have embarked on such 'un-Puccinian' characters as Zola's Abbé Mouret and Daudet's Tartarin had the rights been available. Moreover, he later yearned to make audiences laugh instead of weep, and proved his capacity to do so in his little masterpiece, *Gianni Schicchi*. His incapacity to handle large-scale Verdian or Wagnerian themes, quite apart from a notable weakness in handling male characters, may have limited his portrait gallery far more than any guilt feelings or other fixations.

The frustrations which almost overwhelmed him after completing *Madama Butterfly* cannot be easily reconciled with any lingering Freudian fantasies. He was then in his mid-forties, successful and firmly settled in his ways. The immediate causes of his near-collapse were a crippling car accident, and more seriously in the long term, the unforeseen consequences of his decision to marry Elvira.

Chapter Seven

Puccini worked feverishly on *Madama Butterfly* throughout December 1902. He had almost completed orchestrating Act One when Illica arrived to discuss re-writing the second act without the Consulate scene. The composer seemed confident enough but he looked abnormally pale and kept stroking his throat as if in pain. Although cracking jokes until the last bottle was drained, he left Illica with an impression of forced gaiety.

Fosca's marriage had aggravated her mother's sense of isolation, and Puccini, now approaching the difficult half-way stage of his score, offered little comfort. He would lock himself away for hours and only emerge for snatched meals, often hurrying off without warning to shoot game or, as Elvira feared, to meet some new light o' love. She had almost reached breaking point when word came unexpectedly from Lucca that her husband had suffered a seizure and seemed unlikely to survive.

Naturally enough, she welcomed the prospect of at last being free to marry Puccini, but soon learned with horror that Narciso had made a will in which he cursed her for having so shamelessly betrayed him. Although not a religious woman, she was deeply superstitious and decided in a panic to beg his forgiveness. On 25 February 1903 she set out nervously for Lucca in the chauffeur-driven Clement with Tonio, then home on a brief school holiday, and Puccini, who had taken the opportunity to consult a throat specialist.

He was reassured by the doctor and in high spirits, but Elvira was weeping hysterically when he arrived at the house of Alfredo Caselli. It seemed that Narciso's relatives had driven her from the door as 'a faithless whore'. After serving an excellent dinner, the pharmacist invited them to stay the night as a heavy mist had crept in to make the frosty roads even more dangerous. Puccini, however, was impatient to resume his usual night's work on *Butterfly*.

Their chauffeur took the wheel but drove incautiously fast to please his employer. The night was moonless and the steep Quiesa Pass a slippery hazard. Four miles out of the city the car skidded off the road and plunged down a fifteen-foot embankment before striking a tree and overturning. Elvira and Tonio were slightly bruised but the chauffeur had a severe leg injury. Puccini was trapped under the car and fortunate indeed to avoid suffocation from the escaping fumes. Elvira and Tonio helped him to the nearby house of a village doctor who gave first aid and swiftly diagnosed a compound fracture of the right leg. They stayed the night but Puccini refused to go to hospital. At La Piaggetta, where they had been driven next morning, he was strapped to a raft and punted across the lake to Torre del Lago. Semi-conscious and in considerable pain, he kept repeating, 'Poor Butterfly! My poor Butterfly!'

The leg was imperfectly set and gave him much discomfort. There seemed no end to his misery. A surgeon, summoned from Milan, slipped on his way to the railway station and fractured his own thigh! Another doctor re-set the leg, but the delay resulted in wastage of the muscle. A tumour developed and healed so slowly that a specialist had to be called in; then a urine test disclosed a diabetic condition. Puccini was at once put on a diet of five sugar-free meals a day with Karlsbad water and small doses of strychnine. Bedridden and depressed by this latest misfortune, he wrote gloomily to Illica, 'Addio tutto, addio Butterfly, addio vita mia!' Ricordi, Giacosa, Caruso and de Lara tried to rally him with cheerful letters but others, notably in Lucca, saw the hand of a wrathful Deity who had literally brought the *maestro cuccumeggiante* (composer of whores' operas) to his knees and spared blameless Narciso, now making an almost miraculous recovery.

After some weeks he could wheel himself to the piano in a bathchair but his flow of orchestration had lost its early impetus. He had a terror of being left with a permanent limp and also became aware of an alarming increase in weight during this period of what he called 'semi-nursery'. Looking out on the lake, so tantalisingly near yet unapproachable, he tortured himself with the prospect of never again enjoying a day's carefree shooting. His melancholia and irritability placed a heavy burden on Elvira, who nursed him with devotion and ingeniously replaced the forbidden foods with tempting dishes. She became gentler and less self-absorbed while he was utterly dependent on her and, of course, denied all chance of amorous excursions. Ricordi seized the opportunity for a fatherly homily, urging him to mend his ways and not tempt the fate of another composer whose last years had been wrecked by syphilis. 'Puccini, who could have been the modern Rossini, has been in the way of becoming the unhappy Donizetti', he warned solemnly.

The scoring of *Butterfly* slowly gathered momentum and, although he could only hobble about with two sticks, the leg was appreciably stronger. By early summer he already itched for a change of scene, but Chiatri was too inconvenient in his condition. He had hopefully offered to share part of the cost of continuing the road up to his villa, but the local council was unsympathetic to motorists and firmly rejected his proposal. He soon found a far more attractive and accessible alternative at Abetone, now a popular winter sports resort but at that time an unspoilt Apennine village perched on the lower slopes of Monte Cimone. Set among beautiful fir, chestnut and beech-woods, often carpeted with wild strawberries, its altitude of 1,550 metres offered summer coolness and panoramic views of peaks and valleys, with even the occasional glimpse of a rare herd of the moufflon sheep originally imported from Sardinia. It was also reassuring to be within easy driving distance of the mountain spa at Boscolungo whose doctors could keep an eye on the leg and test his urine regularly. In the villa, with Elvira in attendance almost around the clock, he worked steadily on his opera and had completed the *intermezzo* for Butterfly's night vigil before they returned to Torre del Lago early in September. He now felt confident enough to promise Ricordi the entire score in ample time for the première scheduled for La Scala in mid-February 1904.

His leg still troubled him and he sometimes grew crusty over his diet, but Elvira remained sweet-tempered through all his see-saw moods. Without cause for jealousy—he was unable even to slip away to the Milan apartment because the stairs tired him—she almost glowed with a new-found sense of security and well-being. In the lamplight Puccini again saw the face of the woman who had first touched his heart while her husband snored in his armchair. Their lovemaking became more tender and serene than the passionate couplings which had so often reconciled them in the past.

The sweet-sour langour of convalescence encouraged fantasy on both sides. Elvira was luxuriating in a second honeymoon, while Puccini interpreted her calmness as almost a rebirth. She pleased him by discarding her dowdy gowns for ribbons and furbelows, even engaging a sixteen-year-old village girl as maid-of-all-work. Doria Manfredi was no beauty but her parents, aware of Puccini's reputation and Elvira's waspish jealousy, had consented with some reluctance. The arrangement proved surprisingly successful. Doria was a gentle and retiring girl with a nunlike serenity of manner. She helped nurse Puccini, who gave no sign of sexual interest and merely thanked her politely when she picked fresh flowers daily for his room. She also relieved Elvira of laundering and ironing, waited respectfully at table and never indulged in village gossip. She was soon accepted as a member of the household and helped to fill the gap left by Fosca.

Her presence had made it easier for Puccini to depart for Paris in October. Elvira raised no objections and for once did not plead to accompany him on what, he assured her, would be a short and useful trip. There were two reasons for breaking off in mid-opera; he had been invited to attend rehearsals for the opening of *Tosca* at the Opéra-Comique, which would also enable him to consult a French orthopaedic surgeon about his slow-healing leg. Hopefully, he had packed his notes for the uncompleted second act of *Butterfly*, but found little

opportunity to work. Paris depressed him, as always. The cold
rainy weather affected his leg muscle, but massage and electrical treatment, night and morning, brought some relief.
Rehearsals went smoothly although the conductor, André
Messager, a fanatical admirer of Massenet, plainly resented this
foreign usurper. Sardou did not improve the atmosphere by
bouncing into the theatre and behaving as if he were librettist,
composer and stage manager. 'I half expected him to push the
conductor out of the pit and seize the baton himself', Puccini
reported sardonically to Milan.* *Tosca* opened to an ovation
on 13 October. Most of the French critics, however, echoing
Italian colleagues, condemned the subject as unsuitable for an
opera. Sardou took this as a personal attack and thundered
back in *Le Figaro*, 'A play which has been given three thous-
and times is always right.'

Puccini returned thankfully enough to Torre but kept
brooding on the French surgeon's gloomy verdict that he
would be unable to walk without sticks for at least a year. 'My
life is a sea of sadness and I am stuck in it', he wrote
self-pityingly to Illica. This mood vanished with the purchase
of a new Lancia, followed soon after by the death of Narciso,
who had naturally disinherited Elvira but without curses or
reproach. There seemed no longer any bar to her second
marriage and the long-hoped-for legitimisation of Tonio, but
Puccini waited until the *Butterfly* score was despatched to
Milan on 27 December. Four days later, precisely three years
since he and Elvira had stood together on a hotel balcony in
Rome to toast the new century, he sent a comic drawing to
Ricordi and a few other intimates. With Elvira floating by his
side in the clouds and flanked by angels, he depicted himself in
a loincloth of music paper with a toy model Lancia slung over
his shoulder. He issued no wedding invitations and kept the
date secret.

* During this visit he saw a performance of *Pelléas et Mélisande* and was
sardonically amused by the backstage acrimony. Maeterlinck had
nominated his wife, Georgette Leblanc, for the leading rôle but had been
overruled by the composer in favour of Mary Garden.

They were married in Torre del Lago at 10 pm on 3 January 1904. Elvira's sister was matron of honour, her husband and the local doctor signing the register as witnesses. Nobody else was asked and the priest had been sworn to secrecy. To avoid riotous interruptions from bohemians like Pagni, the bridegroom prohibited the playing of organ music and even had the front windows screened to conceal any light.

In legalising their union he could reasonably claim to have compensated Elvira for much self-sacrifice and humiliation during their twenty years together. No doubt he also imagined that their relationship would not change significantly or only for the better. Apparently he expected his abnormally jealous mistress to glide smoothly into the rôle of an equally devoted, but less demanding, spouse. If so, he was quite remarkably myopic about Elvira's character and disposition in imagining that, once freed from insecurity, she would automatically grow more tolerant of his own weaknesses. He had minimised the effects of her approaching menopause and could also have been misled by their recent months of comparative harmony. Whatever the reasons for his optimism, he was guilty of an almost classical misjudgment in ignoring the possibility of her becoming even more rabidly over-possessive as his legal partner.

For the present, however, nothing concerned him but the excitement of staging *Butterfly*. A few days after the wedding he was driven to Milan in the Lancia, still tangy with new leather, and soon absorbed himself in rehearsals. He seemed to have lost all dread of La Scala and saw no possibility of failure. His one regret was the absence of Toscanini from the pit. The Maestro, long unpopular with singers and musicians alike for his uncompromising severity, had continued to infuriate audiences by disallowing all encores. After the final performance of the previous season he took a storm of hisses from the claque, soon joined by his own orchestra. He snapped his baton on the desk and tossed the pieces into the stalls before stalking out of the theatre, vowing never again to conduct there.

Puccini deplored his departure but could sympathise with the audience. Others, like Melba, took the opposite view. As Puccini's guest at a performance of *Tosca* in La Scala, she was horrified when the soprano came forward after the prayer to acknowledge the applause and sang it all over again. 'It's disgraceful,' she protested to the composer. 'The Germans would never allow such a thing.' He reminded her with a shrug, 'If there is no *bis* in Italian opera, there is no success.'

While reasonably satisfied with Campanini as substitute conductor, he was hungry enough for Toscanini's approval of his score to visit him some days before the première. The Maestro became suspicious when Puccini played over only a few melodious excerpts. His doubts were confirmed after a quick glance through the manuscript. It seemed obvious to him that the composer had blundered in confining his opera to two acts; the first weak and long, the second stronger but running to an estimated eighty minutes. 'I thought at once this length is impossible,' he recalled. 'For Wagner, yes! For Puccini, no!' He was also doubtful of its musical qualities and would later ridicule Ricordi's inflated claims for the opera as worthy to rank with *Traviata*; 'Puccini was very clever, but only clever. Look at Cio-Cio-San. The poor woman has been waiting for years. She thinks he is returning at last. Listen to the music. Sugary. Look at Verdi in *Traviata*. Listen to the agitation of the music, the passion, the truthfulness.'

Since he would not be conducting and might therefore be accused of professional bias, he kept his views to himself and complimented Puccini on a piece which obviously had all the hallmarks of a popular success. He was genuinely convinced that Rosina Storchio would make an ideal Butterfly and earn more than enough encores to satisfy even the greediest of her admirers.* However, although he would have liked to applaud the beautiful young soprano, whose career he had promoted at La Scala and with whom he was currently enjoying a

* She had sung the rôle of Mimì Pinson in the world première of Leoncavallo's *La Bohème* in Venice, her native city, but was even more acclaimed for her Violetta in *La Traviata*.

romantic liaison, nothing would induce him to set foot in the opera house.

Gatti-Casazza privately shared Toscanini's adverse view of the *Butterfly* score, but he spared no expense and had commissioned Jusseaumme of Paris to design the scenery. His own misgivings melted at rehearsals when even hardened stagehands would stop work and listen spellbound to the melodies. After the dress rehearsal the entire orchestra rose to its feet and applauded Puccini, who embraced Rosina Storchio with such warmth that the Galleria soon buzzed with absurd rumours that she had deserted Toscanini.

Her large seductive eyes and gay coquetry were enough to turn any man's head, but on stage she was wholly professional and meekly took criticism from Tito Ricordi and Campanini. Puccini had admired her Musetta in Rome's production of *La Bohème* and considered her graceful style, backed by a voice of true lyrical quality, foolproof assets for Butterfly. Nobody dared hint, in his presence, that her sparkling vivacity seemed rather more suited to Violetta or Donizetti's gayer heroines than to Cio-Cio-San. On the morning of the opening performance he sent her an effusive note; 'My good wishes are superfluous! So true, so delicate, so moving is your great art that the public must succumb to it! Through you I am speeding to victory! Tonight then—with sure confidence and much love, dear child!' A few hours later, he again wrote to her, 'We are obliged to make you die on the stage but you will, with your exquisite art, make our opera live forever. Puccini.'

He seemed almost as pleased with the other principals. Giovanni Zenatello, his Pinkerton, was a blond, personable tenor with an upper register recalling de Reszke in his prime. Giuseppe de Luca lacked Scotti's menace as Scarpia, but his virile interpretations of Wagner had won him a following at La Scala. He seemed a foolproof Sharpless.

With such artists and an orchestra directed by the well-liked Campanini, it is not easy to explain the almost virulent hostility which began to build up locally. For this the Ricordis, father and son, were partly responsible in barring the critics from all rehearsals. Tito relished hush-hush publicity which could stimulate gossip, but this time it boomeranged disastrously, and Puccini had also been unhelpful in pointedly avoiding the Galleria. He refused interviews and, even more unwisely, cold-shouldered the all-powerful claque some of whom had neither forgiven nor forgotten Franchetti's 'victimisation' over *Tosca*. A dangerous underswell was therefore threatening the new opera if it failed to live up to La Scala standards or the Ricordis' extravagant hopes. Moreover, Leoncavallo and Mascagni each had admiring coteries who thought Puccini overrated and would not hesitate to make themselves heard.

Puccini himself, usually prone to pre-opening nerves, seemed oblivious of any resentment. Rehearsals had gone so smoothly that he was almost anaesthetised to the possibility of failure. Euphoria had even prompted him to make the quite unprecedented gesture of inviting three of his sisters to share his triumph. They arrived, obviously ill-at-ease in their provincial hats and dresses, but greeted Elvira with affection now that she had at last achieved marital respectability. With Tonio also present and looking handsome in new evening clothes, the family gathering comforted Puccini almost as much as the box-office receipts of 25,000 lire, a record for any opening in La Scala's long history. It was nevertheless unfortunate that Gatti-Casazza's heavy production costs had tempted him to raise the price of all tickets.

The house was thick with celebrities, many from Rome and other cities, when Campanini raised his baton sharp at eight-thirty. Puccini stood in the wings with his son and began sweating nervously during the opening scene. It was played in almost eerie silence. Shouts of '*Bohème*! Again *Bohème*!' came from the gallery, who recalled a passage from the third act of that opera. Storchio was shaken but ignored derisive cries from a gallery heavily infiltrated by the claque. They were hushed with difficulty by patrons in the more expensive seats, but they too became restive at the slowness of the early action. The novelty of Puccini's subtle harmonies was all but lost in jeers which unsettled the more serious-minded members of the audience. Even the enchanting love duet extracted only a mild spatter of applause, mingled with renewed parrot cries of '*Bohème*!' The act ended to more boos than bravoes.

Mascagni stood up to applaud but Giacosa, marooned with his family in the orchestra stalls, blubbered like a child. Puccini was persuaded to limp on stage and take two curtain calls with Storchio and the other principals. Again the hisses and catcalls blotted out the few handclaps. Nervous and pale-faced, he hurried back to the box where his sisters and Elvira were quietly weeping. Nobody arrived to offer comfort, and Tonio had to bite his tongue as he pushed his way through corridors swarming with sneering critics and their toadies.

Act Two, running to almost an hour and a half, stimulated the vicious claque to complete what Puccini justly described next day as 'a lynching'. Storchio was singled out for a tasteless act of sadism almost unique in operatic history. When a draught from the wings unluckily distended her kimono, it prompted jeers of 'Butterfly is pregnant! Ah, the little Toscanini!'* She dissolved into tears but managed to sing 'Un bel dì' movingly, although without any applause for either that or her Letter Scene with de Luca. Some of the audience, fidgeting impatiently over the inordinate length of this act, indulged in still more horseplay when, after Butterfly's night vigil, she greets the dawn with her child and Suzuki. Tito Ricordi, aiming at a charming stroke of atmospheric realism, had arranged for bird-whistles from different parts of the house. The twitterings cued off a cacophony of barking, braying and mooing from the claque. Nothing could survive such an exhibition. The final curtain fell to laughter and whistles, neither Storchio nor the composer daring to take a call.

* Storchio later bore Toscanini's child, a sickly deaf-mute boy who died, aged sixteen. She was buried in the same grave at the Monumentale which Toscanini often visited.

He stood in the wings, chewing his nails and smoking furiously, ignoring protests from the firemen. Tonio embraced him and cried brokenly, 'Oh! father! My poor, dear father!' Together they hurried to Storchio's dressing-room where she was sobbing hysterically. They could still hear the hubbub from the auditorium but missed a solo performance by Mascagni who went before the curtain and, dabbing his eyes, harangued the audience for their behaviour. Gatti-Casazza and others thought he was shedding crocodile tears and looked on sceptically when he kissed his rival composer and declared, 'Your opera has fallen, but it will rise again.'

Puccini fled to his apartment and refused to touch any of the food which Elvira had prepared after hastily cancelling the 'celebration' supper at the Cova. He sat in almost complete darkness, knuckling a tattoo on the piano lid. It seemed to express his hatred and contempt for the savages who had raped fragile Butterfly. He accepted well-meant commiserations from Ricordi but was scarcely civil to other callers whose sincerity he suspected. He slept little that night and rose before daybreak. Elvira found him in his dressing-gown, unshaven, and still drumming the closed piano lid. Over hot black coffee he suddenly recalled how Venice had also laughed *La Traviata* off the stage and comforted himself with Verdi's prophetic words after that fiasco; 'I do not believe the final word was spoken last night. They will see it again, and we shall see!'

But the morning papers convinced him that it would be folly to risk another confrontation with the claque. One critic denounced *Butterfly* as 'a diabetic opera, the result of an automobile accident'. Almost all the others, apart from Pozza of the *Corriere della Sera*, always a staunch friend, made no attempt at serious reviewing and merely smacked their lips over his humiliation. The Ricordis together with the librettists, Gatti-Casazza and a red-eyed Storchio, gathered in Puccini's apartment for a council of war which soon became a wake. Storchio swore that she would never sing Butterfly again to an Italian audience, though she sang it once more in

Rome in 1920. Puccini, with her hand clasped in his, insisted on having the opera withdrawn, despite Gatti-Casazza's pleas, and returned his 20,000 lire advance on royalties. He gloomily acknowledged his error in not dividing Act Two, as Giacosa had always recommended, and now proposed revising the opera. But whatever the outcome, he declared firmly, the Milanese 'cannibals' would be denied a second helping.*

Before leaving Milan he wrote to Father Panichelli, 'You will be horrified by the vile words of the envious Press. Never fear! *Butterfly* is alive and real, and will soon rise again.' He also sent Rosina Storchio one of his photographs, tenderly inscribed, and took back with him her own signed portrait which he placed on his piano at Torre del Lago. Soon afterwards she proclaimed both her affection for him and her faith in the opera by having herself painted in the rôle of Cio-Cio-San. He hung the picture over his desk at Via Verdi 4, having wisely decided that Elvira might not welcome it in their villa.

For the next three months he revised the score, rarely emerging except to doze for an hour or two in a garden hammock. The Lancia, on blocks, was lovingly polished and greased by Tonio who had just enrolled for a diploma course in engineering but seemed reluctant to leave home during this melancholy period. Instead he made himself useful by exercising the three dogs, attending to his father's correspondence and polishing the riding boots which he still wore during working hours, although his lameness precluded any shooting. Tonio also comforted his mother when Puccini acted more offhandedly than usual or had splenetic fits at being housebound and condemned to a tiresome diet.

His temper improved as the revised *Madama Butterfly* took shape. Apart from the main task of dividing Act Two by an intermission, he shortened the wedding ceremony and trimmed other superfluous fat in the first act. Although the structural changes and cuts accounted for less than eight per cent of the original score, the overall result sharpened the

* *Madama Butterfly* was not staged again at *La Scala* during his lifetime.

focus on Butterfly and also improved Pinkerton's rôle. Ricordi approved the revisions and swiftly arranged for the new version to be staged in Brescia which was convenient enough for the Milan critics but offered a safeguard from any malicious faction. The Russian *diva*, Salomea Krusceniski, would replace Storchio who had already departed with Toscanini for a season in the Argentine.

Puccini went to Milan for discussions with Illica and was particularly touched by a letter among the pile of correspondence awaiting him in Via Verdi. It came from a book-keeper who had attended the première and announced that he had christened his new baby daughter, 'Butterfly', to demonstrate his disgust with the rabble who had dared to hiss such an enchanting opera. Puccini good-naturedly invited him and his wife to call at his apartment and though astonished when they arrived with the baby and a host of other relatives, he served them coffee and cakes and presented his 'godchild' with various keepsakes, including a signed portrait.

He stayed some days with Illica who chanced to have another house guest, one 'Signor Tom Beecham', a little Englishman with a nervous facial twitch and a chronic sniff. He was introduced as a promising conductor who had completed the score of an opera about the life of Christopher Marlowe. Illica had written the script but thought the young aspirant would need all the magic of his 'lucky horseshoe', with which he always travelled, to interest any impresario. Impatient to get back to Torre del Lago, Puccini was barely civil except to Beecham's pretty wife, Utica, whose broken Italian amused him. Beecham later recalled, 'I never like him too well', but he enthused over the reshaped score and libretto for *Butterfly* which he declared to be 'a marvel and a miracle' when Puccini had played a few excerpts to entertain them.

Early in May he left to attend rehearsals in Brescia, after sending Rosina Storchio an affectionate note: 'I think of you so much! I am always seeing you in your charming present-ment of *Butterfly* and hearing again the sweet little voice which has such a sure way to the heart . . . How I should like

123

to be there with you!' But he was delighted with Krusceniski, who had partnered Caruso in *Aida* during his first St Petersburg season. Her Cio-Cio-San had a dramatic quality which more than compensated for her predecessor's 'sweet little voice'. Zenatello had also recovered from the earlier disaster and now sang confidently, helped by felicitous new lyrics like 'Addio fiorito asil' in the second part of Act Two. The chorus displeased Puccini but he praised Campanini's painstaking handling of the orchestra and, above all, Tito Ricordi's determination to perfect every production detail. No attempt was made to rocket seat prices although the Teatro Grande had been besieged for days before the opening. The critics all arrived in good time from Rome, Milan and Naples and were handled with kid gloves by Tito, who nevertheless appreciated assurances from Boito and other admirers that they would counter any hooliganism *à La Scala*.

There was no call for their services on the night of 28 May. From Pinkerton's first entrance until Butterfly's death scene every aria and duet was warmly approved, and the entire love duet had to be repeated before the opera could continue. After the first act Puccini was mobbed in his box by backslapping friends, led by Boito. The scenery earned a round of applause from an uninhibited audience who stood up to demand encores for 'Un bel dì', the reading of the letter and the Flower Duet. The house approached near-hysteria after the Humming Chorus and as the curtain descended to roars of 'Puccini! Puccini!', he limped excitedly on stage without his stick and was only saved from falling by Zenatello's stout arm.

It was a night of 'real and unqualified triumph' as he reported joyfully to one of his sisters. He received a hero's welcome in Torre del Lago where he entertained his bohemian friends night after night with songs from *Butterfly* and their lasting favourite, *La Bohème*. Elvira masked her distaste and only lost her temper when she overheard Pagni refer to her as 'the policeman'. Always sensitive to her large hands and feet, she took even more offence at this reference to her jealousy, and it was months before the painter was allowed back into the villa after making a tongue-in-cheek apology.

For a while Puccini was too busily enjoying his success to philander. With so much mail to answer and an avalanche of requests for autographed pictures, there was barely time for snatched drives to Viareggio in the Lancia or occasional speedboat dashes across the lake to see the Marchese Ginori. The village postman unloaded a daily sack of admiring letters but none so welcome as Rosina Storchio's news that *Butterfly* had taken Buenos Aires by storm. Tito Ricordi sent excited reports of provisional bookings for almost every Italian opera house, as well as requests from Covent Garden, Paris, Cairo and the United States. Almost every living soprano now seemed eager for the chance to sing Cio-Cio-San. All Puccini's previous heroines had been given scope for thrilling climaxes and crescendoes, but Butterfly's lyrical moments were exceptionally well prepared by dramatic effects like the cannon-shot announcing the arrival of Pinkerton's ship.

Puccini would soon discover, however, that more than vocal technique was needed to interpret his exquisite little geisha. He had been flattered by a gushing note of congratulation from Melba who hinted coyly that she might be available for Covent Garden, with Caruso 'of course' singing Pinkerton. She suggested an early meeting to run through the score. With memories of her excellent Mimì, he went to Venice where she was staying in a magnificent *palazzo* as the guest of an English friend. It quickly emerged that the queenly Melba, despite a voice of remarkable purity, lacked both the passion and acting ability for the title-rôle.* He was courteously non-committal but, after his beloved Storchio and the recent impact of Krusceniski, it seemed almost ludicrous to imagine this imposing Australian as a broken blossom.

* Melba was similarly thwarted in her hopes of singing Tosca. She made a creditable recording of 'Vissi d'arte' in 1907 and, four years later, still hoped to make her début in the title-rôle before an Australian audience. However, her sudden indisposition gave the part to her rival, the Polish soprano Wayda, who won such an ovation that Melba dared not risk comparison and never attempted the rôle.

Although Melba would later declare (quite without foundation) that he had written the opera specially for her, she could not convince herself that the leading rôle was within her dramatic range. After a mercifully short but embarrassing recital, she threw the score across the room in exasperation.

Deciding to spend a few days in Abetone, Puccini still found walking difficult. He had a check-up for his diabetes in Boscolungo and was soon home again, restlessly pacing the studio like a caged lion before feeding time. 'Shall I ever find a subject?' he wrote plaintively to Ricordi, who prodded him to attempt something more substantial than the lightweight *Butterfly*. He suggested *William Tell* but Puccini was reluctant to compete with Rossini's masterpiece. 'If I were to do it,' he wrote back, 'I should again be a mark for the thunderbolts of all the Italian critics. Poor, crushed Butterfly! With what feline rage did they hurl themselves upon her!' He urged Giacosa to search his files for 'something that will make people really laugh . . . instead of dramas of death and languor', but the poet's elephantine frame was now so pitifully ravaged by disease that he lacked the strength even to travel to Milan for a conference. Illica was also less amenable than usual, having already drafted a scenario of over a dozen scenes for *Marie Antoinette*, at Ricordi's prompting, without sparking much reaction from the capricious composer. He ignored the plea for a comic subject and offered instead to draft something on Hugo's *Hunchback of Notre Dame*. This also fell flat as Puccini had by now become intoxicated with the idea of attempting three one-act operas based on tales by Gorki. He had heard Chaliapin sing Méphistophélès in Gounod's *Faust* and thought him ideal for one or more of the leading rôles, but Ricordi squelched the whole plan. In his practical view no miscellany, however attractive, could compete with a big subject worthy of Verdi's legitimate successor.

With so many libretti being hatched and quickly addled, Puccini welcomed the relief of visiting London in October for a six-weeks' season at Covent Garden, opening with *Manon Lescaut*. There would also be five performances of *La Bohème*, now established in the London repertoire and a particular favourite of King Edward and Queen Alexandra, even without Melba. Some wealthy Neapolitan patrons had subscribed £20,000 to send a San Carlo company, directed by Campanini, with Rina Giachetti, the sister of Caruso's mistress, as leading soprano. Caruso had no love for San Carlo—he never again sang in Naples after being hissed there in 1901—but Rina needed support for her London début, and the Covent Garden management had hinted bluntly that only his name could ensure success for a rather 'scratch' company.

That visit was something of a revelation to Puccini. He had of course heard of Caruso's triumphs at Covent Garden and the Metropolitan New York, but blinked incredulously when long queues formed for tickets in an off-season. Caruso's presence was apparently enough to guarantee capacity houses whatever the opera or the quality of his fellow-artists. Moreover, his records were now bought by thousands of gramophone addicts, with 'Che gelida manina' and 'E lucevan le stelle' approaching the phenomenal sales of Leoncavallo's 'Vesti la giubba'.

Puccini had just taken refuge in one of the new river suites at the Savoy, from which Monet had painted his 'Waterloo Bridge' a few months earlier, when the tubby little Neapolitan, newly arrived from Berlin, bounced in to welcome him. He looked anything but the nervous young 'street singer' who had once pleaded for his chance to sing Rodolfo with a third-rate company in Leghorn. He was portlier, sleeker and raffishly self-confident in a silk shirt and morning clothes cut by a Savile Row tailor to whom he had been introduced by Scotti. A ruby glowed on one of his fingers and he took care to display the diamond-studded cufflinks presented to him by the Tsar Nicholas II. From a gold cigarette case bought at Tiffany's during his last visit to New York he offered thickly opulent Egyptians. He sympathised with Puccini over the brutish La Scala claque and seemed genuinely flattered at the prospect of singing Pinkerton in the première of *Madama Butterfly*, scheduled for Covent Garden's next season. He chuckled at Puccini's wry account of Melba's disastrous 'audition' in Venice and warmly endorsed Tito Ricordi's provisional booking of Emmy Destinn, whom he had partnered earlier that year in London.

They enjoyed supping in the Café Parisien, which had replaced the Savoy Grill, but after rehearsals both preferred the less formal Pagani's. The tenor would boast uninhibitedly of his luxurious villa in Castello, near Florence, where his second son had been born the previous month and named Enrico Caruso, Jr., in the American style. He was still devoted to his mistress, Ada Giachetti, but did not object to broad hints about his more than professional interest in her younger sister, Rina. Slyly prodded by his friends, he regaled them with love letters from admirers who offered themselves body and soul. This encouraged Tosti, with Puccini's willing connivance, to organise an elaborate hoax. Day after day Caruso began to receive passionate requests for a rendezvous from a young woman whose portrait, loaned by a Baker Street photographer, revealed an English golden-haired beauty in her delicious prime. One night, while tucking into a mammoth bowl of spaghetti at Pagani's, Caruso was handed a bogus telegram from the lady who threatened to throw herself under a train unless he met her under the station clock at Victoria Station at eleven o'clock. Tosti and the other conspirators kept straight faces when he pocketed the wire and, hurriedly making his excuses, snapped up a hansom cab. After waiting two hours in the draughty station he drove back to the Savoy.

Next day he had a severe head cold which affected his voice for the opening of *Manon Lescaut*, but the audience was sympathetic and Rina Giachetti duly registered a triumph. Within a few days he was singing with the familiar magic and even indulging in characteristic prankishness. In *Bohème*, Pasquale Amato was about to go for medicine for the dying Mimì but could not get into his overcoat as his fellow-Neapolitan had sewn up the sleeves. Like everyone else, Puccini was laughing too much to scold the tenor who apologised for his behaviour, but the following night he again injected a little light relief, this time with Arimondi as the victim who, after singing the Overcoat Song, put on Colline's stovepipe hat which Caruso had half-filled with water.

In Italy Puccini might have been less amused by these liberties, but the rapturous welcome for every production mellowed him. In that short season twelve performances of his operas had been given, far exceeding that of any other composer, even Verdi himself. London lifted his spirits. He loved bowling about the streets in a hansom, although much intrigued by the first motor-buses to appear in the Strand. He saw Réjane arriving in her vast mustard-coloured limousine in the Savoy's rubber-paved forecourt, and was almost tempted to buy himself a Rolls-Royce. Instead he shopped for silk cravats and dressing-gowns in the Burlington Arcade and selected a handsome scarf for Elvira. He also followed Caruso's example by ordering new suits from a Savile Row tailor who proposed an ingenious device for camouflaging his limp, with lead weights sewn into the left trouser leg so that the cloth hung straight to make the curvature almost undetectable.

Justifiably suspicious of effusive critics and rival composers, he had always avoided receptions in Milan and Paris, but the atmosphere of London enchanted him. He was coddled by the Savoy management and found it easy to relax in the homes of Anglo-Italians without being irked by language difficulties or professional intrigue. The Tostis' house in Mandeville Place became almost a second home. In their drawing-room one evening, after the host had entertained his guests with ballads of his own composition, he met one of Tosti's former pupils, the wife of David Seligman, a merchant banker.

The Seligman dynasty, like the Rothschilds, had soared to wealth from humble origins. A Bavarian ancestor had sailed steerage to the United States in 1837, soon followed by several brothers. One of them established a store in San Francisco, the only brick building in town, and thus escaped

129

the fire of 1851. The clan prospered rapidly after receiving a lucrative contract to supply uniforms for the Union Army during the Civil War. Within a few years the clothing firm had expanded into an international banking and brokerage house with substantial interests in American railroads. Joseph Seligman, the founding brother, acted for a time as confidential financial adviser to President Ulysses S. Grant, and in the 'seventies the firm, together with the Rothschilds and Morgans, issued US Government Bonds amounting to $1,000,000,000. The New York bank of J. and W. Seligman was founded in 1862. Other members of the family headed branches in San Francisco, Paris, London and Frankfurt, basing their policy on an equal division of all profits and losses between the eight brothers. The London branch came into being in 1864, the year of David Seligman's birth. His younger brothers were Edgar, later British Amateur fencing champion and Olympic gold medallist, and Herbert, a Regular Army officer who rose to the rank of Brigadier-General in the 1914 War.

When Puccini first met David Seligman he was a highly respected figure in the City of London's merchant banking echelon. A tall man, heavy-set, with a military-looking moustache and high-bridged nose, he looked a trifle out-of-place among Tosti's semi-bohemian guests. He had a faraway look and smiled to himself as if remembering some private joke. That night he wore stylish evening clothes and a white waistcoat with large gold and onyx buttons. Both in dress and manner he had a sombre elegance which made a perfect back-cloth for his vivacious wife.

She was not beautiful by conventional standards, but Puccini approved her slender waist, expressive Jewish eyes and superbly coiffed thick chestnut hair. Her fashionable clothes and jewellery proclaimed admirable taste. Then in her middle thirties and older than Puccini's usual bedmates, she appeared to be happily married to an easygoing man who did not share her musical interests but gladly indulged her whims.

She had two sons but seemed far from domesticated.

Within a few minutes, speaking in fluent Italian, she told Puccini that she often sang at charity concerts, usually accompanied by Tosti. That September she had performed at Cannes in aid of the Russian wounded and also in St Moritz, giving songs by Tosti and Rubinstein. She avowed her passionate love of Florence which she visited at least once a year, and talked sensibly about opera houses and conductors, with flattering reference to *Manon Lescaut* and, in particular, *La Bohème*, her special favourite.

She was of Sephardic descent. Her great-grandfather had been prominent in Jamaican public life and taken a pioneer rôle in emancipating the slaves on his estate in Montego Bay. His son, educated in England, became a distinguished advocate, a member of parliament, and was knighted on Gladstone's recommendation. Sybil had inherited her looks and musical talent from her mother, Zillah Beddington, one of the finest pianists of her day and a prominent London hostess. She often gave recitals at her mansion in Hyde Park Square where she entertained composers, musicians and celebrated artists like Sir John Millais, whose portrait of her was exhibited at the Royal Academy.

Sybil followed the tradition with even more success. She kept open house in Upper Grosvenor Street for leading members of the Italian colony and always welcomed visiting artists such as Caruso, who often turned down handsome fees to sing at private parties, but confided to Puccini as they drove back to the Savoy after the Tosti reception, that he willingly made an exception for 'cara Sybil', asking only 'a plate of spaghetti' for his services. He was in good company for Melba, Patti, Kreisler and Paderewski performed at the Seligman soirées for influential music-lovers like Lady de Grey, Alfred de Rothschild and other Covent Garden box-holders.

Anxious for news of a libretto for his next opera, Puccini had already made arrangements to return to Italy but had underrated both Sybil Seligman's appetite for celebrities and his own personal charm. As there was no time to organise a full-dress reception in his honour, she persuaded him to delay

131

his departure to dine at her house. He ignored Tosti's teasing glance as he kissed Sybil's hand before taking his leave. Her smile had been warm and openly inviting, giving promise of more than social acquaintance.

A fascinating creature, Puccini had decided lazily; rich, poised and obviously ripe for a flirtation uncomplicated by an over-possessive husband. In short, a woman wholly outside his previous experience. Nevertheless, apart from writing a note of thanks for the dinner party, he quickly dismissed her from his mind.*

* He was still unaware of her position in European society. Reporting on her visit to the Villa d'Este in September, a *New York Herald* (Paris edition) columnist had enthused, 'I saw pretty Mrs Seligman from London in a charming toilette of rose batiste with Valenciennes insertion and a yellow straw hat trimmed with flowers and green leaves. With her were her two lovely children. Already people are begging her to sing, since she has the most beautiful voice ever possessed by an amateur. At a charity concert got up at St Moritz by Princess Stéphanie, 300 tickets were snatched up at once.'

Chapter Eight

In Torre del Lago, while waiting for a suitable libretto, he amused himself with a new motorboat christened *Butterfly*, one of the few luxuries he had permitted himself despite mounting royalties from his operas. His domestic economy reflected surprisingly little change. Elvira continued to keep a good table on her modest allowance from which she secretly managed to assist her daughter. Puccini had now reconciled himself to Fosca's mediocre marriage and took a delight in her baby Franca, who would coo and purr on his knees while he rattled off little tunes on the piano. He used to limp beside her perambulator, often followed like a Pied Piper by the village children, who scrambled for sugared almonds and coins from two bags slung over his shoulders.

He seemed at peace, rocking lazily in his garden chair, with a cloud of bright butterflies fluttering over the flowers, and ducks quacking from the lake to remind him that soon he would be able to throw aside his stick and go shooting. The maiden voyage of *Butterfly*, garlanded and hung with lanterns, had been celebrated at the annual water carnival when she sped among a flotilla of fishing boats, canoes and rafts to roars of cheers. At *festas* the village band always gave an entire concert of Puccini favourites. Afterwards he would stop for a laugh with old acquaintances, among them a shambling hulk of a man who would sweep off his hat and kneel like a feudal serf until Puccini raised him gently to his feet to whisper some coarse Tuscan quip into his ear.

His name was Smeriglio, formerly a convict in the local penal colony. Working on the roads, manacled like his companions, he had once burst into a Neapolitan ballad as they passed Puccini's villa. The composer, amazed to hear such a beautiful tenor voice, rushed to the window and soon learned that the singer was serving a sentence for attempted murder.

On impulse he wrote to Queen Elena imploring her to release this caged songbird. His own prestige must have influenced the royal family, then in need of favourable publicity, and he had no doubt exaggerated the talents of his unexpected discovery, but Smeriglio was quickly pardoned and settled down in Torre del Lago to work as a builder's labourer. He married a young widow and sired a brood to whom Puccini played kindly godfather. The story, repeated for years in the village, gave him a reputation for quixotic generosity. In fact he would never conquer an innate niggardliness except for indulging his taste for well-cut clothes, guns, boats and motor-cars. He wrote often to his sisters and would enquire solici-tously about nephews and nieces, but his birthday and marriage gifts were on a modest scale. He gave generously to the con-vent where his sister Iginia had become Mother Superior, but his other religious contributions were rare and usually co-incided with an attack of depression. Like many another lapsed churchgoer he enjoyed the society of priests when he had lost his awe of them and overcome his dread of eternal damnation. Father Panichelli, who understood him well, did not pay much account when he once remarked gloomily, 'Give me back my faith and I will give you *Tosca*.'

He had a morbid preoccupation with death and used to cross himself superstitiously or pay a hasty visit to his mother's grave whenever his date of birth happened to be mentioned in some newspaper article. A cunning priest from the neighbour-ing village of Quiesa even extracted 500 lire for a new church bell by ringing the cracked one so loudly that Puccini shut his ears and pulled out his wallet, but street musicians and others who played his songs in the hope of a fat tip were usually disappointed. Quite exceptionally, while sipping drinks out-side a café in Viareggio with Galileo Chini the painter and scenic designer, he rewarded a strolling accordionist with a 50-lire note for playing 'E lucevan le stelle'.

Although his taste for creature comforts and privacy made it almost obligatory to stay at the most exclusive hotels when travelling abroad, he would complain bitterly of heavy bills.

He was therefore delighted by an invitation from South America to attend a summer season of his operas in 1905. His fee would be 50,000 francs (£2,000), plus first-class steamship tickets and hotel accommodation for Elvira and himself. Knowing that even a boat trip on Lake Massaciúccoli often made her queasy, he was taken aback by her eagerness to accompany him, but could not this time plead expense. Of late there had been fewer quarrels but since his return from London, dapper in new clothes and with a number of smoking jackets and silk dressing-gowns, Elvira had not failed to notice that he took more pains over his *toilette* whenever he went off to see Ricordi or paid visits to theatres staging any of his operas. He constantly used a tortoiseshell moustache-comb bought in Bond Street and had an irritating habit of raising his eyebrows in mock martyrdom whenever she had one of her raucous coughing spells. She argued that the ocean trip might benefit her bronchitis, but he guessed that the presence of Rosina Storchio and other possible charmers in Buenos Aires had persuaded her to brave the Atlantic.

The South American junket would give him an opportunity to see *Edgar* performed again. For this production he carefully revised his original score, notably the orchestration in Act Two, and introduced a new duet for Edgar and Tigrana among other improvements. Unfortunately the trip would clash with the Covent Garden production of *Madama Butterfly* which he would have liked to supervise. While visiting Milan that February he wrote warmly to Caruso, 'I learned of *Tosca* and *Bohème* at the Metropolitan and it pleased me so much to hear the echoes of the successes—mostly obtained through you and your merits! In London you will sing Butterfly. I hope very much for your collaboration with Destinn and Scotti—I can hear you, I can see you in that part, which not being as lengthy a one (less work for you to learn it!) has, notwithstanding, the need of your refulgent voice and of your art . . . I thank you and I greet you.'

*   *   *   *

Elvira, as he had feared, was seasick but quickly recovered her spirits in Buenos Aires where they were cheered, night after night, at the Teatro de la Opera. The Italian colony swamped them with banquets, bouquets and receptions, and Puccini would lock himself into his hotel suite rather than face the street crowds, but Elvira thrived on this show of affection after her isolated months in Torre del Lago. He only came to life in the theatre and shared Storchio's delight in the public acclaim for her Butterfly. It helped to console him for the politely formal reception of *Edgar* even with his improved score. The other operas, *Manon Lescaut*, *La Bohème* and *Tosca*, all won roars of approval which lured him on-stage, garlanded like a hero, for repeated curtain calls.

He was even more excited by newspaper reports of the Covent Garden première which had been lavishly staged in the presence of Queen Alexandra.* Emmy Destinn, of whom it was said that 'she looked like a cook but sang like an angel', lacked Storchio's ideal physical qualifications for the rôle, but she commanded superlative high notes and brought such pathos to her portrayal of the fifteen-year-old bride that her height and plumpness seemed to dissolve. Herman Klein of the *Sunday Times* wrote rhapsodically; 'The tears drawn by Emmy Destinn from every eye in her inspired creation of Cio-Cio-San constituted the real baptism of the new work.' Caruso and Scotti both sang superbly but, even after their departure for the next Metropolitan season, the Covent Garden management still felt justified in nominating the opera as their chief autumn attraction. They engaged Rina Giachetti for Butterfly, with Zenatello in support, under Mugnone's baton and cordially invited Puccini to attend rehearsals. Negotiations were soon afoot to stage the opera in Paris, and Tito Ricordi would supervise a coast-to-coast tour of the United

* Among the many London Italians who had queued patiently for gallery seats was Lorenzo Barbirolli, then first violin at the Empire Theatre in Leicester Square, and his five-year-old son John, who would make his Covent Garden début as guest conductor of *Madama Butterfly* on 30 June 1928.

States by a company singing an English version, with Florence Easton in the leading rôle.

Back from South America, Puccini began harassing his associates for news of any potential libretto, but Illica still smarted over his abortive labours on *Marie Antoinette* while Giacosa was dying slowly and painfully of cancer. In Ricordi's view the most promising candidate seemed to be a salacious tragic-comic novel, *La Femme et le Pantin*, by Pierre Louÿs, some of whose work had already been successfully set by Debussy. The novel's frankness had shocked but enthralled readers, and a dramatised version by the French playwright, Maurice Vaucaire, swept the Continent. The central character Conchita is a wanton who, like Carmen, had worked in a cigar-factory before turning temptress. Her *pantin* (puppet) is a wealthy aristrocrat whom she teases sadistically, without satisfying, even indulging in lovemaking with a younger man in his presence. When the puppet suddenly refuses to be manipulated and instead gives her a brutal thrashing, she forms a masochistic passion for him. This love-hate relationship, unsavoury but obviously dramatic, attracted Ricordi enough to begin negotiating for the operatic rights while Puccini was away in England for *Butterfly*'s second season.

That London visit not only renewed and consolidated his acquaintance with Sybil Seligman but furnished him with an unexpected source of libretti. She had very soon asked him to dine and, sympathising with his hunger for subjects, volunteered several suggestions. He rejected *The Last Days of Pompeii* but was perhaps too off-hand in dismissing *Anna Karenina* which might have been more rewarding. Kipling's *The Light that Failed* interested him, but he did not think it worth seeing on the stage and preferred to rely on Sybil's résumé of the plot. Although little of her advice would ever bear fruit, he had gratefully seized the advantage of having such an enthusiastic cultured woman as his London 'scout' and go-between.

He dined often with the Seligmans but declined Sybil's impulsive invitation to stay with them instead of the Savoy where, she argued disingenuously, his diet might not receive the necessary attention. She instructed her own cook to prepare appetising sugar-free dishes and cakes made with saccharine, but Puccini was too wary of sacrificing his independence or arousing Elvira's suspicions to move out of his hotel. Thus he could enjoy his shopping tours and even flirt a little with the charming Mrs Seligman without openly compromising himself. It was easy enough to fan her obvious infatuation while pleading, reasonably enough, that irregular rehearsals and his social engagements with Tosti and other friends made it inconvenient to use her home as a base.

Unusually cheerful throughout this visit, he even took time off from rehearsals of *Manon Lescaut* to give a short interview in the wings. When the reporter happened to raise his voice, he put a finger to his lips and whispered with mock severity, 'Let us please step quietly—like butterflies!' At the end of the short season, during which *Madama Butterfly* had been played eleven times to capacity, a supper in his honour was given at the Savoy by the company, including Mugnone, Rina Giachetti, Zenatello and de Marchi, his first Cavaradossi. Melba, Lady de Grey and other leaders of London society were present, and a most elaborate menu had been designed with the composer's portrait framed by bars of music from his operas. There was much laughter at the red-faced management's printing error in describing him as 'Maestro *Giovanni* Puccini', but although he took this gaffe with good humour he was less amused when one of the guests repeated the joke that all lazy tenors adored the second act of *Butterfly* because Pinkerton hardly reappears on stage after having abandoned his geisha.

He paused briefly in Milan to see Ricordi and Illica before hurrying off to Bologna where Toscanini was directing *Butterfly*. The singers and production seemed to him below par but the performance had been acclaimed, a woman in the audience fainting with ecstasy at the climax. Puccini thought Toscanini had taken a number of unjustified liberties with the score but he was too nervous of antagonising him to protest.

However, he made an excuse not to attend the opera's next performance in Turin under his baton.

Elvira welcomed him back affectionately but had to endure an exuberant account of his social triumphs in London. She was soon mollified by the gift of a handsome woollen stole which Sybil Seligman, no doubt appraised of her jealous disposition, had swiftly mailed with a message of good wishes. Puccini replied, 'Elvira sends you her fondest love . . . How I remember everything—the sweetness of your character, the walks in the Park, the melodiousness of your voice and your radiant beauty.' Admiration did not blunt his critical faculties. He had dutifully struggled through a French translation of the Kipling novel and pronounced it 'no good'. He was also against adapting Tennyson's *Enoch Arden* but tactfully complimented Sybil on being 'so clever and intelligent'.

She may already have become emotionally involved, but behaved with the decorum and touch of guile expected from a rich woman of the world. At Christmas she sent Elvira a tasteful trinket, with a gold pen and letter-case for 'dear Giacomo'. Her New Year's greeting card ended with a casual postscript mentioning that she would as usual be spending February on the French Riviera with her husband and younger son Vincent. It is not clear whether she or Puccini hinted that *Manon Lescaut* was being performed in Nice that month, but it provided a cast iron excuse for a rendezvous. The Ricordis regarded this production as so unimportant that their Milan office had difficulty in even establishing the exact opening date, but Sybil had energetically tracked it down. The Puccinis arrived too late for rehearsals and went straight to the theatre after a quick change. They shared the Seligmans' box and dined with them afterwards at the Café de Paris.

It was an altogether pleasant and surprisingly congenial meeting, considering the disparity in background of the quartet and, above all, Elvira's ingrained shyness of strangers. To Puccini's relief, she showed no awareness or resentment that her heavy bust and somewhat dowdy wardrobe compared unfavourably with the Englishwoman's slenderness and chic.

Sybil had brought several Worth creations in his newest pastel shades and seemed to have an unlimited stock of matching hats and lacy parasols. At night she dazzled in jewels with low-cut gowns which did justice to an exquisite neck and shoulders, but Elvira's thick hair had benefited from a visit to the hotel coiffeur and, as always, she carried herself with admirable majesty. She took at once to Vincent Seligman. As they strolled on the Promenade des Anglais, he grabbed her arm excitedly to point out boats on the horizon or some chauffeur-driven limousine with a coronet on its gleaming panels. His father, dapper in a college blazer, razor-creased white ducks and a yachting cap, chattered amusingly in fluent but heavily-accented Italian which Elvira gave up trying to correct. Puccini had made no concessions to the balmy Riviera weather. With his chronic fear of colds and draughts he wore an overcoat with the collar turned up, as standard a sartorial trademark of his as the Homburg cocked at an angle. His suit of thick dark blue cloth with pinstripes was one of several cut for him in Savile Row. His leg was stronger but he still leaned heavily on his stick clasped in lavender-coloured kid gloves.

As he was now fretting for news of *La Femme et Le Pantin* the holiday had to be brief. The couples parted with genuine regret on both sides. The Puccinis were still unpacking when a magnificent box of flowers arrived for Elvira with an affectionate card. Puccini wrote back gushingly, 'How we miss Nice, and above all our beloved and unforgettable Sybil! Not a minute goes by that we don't talk of you!' He was exuberant now that the way had practically been cleared to acquire the operatic rights in the Louÿs novel which Illica had provisionally agreed to translate from an adaptation by Vaucaire.

Ricordi had meanwhile arranged for d'Annunzio to visit Torre del Lago and discuss ideas for future libretti. This had become an urgent problem with Giacosa's doctors offering little hope of recovery. Ricordi was therefore desperate for a replacement. It so happened that d'Annunzio had

recently adapted one of his Abruzzi dramas for a piece by
Franchetti which La Scala would put on. Inflamed by operatic
fever, he needed little enough persuasion from Ricordi to visit
an old acquaintance, now the most popular composer of the
day.

Reeking of scent, he was squeaking out ideas almost before
he had peeled off the snow-white gloves. He jingled ancient
coins in his pockets ('to renew their patina from the heat of
my body'), but Puccini guessed that more than body heat
would be needed to restore his finances. His mistresses, marble
bathing pools and housemaids coiffed and costumed in the
Greek style had all but bankrupted him. This sudden passion
for writing libretti was obviously a desperate move to head off
an army of moneylenders.

He quickly outlined the plot of his play, *La Parisina*, a
subject which had once attracted Donizetti. At dinner Puccini,
dizzy at the prospect of collaborating with the illustrious poet,
recklessly promised him 20,000 lire (£800) on delivery of the
libretto, without taking the precaution of consulting Ricordi.
D'Annunzio departed in excellent humour, announcing gaily
that he proposed breaking his return journey to call on Ouida,
'the mad old Englishwoman', all of whose novels about
English high life he had read in translation. Blind in one eye,
swathed in shawls and wearing a bonnet like Queen Victoria,
she lived across the lake in a tiny ramshackle villa, guarded by
savage dogs whom she refused to muzzle. It was known that
she starved herself to feed them delicious scraps. The name of
'Ouida' meant little to Puccini, who had quite forgotten that
the music critic of the *Corriere della Sera* had once mentioned
a story of hers as a possible operatic subject. He declined to
accompany d'Annunzio, explaining that the crazy creature
would probably set her dogs on him as she disapproved
fanatically of hunting and bombarded the newspapers with
letters attacking vivisection.

He next met d'Annunzio at La Scala where he and Elvira
shared a box with the Tostis for the opening of Franchetti's
opera, an unhappy near-disaster for the composer who had to

fight back the tears when Puccini was given a standing ovation by the fickle claque as he left the theatre. D'Annunzio's ego had also taken a rap. He held all his work in such esteem that the bells of his local church used to be rung to celebrate the completion of every new poem. Although he could not be blamed for Franchetti's mediocre score, he was unaccustomed to failure and therefore warmed even more to the chance of recovering his prestige through the Maestro from Lucca. But his outline for *Parisina* did not enthuse Puccini, who expressed far more interest in a hasty alternative offer to adapt one of his poems, *La Rosa di Cipro*. By now d'Annunzio was so short of cash that a moneylender had to be cajoled into advancing a loan entirely on the strength of his 'arrangement' with Puccini.

While the poet was feverishly working on his script, an agreement had at last been signed for Pierre Louÿs' novel. The opera would be called *Conchita* after its nasty heroine. But despite two such promising subjects in the making, Puccini had become unusually restless. After a few days in the mountains with Tosti, he paid an unannounced visit to Caruso's baronial Villa Bellosguardo at Signa, forty miles from Florence. The tenor, still shaken by his experience of the San Francisco earthquake, was surrounded by sympathetic friends, like the conductor Mugnone, and a host of relatives. Puccini dutifully inspected the magnificently landscaped gardens (so much more impressive than his own home-made patch at Torre!), but was relieved to escape from what seemed to him a noisy extravaganza of flamboyance and vulgarity, with most of the guests obviously sponging on Caruso's good nature. He was not perhaps too well qualified to judge the tenor's excellent taste in assembling such fine examples of sixteenth century Italian furniture and objets d'art, but accurately assessed the character of Ada Giachetti, whom he had always instinctively disliked. An overdressed haughty chatelaine, she looked so discontented that Puccini found it easy enough to credit the rumours about her many lovers, including a young chauffeur who swaggered like a Sicilian bandit.

Before taking his leave, he politely invited Caruso and his mistress to visit him at Torre del Lago and a day or two later was genuinely delighted when the singer arrived alone, explaining that he needed to relax before his strenuous season at Covent Garden. This did not prevent Puccini from indulging in some mischievous cruelty at his expense. One night they had dined and wined exuberantly, with Pagni and other local bohemians coming in afterwards for cards. They soon turned from *scopa* to poker which Puccini and Caruso both enjoyed, although the tenor's expressive features made him an inevitable loser. At dawn, after very little sleep, he was shaken awake and persuaded to go out duck-shooting. Lured on to the marshes by Puccini, who had swiftly punted off with Manfredi, the little tenor waited several hours for them to return. He arrived back at the villa, half-frozen and plastered with mud, but triumphantly displaying his entire bag for the day; a single tiny quail. Puccini begged forgiveness and promised to entertain him to a full-scale supper at Pagani's as a peace-offering.

His sudden decision to visit London that May was ostensibly to see Caruso's Pinkerton for the first time, but one can surmise that he needed Sybil's soothing company while his various libretti were slowly incubating. He checked in as usual at the Savoy but was soon dining regularly at the Seligmans and joining Sybil on shopping excursions. During her husband's absence in the City they would often be closeted in her drawing room, discussing operatic plans and perhaps more tenderly personal matters. She had unearthed yet another possible subject, this time Oscar Wilde's unfinished one-act melodrama, *A Florentine Tragedy*, which Puccini liked enough to approve her approaching Robert Ross, Wilde's literary executor, who happened to be a friend of hers.

In the Seligmans' box at Covent Garden he saw Caruso in *Rigoletto* but was naturally more concerned with his Rodolfo. His partnership with Melba melted every heart, including Puccini's, who went backstage to embrace them. But this exhilaration faded quickly during the rehearsals of *Butterfly*.

Although full of praise for Caruso's fine legato singing as a surprisingly plausible Pinkerton, with Destinn and Scotti both in superb voice, he was disappointed in the orchestra and complained peevishly to Campanini. The whole production seemed mediocre and unworthy of camparison with others he had seen in Italy and South America. He duly supped Caruso at Pagani's but did not stay for *Tosca* in which the tenor triumphed with Rina Giachetti in the name part and Scotti as Scarpia. Next morning Caruso awoke to such a chorus of newspaper praise that he rushed out to a Piccadilly gunsmith's and sent the composer an expensive sporting rifle.

It was not Puccini's only gift. After seeing him off at Folkestone, Sybil despatched a handsome walking stick and a picnic basket which he promised would remain unused until she arrived with her sons for a holiday in the autumn. 'We'll give it its first outing together in the cool shady woods at Abetone', he wrote from Milan. Elvira was busy 'from morning till night' with Fosca, but she thanked Sybil for a magnificent cushion.

They were now exchanging letters at least once a week. Sybil's have not been preserved, as Puccini kept little more than business correspondence to avoid inflaming Elvira's jealousy, but his own letters to Sybil clearly testify to their growing friendship. He was already confiding details of his movements, his state of health, and the progress—or lack of it—on the many scripts in preparation. He now urged her to send him the Wilde translation and synopses of any other current plays with operatic possibilities. At the same time she was left in no doubt that their friendship went deeper. That spring he wrote from Milan, 'It seems to me that you are the person who has come nearest to understanding my nature—and you are so far away from me!! I am sending you a little photograph to remember me by—a thousand affectionate thoughts for that exquisite and beautiful creature who is the *best friend* I have.'

Puccini's characteristic Homburg, slightly tilted, and upturned coat collar
were later reproduced in Prince Paul Troubetzkoi's lifelike statuette.

Puccini in his study at Torre del Lago. Chainsmoking throughout the night, he usually composed at a Förster upright piano, with damper, and a sidetable covered with his notes. Here at midnight, 10 December 1895,

he ended Mimi's death scene, weeping hysterically. 'It was as though I had seen my own child die', he recalled.

Puccini never lost his taste for shooting wildfowl and duck on marshy Lake Massaciúccoli. He even worked in hunting regalia, with a gun beside him, ready for a dawn excursion.

Giulio Ricordi, Puccini's publisher, remained a friend and understanding guide over the years. His allowance of 300 lire (£12) a month kept the composer alive until his triumph with *Manon Lescaut*.

At the wheel of his first car, a Clement, with the chauffeur, Ultimo. An
early motoring enthusiast, Puccini liked driving at high speed. Returning
from Lucca one night in February 1903, he crashed. The accident held up

Madama Butterfly for several months and also left him with a permanent limp. He continued to buy faster cars. His last: an 8-cylinder Lancia.

Shipboard send-off before the Puccinis sail for summer season in Buenos Aires. His fee for attendance: 50,000 francs (£2,000). Standing beside Elvira (l. to r.), Illica and Toscanini.

PART THREE

Sybil

Chapter Nine

Puccini's long-lasting association with Sybil Seligman has inevitably stimulated speculation and a spicy whiff of scandal. Most of his Italian biographers, although generally unsparing of highly-coloured and often scabrous accounts of his philanderings, seem unusually reluctant to cast her as a *femme fatale*. Their reticence may have stemmed from libel fears during her lifetime (she survived until 1935) or an over-reliance on the composer's letters to Sybil, edited and published by her son Vincent, three years after her death. They echo Puccini's own insistence that they were only 'affectionate friends, full of good and sincere feelings towards each other.'

It is possible that Sybil's letters might have presented a different picture had they been preserved. Moreover, it has long been inferred that Vincent's emphatic denial of anything improper in his mother's conduct could be explained by an anxiety to sanctify her memory, backed by his somewhat naive view of Puccini's character. Only a blinkered hero-worshipper could write so uncritically of the composer's 'true nobility of character, his patience, his long-suffering, and his amazingly forgiving spirit.'

The present writer shared these misgivings about a unilateral correspondence, 'selected and edited' by a loving son, until it became possible to study the unused letters, which Vincent Seligman decided against publishing. They are, for the most part trivial, often repetitive, and give no hint of any sexual attachment, although confirming that the early ones were far more ardent in tone than those that followed. But this could be explained by Puccini's Latin weakness for paying extravagant compliments, particularly to an attractive hostess who had flattered his ego and could promote his interests, through Lady de Grey and others of influence, with the Covent Garden management.

147

Nevertheless, one cannot altogether rule out the possibility that Sybil became his mistress for a brief period. Mosco Carner, whose views are always entitled to respect, cites the authority of her sister Mrs Violet Schiff, in asserting that 'it began as a passionate love affair and only with the years developed into one of the few genuine friendships which Puccini was able to form; it lasted to his death.' Against this, the factor of sisterly rivalry must be taken into account. Sydney Schiff was a gifted novelist, editor of *Art and Letters* and later translator of Proust's *Le Temps Retrouvé*. His wife became a patron of art, literature and music, both in London and Paris, but the effete Proust whom she adored, was hardly as prestigious a scalp as Puccini. One can assume, not too uncharitably, that her retrospective view of Sybil's morals may have owed something to the brisk taste for gossip which she indulged in later years. But in fairness to her, others formed a similar impression during Puccini's first visits to London when he escorted Sybil to the Tostis and informal Sunday luncheons at Luigi Denza's house in St John's Wood. They behaved decorously but somehow suggested a tender understanding which, reinforced by the composer's notorious reputation for philandering, hinted at rather more than an innocent friendship.

If an *affaire* started after their second meeting in 1905, it could have flourished only during Puccini's subsequent trips to England. Although Sybil had the means and inclination to travel at will, she seldom went abroad without her husband or one of her sons, usually Vincent. Any rendezvous in Italy, where Puccini's name and fame would have made secrecy virtually impossible, must sooner or later have come to Elvira's sharp ears. Relatives and malicious gossips primed her with tittle-tattle about his infidelities, but apart from a brief show of irritation on Elvira's part some years later, when she was almost deranged by menopause, nothing remotely suggests she ever suspected them of misconduct. Over the years both the Seligmans gave constant proof of their affection for her with gifts and tender messages of sympathy whenever she was sick or worried about her children.

It should not, however, be overlooked that while Puccini's celebrity and affluence had given him social poise, Elvira remained a simple bourgeoise to whom Edwardian England was as remote as Tibet. She was far more likely to be affronted by his local wenching than any suspected rustling from boudoirs hundreds of miles away. The standards of London high society, where wives now smoked in public and sometimes dined alone with lovers or men friends, might have shocked her, but few in Sybil's own circle would have been scandalised if she had visited Puccini's hotel suite, presumably to discuss libretti, or even received him at home when her sons were away at their boarding schools and her husband busily discounting bills in the City.

David Seligman played the rôle of *mari complaisant* with unruffled dignity and for the best of reasons encouraged the friendship, innocent or otherwise. Like most rich Edwardians, he enjoyed food, drink and baccarat, but women were his principal form of relaxation. Ironically, he maintained his corps of mistresses without in any way tarnishing a serene picture of domestic bliss, whereas Puccini, despite the traditional latitude demanded by Toscanini and many other Italian husbands, not only acquired a libertine's reputation but was never immune from his wife's jealous tantrums. But perhaps David Seligman was more deserving! In contrast to Puccini, who did not believe in impoverishing himself like Scotti to make conquests, and was never tempted to follow Caruso's unfortunate precedent in maintaining a full-scale ménage for Ada Giachetti, the banker behaved generously towards his women. Years after his death, his family continued to pay one white-haired ex-charmer an annuity of £700 a year.

He had some justification for his extra-marital adventures. After the painful forceps delivery of her first baby Esmond (which may have contributed to his lifelong epilepsy), Sybil developed such a distaste for sexual intercourse that her younger son Vincent once declared laughingly that his own birth

149

almost qualified as an immaculate conception. In this context, even taking Puccini's charm and physical magnetism into account, the theory of a passionate liaison becomes even more remote.

Nevertheless, a fully platonic friendship seems quite out of character for a man of his temperament. His attitude to women was flagrantly amoral; he once declared, 'On the day when I am no longer in love, you can hold my funeral.' But his amours were rarely anything but brief, explicit and uncomplicated by deep emotion. At times of creative stress, over-anxiety or frustration he emulated d'Annunzio's eroto-mania and had a similar intolerable need for 'something fleshly, something that resembles a carnal assault, a mixture of outrage and intoxication' (*Le Faville del Maglio*). However, he had no taste for leading actresses or aristocratic nymphoman-iacs, preferring chorus girls, waitresses and other readily-available admirers whom he picked off with as little emotion as the wildfowl on Lake Massaciúccoli. But, unlike the promiscuous poet, he was fortunate in not siring any illegitimate children and, even more remarkably, escaped syphilis.

His melancholia demanded relief in violent sex, slaughtering birds and driving high-powered cars at reckless speed. After a tiff with Elvira, or even some unkind review of one of his operas, he would summon his chauffeur Ultimo and drive off angrily to Milan or Rome, but more often than not turn back for Torre once he had calmed down. He tired of women just as quickly. Richard Specht aptly describes him as 'a male siren who sips each flower and changes every hour'. He enjoyed a few non-scandalous friendships with singers too fat (like Tetrazzini) to attract him physically and, in the case of Gilda dalla Rizza and others, happily married or otherwise unwill-ing to succumb to his charms. But Sybil Seligman was uniquely qualified, socially and intellectually, to remain a devoted confidante for the better part of twenty years once their first ardour, if any, had subsided. Distance undoubtedly helped to keep them together, and Puccini's letters often confirm the joy of reunion after long periods apart.

Within a few months of their pleasant Riviera interlude, the two families met again at Abetone in August 1906. Elvira, plainly more at ease in familiar and unsophisticated territory, made the Seligmans warmly welcome. As the lodge was too cramped for visitors, they stayed at the so-called Grand Hotel in the village. The boys (Esmond, with fair ringlets and more aesthetic than his high-spirited brother) amused themselves by feeding wild strawberries to a tame bear and Puccini's chauffeur took them on perilous drives over the steep Apennine passes from which they usually returned smiling but shaken, Esmond giving his brother 'Vini' (Vincent) an object lesson in Etonian fortitude although by far the more nervous of the two.

They swam, picnicked and often dined al fresco on delicious food prepared by Elvira who saw nothing amiss when Sybil spent hours in the garden with Puccini, reading out passages from Wilde's *Florentine Tragedy* and translating as she went along. He seemed more excited, however, by a visit to d'Annunzio, who was staying at nearby Pietrasanta and had promised to deliver the first two acts of *Rose of Cyprus* within a few days.

This euphoria dissolved almost before d'Annunzio had finished reciting from the manuscript in his high-pitched voice. Puccini toyed with his fountain pen, a gift from Sybil, and continuously smoked Turkish cigarettes from the casket she had brought him.* He professed to be overwhelmed by poetry too powerful for his own talent, but d'Annunzio saw through the stammered compliments. He departed without his hoped-for fee of 20,000 lire for months of wasted effort. To his credit, although confessing to a friend that his 'sterile contacts with the Maestro from Lucca' had caused him serious difficulty over a promissory note, he did not indulge in

* Sybil's father was one of the Beddington family, who founded the Abdulla cigarette and tobacco company.

malicious reproaches. Understandably, however, he shrugged off a letter in which the composer begged for a third outline, 'a more humble one suited to my strength'.

Within a few days Puccini welcomed a less disappointing visitor, Maurice Vaucaire, who had arrived from Paris with the libretto of *La Conchita*. Soon afterwards, on 2 September, they received news of Giacosa's death. Puccini retreated to his study for several hours and emerged, still weeping, for solace from Elvira and Sybil. He spoke brokenly of the playwright whose inspiration and sympathy had steered his operas through so many dark tunnels. But he recovered quickly and implored Illica to lose no time in translating and adapting Vaucaire's manuscript. The first draft proved unsatisfactory and Puccini already lamented the loss of Giacosa, who had so often curbed his brilliant but slapdash partner. In fact he had himself gone cold on 'the cursed Spanish slut' (Conchita) and found the sordid plot increasingly repellent. He turned back to Wilde's *A Florentine Tragedy*, which suddenly struck him as a possible rival to Richard Strauss's *Salome*. Without consulting Ricordi, he urged Sybil to arrange for a translation.

Relations between publisher and composer grew strained for the first and only time. The fault was not entirely Puccini's. Ricordi, now ailing and irritable, had hoped to groom his son for the succession while continuing to hold the reins, but Tito disliked sitting behind a desk in Milan. He departed huffily that autumn to supervise the Savage Company's *Butterfly* tour of several American cities, soon threatening to resign altogether from the firm. His father did not take this too seriously but Tito was sufficiently in earnest to ask Puccini and others to send testimonials which might help to set him up as an impresario in New York.

This family crisis had disturbed Giulio Ricordi, normally the most urbane of men, but he had every justification to resent Puccini's jackdaw pecking at half-a-dozen libretti and his cavalier treatment of d'Annunzio and Illica, both of obvious potential value after Giacosa's death. Ricordi plainly doubted Sybil's eye for suitable operatic subjects and thought so little of Wilde's play that he wired Illica, 'Throw Florentine stupidity into fire'. As *La Conchita* still seemed to him the most promising candidate on offer, he had commissioned Puccini to set it for a fee of 70,000 lire, payable in three instalments, with a royalty of thirty-five per cent of all rentals and royalties 'after deduction of the usual agent's fees'.

Puccini signed but very soon had second thoughts about the plot. It seems that he had also, perhaps flippantly, objected to giving up the usual sixty-five per cent of proceeds. On 19 November Ricordi replied in a rare outburst of sarcasm, 'All right—kick out that bloodsucker of a publisher, who is swimming in his millions . . . Up to now, Butterfly is a liability . . . What with the administrative expense, the personal representation, the voyages, more voyages, regal suites, banquets, and all the other incidental nuisances.' However, he reminded his 'Giacomo, Doge and Imperator' that he would always be like a son to him.

Tempers cooled off when Puccini received an invitation to attend rehearsals of *Butterfly* at the Opéra-Comique. Ricordi hoped that Pierre Louÿs and Vaucaire might together revive the composer's zest for their project, but he had become too involved in maddening difficulties over *Butterfly* to think of anything else. Albert Carré the manager had been difficult enough during the first French production of *La Bohème*. Now the henpecked husband of the prima donna who would sing Cio-Cio-San, he sided meekly with her when she demanded cuts to make the rôle less exhausting. Puccini soon decided that 'Madame pomme de terre' lacked the charm and voice for his geisha, but he could do little as Carré owned the performing rights throughout France for the next two years and would clearly not hesitate to shelve them altogether unless the pampered prima donna had the last word.

Puccini bit his lips and tried to keep the peace by flattering Marguérite Carré, like everyone else, but his half-hearted compliments did not deceive her. She bowed curtly when they met and would rarely speak a civil word to him. Carré took his cue from her while André Messager, the resident conductor, now showed naked hostility. Himself the composer of *Madame Chrysanthème*, an operetta based on Loti's geisha heroine, he considered that Puccini's wedding ceremony and final love scene were lifted from his own work and stiffly declined to conduct the new opera, handing his baton to a far less experienced newcomer.

While rehearsals creaked on, with the prima donna tiresomely exacting and the second-rate orchestra demoralised without Messager, Puccini grew testier. He complained to his sister Nitteti of his 'accursed diabetes' and asked Sybil to send him some elixir to raise his spirits. When away from the theatre he mooned about the hotel room in pyjamas, cursing the rain which seemed to coincide with each of his trips to France.

Elvira had been quite unable to resist visiting Paris for the first time. She prattled on about the shops and gay boulevards but cross-examined him suspiciously whenever he went out alone to some tedious reception. He could not refuse an invitation to dine at the Italian Embassy to meet Clemenceau and other prominent Frenchmen, but soon left. His habit of flitting among guests and quickly vanishing earned him the nickname of 'Monsieur Butterfly', but it was given and received without affection. After one interminable *soirée* with coquettish but ancient duchesses irritating him even more than the offhand critics, he scribbled a note to assure Sybil that he pined to see London again, 'in spite of the fog'. Soon afterwards he asked David Seligman to permit her to come over for the opening of *Butterfly*, adding politely, 'And why don't you take a run over to Paris, too? It would give me so much pleasure to see you.' Sybil arrived alone but had to leave two days later when her husband wired that Vincent had been hurt during acrobatics in his school gymnasium. She stayed by his bedside, night and day, but an operation proved unnecessary and she promised to return for the première, now scheduled for 28 December as Marguérite Carré had contracted a sore throat. This postponement infuriated Puccini, who had meantime made arrangements to sail for New York early in January and disliked being rushed.

Tito Ricordi had enthusiastically reported that the *Butterfly* (in English) tour was ending a six-month run of over 200 performances. It stimulated the Metropolitan to schedule four Puccini operas, with the first performance in Italian of *Butterfly* to follow *Manon Lescaut* as highlights of the 1906–7 season, the most critical in its history. The management had suffered heavy losses from the San Francisco earthquake which wrecked a profitable tour, destroying valuable scenery and costumes. Receipts had slumped, year after year, due to a stale repertoire and shabby, under-rehearsed productions. Far more serious, however, was a threat to the Metropolitan's monopoly from the new Manhattan Opera House on West Thirty-fourth Street, where Oscar Hammerstein had engaged Melba at $3,000 a performance and was swiftly arranging contracts for Tetrazzini, Mary Garden and John McCormack to lure audiences from his rival.*

The Metropolitan had countered with a glittering company of established favourites like Caruso, Andréas Dippel, Scotti, Emma Eames and Sembrich (a superb Mimì), but exciting new stars had also been added to the roster. Geraldine Farrar opened the season with a sensational American début in *Roméo et Juliette* and Lina Cavalieri, described by d'Annunzio as 'the most beautiful face on earth', later made her bow in Giordano's *Fedora* having already captivated French audiences with Caruso as her partner. But the harassed manager, Heinrich Conried, still needed some novel attraction to trump Hammerstein's publicity aces. Backed by his multi-millionaire chairman, Otto M. Kahn, he had invited Puccini to 'supervise' *Manon Lescaut* and *Madama Butterfly* for a fee of $8,000, but he was chiefly interested in exploiting his name and not expecting him to direct rehearsals.

The composer had accepted without hesitation. It helped to console him for his sufferings at the Opéra-Comique and also

* The 'Battle of the Opera Houses' is fully described in the author's *Caruso*.

offered escape from a series of acrimonious meetings over *La Conchita*. He had endured the joint importunities of Vaucaire and Pierre Louÿs, whom he derisively nicknamed *Inouï*, the novelist's favourite exclamation of dissent whenever Puccini proposed making 'the Spanish slut' a little more appetising. Illica had arrived in Paris to try and reach a compromise, but quickly saw through the composer's polite evasions. He was not deceived when Puccini broke off one conference with the lame excuse of having to write to Caruso.

The world's newspapers were still buzzing with reports of the tenor's arrest and conviction on a charge of pinching a woman's behind in the Central Park Zoo. But the Metropolitan public had given their idol a heart-warming reception in *La Bohème*, his first appearance after a scandal which had threatened to end his career in America. 'A put-up job by some hostile impresario,' declared Puccini, presumably with Hammerstein in mind. However, he did not share Sybil's intensely emotional reaction to the affair. Their sexual liaison may have ceased by this time, if it existed at all, but he had become over-possessive to the point of small-minded jealousy of Caruso, and showed irritation if she dared to speak too adoringly of his voice.

As the *Butterfly* première approached, he became pricklier and more nervous but seemed fairly cheerful when Tonio arrived to celebrate his father's forty-eighth birthday, soon followed by Sybil, who was determined not to miss the opening night. He had confided that 'Mme Carré . . . seems to me like a woman who wants to be sick and can't—poor Butterfly!' However, she sang competently and her personal following helped to ensure a warm reception for the opera. The critics were more restrained, but *Butterfly* attracted such capacity houses that, on the third night, Tonio had to stand throughout the performance and the composer himself was refused a box. By now he was impatient to leave Paris, although far from relishing the prospect of spending six weeks in New York with Elvira. Since the Metropolitan had generously offered two first-class return tickets in addition to the fee, he could not plead expense when she offered to accompany him, but his sourness was made plain enough in a letter to Sybil; 'I've secured accommodation on the boat—a cabin amidships and a vomitorium for Elvira.'

With sailing-time only a few days ahead, he made a flying visit to Milan for thick underwear and a fur-lined overcoat as the newspapers were reporting sub-zero temperatures in New York. He snatched a hurried dinner at the Cova with Gatti-Casazza and Toscanini, again in double-harness at La Scala, although the little Maestro had become even more dictatorial. He not only discouraged applause for his own efforts, refusing to take curtain calls, but rigidly upheld his ban on encores. He once fined some ballet dancers for chatting in the wings during a performance. When the easy-going President of the Board, Duke Uberto Visconti, cancelled the fines, Toscanini retaliated by pinning up a notice barring him from the theatre at all rehearsals. He was equally emphatic in his dislike of musicians blocking the audience's view of the stage. A committee was set up, with himself, Boito and Puccini, to consider the whole question. Finally, with Boito dissenting, it was decided to 'sink' the orchestra, which Verdi and Wagner had always advocated.

Puccini sailed for New York in the *Kaiserin Auguste Viktoria* on what turned out to be a nightmare voyage. Elvira was wretchedly seasick and seldom emerged from their luxury suite, while he paced the heaving deck rather than face the ship's band who played extracts non-stop from *La Bohème*. Since few of the officers spoke either Italian or French, and his German vocabulary was mainly limited to 'Auf Wiedersehen', 'Guten Tag' and 'Kotelette mit Kartoffeln', he made no social contact and dodged fellow-passengers who tried to pump his hand. His temper did not improve when the ship was delayed two days by fog and docked in New York a couple of hours before the opening of *Manon Lescaut*, barely giving him time to change into evening clothes.

After the first act he was recognised in the directors' box and welcomed with an exuberant fanfare from the orchestra. The opera had a clamorous reception and he could not fault the performances of Caruso, Scotti and Lina Cavalieri, whose flashing dark eyes and coquettish style exactly fitted the title-rôle. She had a colourfully unconventional background. Raised in a Roman slum, she had once hawked flowers in the Piazza Colonna and sold theatre programmes before emerging as a café-concert singer. Her vivacious manner and Carmen-like looks led to revue engagements at the Folies-Bergère and London's Empire Theatre. In 1900 while in Russia, she married Prince Bariatonsky, who helped to advance her oper-atic career. She had made her début in Lisbon as Puccini's Mimì, followed by Nedda, and quickly became a favourite in St Petersburg, Monte Carlo and Paris.

On the first visit to New York, she turned very naturally to her countrymen for encouragement. Puccini was soon sending bouquets and supping with her at restaurants like Del Pezzo's, which Caruso, the violinist Kreisler and other friends patronised. Kreisler, whom Puccini liked and often addressed as 'L'Amico Fritz', was several years younger but had a similar moustache and was not unlike him in looks. He amused them, if not his redheaded American wife, by recalling that through-out his European tours he was constantly addressed as 'Maestro Puccini' and pestered for his autograph. He swore that in a Rome café a crowd of girls had encircled him, planted hot kisses on his lips and refused to believe that he was not the creator of La Bohème.

As Elvira preferred to huddle in their warm tenth-storey suite at the Hotel Astor rather than face temperatures of thirteen below zero, Puccini had more freedom to escort Lina Cavalieri, with Scotti acting as discreet chaperone at their frequent rendezvous. At a Metropolitan concert for Conried's annual benefit, Puccini sat alone in the soprano's box where she joined him after singing an aria from Mefistofele. This preceded the first American production of Richard Strauss's Salome which had already stunned but titillated German audiences. Geraldine Farrar had been offered the leading rôle but some sixth sense had warned her off. Olive Fremstad was less fortunate. Many in the stalls and several Diamond Horseshoe Dowagers stalked out of the theatre even before the curtain fell to outraged hisses.

Puccini was impressed by the sultry atmosphere of the piece and later paid tribute to its subtle symphonic arrangements, but he recoiled from the stage horrors which made his torture scenes in *Tosca* seem almost innocuous. Next morning the entire Press denounced the opera as decadent and grossly offensive to Anglo-Saxon morality. The Metropolitan's land-lords threatened to cancel the lease unless it was withdrawn, and Conried retreated in a panic. Puccini would later deny that this fiasco had influenced his final decision to abandon *Conchita*, but he told a reporter from the *New York Times*, 'I haven't even begun work on *La Femme et Le Pantin*. I have doubts if the American public would accept that after the treatment *Salome* recently received.'

He became even more attached to Lina Cavalieri when a scheduled production of *Tosca* was threatened by the sudden illness of Emma Eames. He persuaded her to deputise although she had never sung the rôle and would have only one or two rehearsals without even an orchestra. His coaching and gentle encouragement extracted an above-average performance. By the time Elvira felt able to face sightseeing, the Metropolitan was already humming with backstage gossip about her hus-band's infatuation. If anything, it made him still more appeal-ing to the interviewers who flocked to the Astor. They reported on his good looks, charm and debonair appearance, one expressing astonishment that his hair was so neatly trimmed. His English was practically confined to 'okay', but he had none of Caruso's vulgar ebullience or the superiority which many European musical celebrities assumed as soon as they stepped on American soil. He signed autographs with a gracious smile, often gallantly kissing the hand of some attrac-tive admirer. The New York weather, cold but sunny, invi-gorated him almost as much as Cavalieri's company. This was a very different composer from the elusive 'Monsieur Butterfly' of Paris. He turned down few invitations and delighted his countrymen by sitting for a special portrait, copies of which were sold in aid of a building fund for an Italian orphanage.

This abnormal bonhomie did not survive the nerve-racking days of rehearsing *Madama Butterfly*. He would have preferred Destinn as the geisha, but she disliked long sea voyages and had refused to cross the Atlantic, so Geraldine Farrar accepted the challenge and engaged a Japanese actress for private coaching. She even shaved her eyebrows, which made her look remarkably odd out-of-doors as the practice was not then fashionable. Whenever Puccini visited her apartment at the old Hotel Netherlands, she would be padding about in a kimono and tight one-toed canvas shoes to perfect her oriental walk. With all this devotion to art, however, she did not at first impress him. Her voice was melodious but seemed smallish compared with Destinn's, and quite often she sang out of tune. He could not fault either Caruso or Scotti but thought the stage-management erratic and began demanding far more rehearsals than the penny-pinching Conried usually allowed. His most savage criticism, bottled up and reserved for the ears of Cavalieri, Scotti and other intimates, was levelled at the conductor Arturo Vigna, whose 'asinine, listless time-beating' made him sigh for Toscanini.

He reported all his woes and anxieties to Sybil but discreetly made only brief mention of Cavalieri ('I liked her in *Manon*; she did it really well'). The soprano not only offered succour and comfort when he left the theatre after hours of wrangling with the singers and orchestra but often watched rehearsals from a box, constantly flashing him encouraging smiles. Elvira paid an unexpected visit one day and must have sensed the familiarity. After he had returned late at night from a reception at Mrs Cornelius Vanderbilt's, she stealthily went through his pockets and in the lining of his silk hat found a note from Cavalieri confirming a rendezvous. Next morning they snapped at each other like angry turtles, but Elvira had to retreat until the all-important première was over.

The dress rehearsal was charged with more than the usual quota of last-minute nerves. Caruso chain-smoked, gargled incessantly and sprayed his throat at short intervals, while Puccini gulped a tonic made up from Sybil's prescription. Vigna held his baton in trembling hands, and Louise Homer (Suzuki) imagined appalling disasters for her twin babies whom she had left in charge of a new housemaid. Only Geraldine Farrar, attended by her devoted but formidable mother, seemed unperturbed. They munched through a stack of free chicken sandwiches supplied by the management and drank hot bouillon from their Thermos flasks, then a rare novelty.

The première was a spectacular triumph, followed by four performances which netted the ticket 'scalpers' enormous profits. This time the audience's enthusiasm was unanimously echoed by the critics. Richard Aldrich saw 'the fine Italian hand of Mr Puccini himself, who has moulded it according to his own ideas and refined and beautified it into one of the most finished performances seen at the Metropolitan for many a long day.' The *Tribune* carried an unusually ecstatic notice from Henry E. Krehbiel, who declared, 'There is nothing more admirable in the score of *Madama Butterfly* than the refined and ingenious skill with which the composer bent the square-toed rhythms and monotonous tunes of Japanese music to his purposes.'

Puccini was gratified, but a sharpish attack of influenza affected his temper. In a letter to Sybil he could not resist an ill-natured gibe at Caruso; 'as regards your *god* (*entre nous*) I make you a present of him—he won't learn anything, he's lazy and he's too pleased with himself—all the same his voice is magnificent.' By the same post he reported gloomily to Tito Ricordi, '*Butterfly* went very well as far as the Press and public were concerned, *but not so as to please me*. It was a performance without poetry. Farrar is not too satisfactory . . .'

In fact she had given the first of over a hundred fine

Metropolitan performances as the geisha. The rôle helped to gain her a vast following, notably among the young 'Gerry-flappers' who aped her fans, slippers and coiffure. They mobbed her, night after night, at the stage-door but there was no shortage of male admirers, one of whom sent her a complete wardrobe of silk kimonos with an exquisitely wrought dagger in a lacquer case adorned by her monogram in Japanese. Scotti also lost his heart but made no headway with the very practical American girl and her vigilant 'Mammina'. Puccini still considered her inferior to his adorable Rosina Storchio and the technically more accomplished Destinn, but he sent her a framed portrait of himself inscribed, 'To the most intelligent artist, Miss Geraldine Farrar, this remembrance of her incomparable Butterfly at the Metropolitan.' She was not taken in and commented acidly in her memoirs, 'He shared our curtain calls and was all that was agreeable, as well he might be, seeing the royalties that came to him from our efforts.'

This seems a touch uncharitable in the circumstances. She was snapped up by the Victor Company to make recordings of *Madama Butterfly* and other Puccini favourites which earned her massive royalties but, for some years, nothing for the composer. Hearing that Caruso's income from gramophone records, with *Tosca* and *La Bohème* arias among his liveliest sellers, now approached $100,000 a year, he wrote sharply to the *New York Herald*, 'While I am heartily glad that my fellow-countrymen like Messrs Caruso and Scotti are not only paid princely honorariums for rendering solos from my operas into recordings but are also allowed liberal royalties on the sale of these records, it seems strangely inconsistent that the composer of these very themes should not be granted slight pecuniary recognition.' Attacking this musical piracy, he also demanded 'the same right to select the medium and the method by which they shall be transmitted to the public as I have in choosing the managers and theatres to produce my operas'.

The piracy was not limited to recordings. As Conried had

first call on Ricordi composers, headed by Verdi and Puccini, Hammerstein turned resourcefully to French operas neglected by the Metropolitan. He bought up rights in Charpentier, Debussy and Massenet in which Mary Garden and Maurice Renaud, the popular baritone from the Opéra-Comique, would soon attract New Yorkers to the box-office, but he did not underrate the Puccini vogue. He desperately wanted Melba to sing Mimì and decided to chance his arm over copyright.

His first task was to secure a copy of the *La Bohème* score, which had never been printed. A dozen handwritten copies were locked away in the publishers' vaults in Milan and only released by Giulio Ricordi's special dispensation. Previously he had allowed touring companies to perform the opera in America on payment of a copyright fee of $150 for each performance, but Hammerstein obviously had no hope of staging one of the Metropolitan's favourite operas. Knowing this, he tracked down a mangled copy of the score but found it too imperfect for use by an artist of Melba's standing. He turned for help to his resident conductor Campanini, who had often directed the opera in Italy and other countries and could interpolate various passages from memory. However, with an injunction imminent, he became too nervous of offending Ricordi or the composer to conduct the 'bootlegged' version himself. A deputy was brought in to lead the orchestra, and Melba, supported by Bonci (hopefully boosted by Hammerstein as 'the new Caruso'), somehow overcame the handicap of a makeshift score.

After only three performances at the Manhattan, the Ricordi office duly secured its injunction, despite protests from Hammerstein and his angry patrons. It gave the opera enormous publicity although Puccini would not comment on the dispute. He was praised for his dignified reticence but had sound reasons to stay neutral. Melba was still very much the queen bee at Covent Garden, and it would also have been foolish to risk antagonising Hammerstein before the court had given its final ruling. However, he chuckled over stories of tickets changing hands at inflated prices for the rival performances.

In the last fortnight of their stay he took Elvira sightseeing which helped to mollify her for the Cavalieri contretemps. That liaison had cooled off on both sides, possibly because the soprano was already putting rings through the noses of various Astor and Vanderbilt scions, who showered her with diamonds. The Puccinis, furred and muffled against the cold, window-shopped but bought only a few inexpensive gifts for Tonio, Fosca and Sybil. Puccini had enjoyed so much hospitality that he did not need to present his letter of credit, arranged by David Seligman with the firm's New York branch, until the very end of the visit. It would have been simple enough to pick up large sums from advertising agencies, but he considered it undignified to endorse various soaps, felt hats, gloves and, above all, kimonos which were swiftly becoming a rage after *Butterfly*. He yielded only once to the bait of easy money after inspecting an almost irresistible motor-boat in a Fifth Avenue showroom. For several days he had fobbed off a wealthy admirer, who kept imploring him to autograph a line or two of his music. Puccini suddenly agreed to write out the opening bars of his Musetta Waltz for $500. He used the cash for a down-payment on the boat which was shipped out to Leghorn.

He toured Chinatown with Elvira and attended various receptions, once shaking hands with Thomas Alva Edison, a memory he would long treasure. At Carnegie Hall he heard an impressive performance by the Boston Symphony Orchestra, the only concert he had time to attend. He also saw a number of Broadway successes, including Belasco's melodrama *Girl of the Golden West*. He told a *New York Times* reporter that he had found the heroine 'very naive and refreshing', but did not seem excited by its operatic possibilities, although the mining camp atmosphere and vigorous crowd scenes remained in his memory.

Impatient to return and finalise arrangements for his next libretto (three frustrating years had drifted by since the com-

164

pletion of *Butterfly*), he cancelled a scheduled visit to Niagara Falls and they sailed on 26 February 1907 after Caruso had entertained them to a farewell supper in the Metropolitan's clubroom, where the management presented Puccini with a silver loving-cup. He would have liked to break his journey at Plymouth and go on to London for a few days but, much to his annoyance, the Seligmans had arranged to stay in Nice for some weeks.

It was not easy to re-adjust to domestic routine. 'I'm rather put out by the confusion at home,' he reported petulantly to Sybil. 'There's nobody to wait, and no cook—Doria has to do everything.' He and Elvira must have been uncomfortably aware that, sooner or later, the selfless little servant would marry some fortunate villager to become another hard-working wife and mother. Nothing remotely suggested that her destiny would parallel that of Puccini's most tragic heroines.

Chapter Ten

Puccini stayed only briefly at Torre. In Paris he had a stormy round of arguments with Pierre Louÿs, who failed to revive his confidence in *Conchita* although heavily backed by the Ricordis. With the Frenchman's excitable threats of a lawsuit still buzzing in his ears, he told Sybil of his 'many days of struggle and the vilest temper'. He soon reverted to his earlier plan for an opera on the last days of Marie Antoinette, but Illica had side-stepped a plea for yet another draft. He took brief comfort when d'Annunzio informed him, 'My old nightingale has awakened with the spring and will gladly sing for you', but the bird remained oddly invisible. Instead he had to endure hysterical demands from Louÿs, who rejected a sop of 4,000 lire as derisory but would later be soothed by Tito Ricordi's purchase of the operatic rights in his novel. Riccardo Zandonai, a gifted young disciple of Mascagni's, was commissioned to write the libretto and set it to music.★

Still hankering for *The Austrian Woman* (Marie Antoinette), Puccini even started collecting music of the French Revolution period, but he was too easily discouraged to fight a lone battle for a subject which might have proved far more fruitful than its shoddier alternatives. It is tempting, though hypothetical, to suggest that Giacosa's taste for history could have tipped the scales. He had so often prevailed over Illica in the past and his judgment had always carried immense weight with Ricordi, but without him Marie Antoinette was doomed. Sybil Seligman's view, for once endorsed by the publisher, proved decisive. She much preferred Belasco's melodrama to the queen's story which seemed to her far too

---

★ His *Conchita*, which Puccini dismissed contemptuously when it opened in Milan in 1911, was later staged at Covent Garden and also enjoyed some success in Paris and the United States, with Zandonai's future wife Tarquinia Tarquini in the rôle of the temptress.

tragic—and over-familiar—for her beloved Giacomo. He finally yielded but not without a mischievous hint that her dislike of *The Austrian Woman* was motivated by the absence of a tenor part for her 'god' Caruso. *Girl of the Golden West* presented no such obstacle. The bandit appeared to be tailor-made for Caruso; Minnie would suit Destinn, Farrar, Cavalieri and almost any other leading dramatic soprano, while most contemporary baritones would seize the chance of singing Jack Rance the Sheriff. Above all, Minnie would make a robust break from his sequence of dying heroines.

Once convinced, he asked Belasco to send him a copy of the play. He discussed it exhaustively with Sybil during his visit to London at the end of June. She offered to arrange for an Italian translation and later supplied him with mid-century American folk music and Red Indian chants which might be useful for absorbing atmosphere. The translation arrived, act by act, and pleased him enough to increase the translator's very modest fee by fifty per cent, but he soon became fretful at Torre and departed moodily for Chiatri. He had now put Abetone on the market, but as no buyers appeared and the Seligmans seemed eager to make a return visit, he decided to spend August there. He demurred, however, at the possibility of sharing Sybil's company. 'Is it true Caruso is coming too?' he demanded sharply. 'Do you think it's a good idea?' The hint was taken. Caruso travelled from England with Sybil and Vincent, but passionately embraced Ada Giachetti at Milan station and drove off with her to his villa.

By the time Sybil and her son arrived at Torre del Lago en route for the mountains, Puccini was able to report excellent progress on *The Girl*. Tito Ricordi had failed to find himself a suitable berth in New York but, still very American-minded, took the new opera under his own wing. He was now enjoying a much freer hand in the firm and assumed such royal airs that Puccini nicknamed him *Savoia*. Tito ruthlessly by-passed Illica and commissioned Carlo Zangarini, a somewhat surprising choice, to write the libretto. He was a promising young dramatist but without either Illica's creative spark or the impeccable sense of construction which Giacosa had brought to all Puccini's libretti since *Manon Lescaut*. However, Tito pointed out that he wrote English fluently and even boasted a Colorado-born mother. Unfortunately, he also happened to be as Italian as macaroni, and with only the haziest notions of the American idiom and the wild and woolly West. But he was an industrious, though slow, writer. Relieved to see another libretto at last emerging, Puccini soon assured Giulio Ricordi that the opera already promised to be a 'second *Bohème*, but more vigorous, more daring'.

After a pleasant holiday month, with Sybil at her most gracious and everyone enchanted by Puccini's new five-seater landaulette, he went off to Chiatri where Zangarini delivered the preliminary draft of his libretto. It seemed reasonably satisfactory. They spent some weeks discussing amendments before Puccini left in mid-October for Vienna to attend rehearsals of *Madama Butterfly*, a novel attraction for Mahler's last season at the Hofoper.

He succumbed at once to a city which seemed to him to possess all the elegance of Paris but without its bustle and artificiality. Everyone at the theatre, down to the youngest stagehand, seemed to be an opera enthusiast without any trace of the surliness which had irked him at the Opéra-Comique. Nevertheless, although he approved a tasteful *mise-en-scène*, the production was inferior to Carré's and quite outclassed by the Metropolitan. The singers were heavy in style and their diction too guttural for *Butterfly*. He thought Selma Kurz over-vivacious and operetta-ish for the geisha, but her celebrated trill could fill any theatre in Austria or Germany.

All his artistic and aesthetic doubts were snuffed out by the audience who demanded ten curtains after the first act, fifteen after the second, and twenty after the third, when he joined Kurz on a stage banked high with bouquets. He was congratulated by the Queen Mother of Spain, who assured him that her daughter-in-law 'is always singing and playing *Butterfly*', as he proudly reported to Sybil.

*   *   *   *

168

This almost mystical reverence for royalty was completely at variance with his apathy towards other celebrities, with the exception of mechanical geniuses like Edison and Marconi. He requested a signed portrait of Queen Alexandra of England which arrived at Torre together with a flattering appeal from Lady de Grey, the intermediary, for *his* photograph. He genuinely admired the beautiful English Queen, but knew the box-office value of royal patronage at Covent Garden where his operas were often chosen for gala performances. He could also be excused for assuming that the Royal Victorian Order, which Caruso now sported among his many other foreign decorations, was as much a tribute to the King's favourite opera, *La Bohème*, as the tenor's supreme art. Above all, he was conscious of his debt to Tosti, recently created 'Sir Paolo', who regularly included Puccini arias and duets in his concerts at Buckingham Palace or Windsor.

The Austrian critics, while not daring to fault Selma Kurz, were far from unanimously in favour. Busoni, who admired Verdi but had little time for other Italian composers compared to his adored Wagner and Liszt, went later in the season and thought the piece 'indecent'. He grumbled at having to pay fourteen kronen for his ticket and left the theatre to walk off his irritation, returning only for the last act. 'I shall never learn to understand the public,' he wrote testily to his wife. 'It will swallow boredom, monotony and unreality as if they were liquid pearls ... The people are taken in by the Japanese decorations and the naval officer in modern uniform.'

Puccini was mobbed by the Viennese public whenever he emerged from the Hotel Bristol. Quite apart from his fame as a composer, stories of his amours ensured a procession of ladies eager for rather more than a scribbled autograph. One morning he was intrigued by a seductive-sounding telephone request for an immediate interview. He agreed at once and, still in pyjamas though freshly shaved and perfumed, awaited his visitor. She was pretty and arrived with a small boy clutching a violin case. Puccini bit his lips, imagining that he would have to submit to a scratchy recital, but the fräulein explained demurely that her brother was on his way to a music lesson and would call for her afterwards. Somewhat perplexed, he went into his bedroom to dress. The girl was smiling and stark naked when he emerged. 'I felt too sorry for the lunatic to send her away', he blandly told Titta Ruffo, who demanded full details. The handsome Pisan baritone, himself a notorious libertine, had become a frequent visitor to Torre del Lago. Before taking up an operatic career, he had studied engineering at the University of Rome and shared Puccini's love of gadgetry and tinkering with cars. He was also an exceptionally gifted raconteur, although far too coarse for Elvira's taste. She was always uneasy in his company and particularly disliked seeing him exchange whispered confidences with her husband.

She had spent a trying winter with a severe bronchial cough that disturbed their sleep, so he tentatively proposed a holiday in Egypt hoping that it might improve her health and perhaps compensate for his neglect. While impatiently awaiting Zangarini's libretto, he killed time and game, much enjoying a week's shooting in Sardinia. He also visited his laryngologist in Florence so often and regularly that Elvira began to have doubts. When the weather was too cheerless for sailing or motoring, he tinkled despondently on his new Ehrbar piano in yellow olive wood, a gift from the appreciative Hofoper.

He had little enough cause for dissatisfaction. *Butterfly* continued to fill houses in Vienna and was equally popular in Berlin and a dozen other German cities, while Madrid already planned a production at the Teatro Reale where he had once hopefully waited for the curtain to rise on *Edgar*. The success of *Butterfly* was enough in itself to reinforce his optimistic hopes of a second Belasco subject, but encouragement came from every quarter. In that year, 1907, performances of his operas had already exceeded two hundred and fifty, with more to come. 'My affairs are going splendidly', he wrote to Sybil, who had just sent him several ties in green which, like all his countrymen, he considered a lucky colour. *Bohème*, *Tosca* and even *Manon Lescaut* (despite Massenet) were playing to huge audiences throughout France and Belgium, but Gatti-Casazza's unexpected decision to stage *Tosca* pleased him even more. Ricordi, however, still feared anti-Puccini bias and also had distinct reservations about the principals neither of whom could hope to match Destinn's rapturous tones and Caruso's passionate artistry. Only the Neapolitan baritone Pasquale Amato, as Scarpia, seemed to command the necessary acting and vocal equipment. Puccini had fewer qualms. Toscanini's virtuoso direction alone guaranteed a subtle yet disciplined interpretation.

Nevertheless, on the opening night of 29 December he had sneaked into the back stalls after the house lights went down, to avoid possible identification by some hostile member of the claque. He was delighted when an attractive young woman took the empty seat beside him and evidently failed to recognise him. She clapped enthusiastically when the curtain fell, but he shrugged with elaborate indifference.

'Didn't you like it?' she asked in surprise.

'No, it's the work of an amateur', he replied, straight-faced.

'Then you must be an unusual ignoramus', she sniffed. 'It's the finest thing Puccini has done.'

He pointed out that some of the best arias seemed to derive from Verdi, while the choruses reminded him strongly of Bizet. He then invited her to supper, but she pleaded another engagement and hurried away. Next morning he read a front-page newspaper article under the heading, 'Puccini's own views on *Tosca*'. The verbatim account of his frivolous self-condemnation was signed by the resourceful dramatic critic, who had followed him into the theatre. The Galleria guffawed but *Tosca* had been received with such ecstasy that Gatti-Casazza rearranged his schedule for several repeat performances.

Zangarini arrived at Torre before the end of January with most of his libretto which Puccini pronounced 'really beautiful'. He and Elvira arranged to sail for Egypt from Naples, which gave him an opportunity to see Richard Strauss conduct the première of *Salome* at San Carlo. 'It was a success but

I don't believe anyone was convinced by it,' he told Fosca. He also scribbled a note to Ricordi repeating his eagerness to start on the new score.

They sailed the following night. The Mediterranean was unkind to Elvira and the round of sightseeing failed to raise her spirits. Armed with two of the latest-type German cameras, Puccini duly captured the Pyramids which left him as apathetic as the camel rides and other routine tourist attractions. They wrote numerous postcards in their room rather than face the street beggars and noisy bazaars. Elvira thought the shops much inferior to those of Milan or Paris and quickly grew homesick, while her husband pined for the Golden West.

His first enthusiasm for Zangarini's libretto soon crumbled. Giacosa and Illica had often enough protested at his vacillations but their professional expertise had always squared the circle. The unfortunate Zangarini, plodding in very alien territory, needed far more than a Colorado-born mother to rescue him. He was too slow for an over-impatient composer and could not absorb the amendments which spluttered in practically every letter from Torre del Lago. That March Puccini had visited Rome for a gala performance of *Butterfly*, followed by a banquet which he sat through without enjoyment. In Milan, still glowering, he informed the Ricordis of his dissatisfaction with 'the wretch of a poet'. Tito blustered but compromised by recruiting Guelfo Civinini, an experienced playwright and editor, who soon took over as sole librettist. He assimilated ideas quickly enough, although his anxiety to meet deadlines made him far less critical than his formidable predecessors, Giacosa and Illica, who seldom gave way without argument and could count on Giulio Ricordi's support in a deadlock. Civinini was denied this invaluable prop; the publisher had now virtually retired to nurse himself and his wife back to health and was no longer available either to mediate or inject ideas of his own.

Facing a task of exceptional complexity with limited outside help, Puccini soon showed his powers of invention by telescoping Belasco's four-act play into three acts. He also devised a new ending with the thrilling man-hunt on stage and Minnie's farewell to the gold-miners. The lynching scene would be set in the vast Californian Forest and, among several other effective improvements, he transferred Minnie's bible-reading class from the play's last act to the first. His eye for pictorial effect and a handling of crowd scenes worthy of de Mille had enabled him to improve on the Belasco original, but with so much spectacle and fast-moving incident there was obviously some danger of producing a play with music rather than an acceptable opera. Moreover, he was not helped by outlandish characters like the bandit and sheriff, while Minnie herself, far tougher in character than any of his past heroines, gave little scope for lyrical romanticism.

His anxiety was reflected in a frenzied restlessness. To escape interruptions at Torre del Lago he retreated to Chiatri and soon complained of the stuffy heat. At Abetone he corrected Civinini's batches of manuscript but a day or two's rainy weather almost tempted him to join Sybil on the Lido. 'Undoubtedly *The Girl* is more difficult than I thought,' he groaned. 'For the time being I've lost my way and don't go straight ahead as I should like ... Write to me, and go on being fond of me, as I am of you.' The much-praised translation of Belasco's play had suddenly become 'vile' and his beautiful piano 'a charabanc'. It had been replaced by another, with a framed portrait of Lina Cavalieri now standing beside Storchio's, which did not sweeten Elvira's disposition.

He wrote few letters except to confide his doubts to Sybil or inform Ricordi of progress. Two months passed before he troubled to commiserate briefly with Caruso on his father's death. His own self-pity left him almost insensitive to the tenor's mental and physical collapse when Ada Giachetti deserted him, after eleven years, for their handsome chauffeur. In a note to Sybil, who was far more distressed by the tragedy, he commented with practical satisfaction, 'Ada has gone off with only one dress and without a penny'.

After a recurrence of throat trouble he puffed joylessly at a pipe Sybil had sent him, but soon resumed his cigarette-smoking. He also drank far too much coffee to assuage the hunger pains left by his diabetic diet. He was once more seeking relief in shooting, cross-country dashes in his car and bouts of lovemaking. Elvira recognised the familiar symptoms which always preceded the pains of composition, but that summer she was herself in exceptionally poor health and less accommodating. All her phobias of middle-aged insecurity had mounted into an over-possessive jealousy which her husband either ignored or ridiculed. Titta Ruffo recalled that he was joking one day with Puccini when Elvira had shouted hoarsely at them, 'What are you two doing down there? What are you telling my husband?' The composer shrugged and murmured sardonically, 'Listen, how dulcet is the voice of Mimì!'

The situation was aggravated by her relatives whom he made even less welcome at Torre while working on the final stages of the libretto. Backed by Leonardi, Fosca's husband, they helped to fuel Elvira's suspicions with sly hints of Puccini's nights errant until she lost all control. Reports of violent quarrels soon circulated in the village. Before long it was being whispered that Puccini's riding breeches always reeked of camphor which was known to be a debilitating drug apart from a moth-repellent. A tragi-comic game of sexual ping-pong now opened. To escape a listlessness caused by diabetes or promiscuity, he turned to a variety of stimulants and elixirs while Elvira, as she later admitted, would doctor his coffee with a counter-aphrodisiac whenever some attractive singer dined with them.

Nobody was safe from her tongue. She began to speak sharply to Doria whom she suspected, quite without cause, of carrying tales back to the village, but the gentle servant sympathised with her mistress's menopause and went about her duties with the usual dedication. Puccini had become aware of an 'atmosphere', but he was too concerned with *La Fanciulla del West*, the clumsy hybrid title suggested by Sybil, to worry unduly about these domestic irritations. During

Elvira's tantrums he would often drive off to Milan for talks with Gatti-Casazza and Toscanini.

Their successful régime at La Scala was now ending. This had come about through Conried's dismissal from the Metropolitan which had continued to show heavy losses against Hammerstein's staggering profit of $250,000 in his very first season. Otto Kahn appointed the singer Andréas Dippel as administrative manager, but a stronger force was needed to check the Manhattan's alarming run of success. Tito Ricordi canvassed wildly for the vacancy and Scotti, an even more unlikely candidate, also asked to be considered, but the board had unanimously approved an invitation to Gatti-Casazza. He accepted, subject to Toscanini's joining him as artistic director, and although the Maestro hesitated he eventually agreed to sign for one season.

The decision gave Puccini a welcome stimulus precisely when he was at last starting to score *Fanciulla* in September 1908. His friends were sailing for America in a few weeks time, but they fitted in a day at Torre del Lago where he played passages for their approval, including the 'Homesickness' theme in the first act. Before they departed, with an emotional exchange of hugs and kisses, it was understood that the opera would be given its world première at the Metropolitan. Moreover, Gatti-Casazza had promised to stage several Puccini works in his first season, although Toscanini insisted on opening with *Aida*.

Sweetened by a brief visit from Sybil, he returned more cheerfully to his task. In his letters to her he again signed himself 'Noti Boi' (Naughty Boy) or, in self-mockery, 'The Successor' (to Verdi), a label which journalists now regularly tagged on to every interview with him. But on 4 October after barely a month of intensive composition, he wrote, 'My life goes on in the midst of sadness and the greatest unhappiness... As a result *The Girl* has completely dried up—and God knows when I shall have the courage to take up my work again!'

He had suffered a nervous shock which left scars for many

years. One night Elvira awoke with a fit of coughing. Puccini's piano was silent and she heard the unexpected sound of voices. Doria sometimes did her ironing after dinner, but this was almost midnight. Seized with a manic fit of jealousy, Elvira rushed downstairs in her nightdress to find Puccini and the girl chatting by the open door leading to the garden. Elvira began shrieking abuse at them and accused Doria of being her husband's mistress. He tried to calm her but his protestations of innocence brought another torrent of such vile language that the girl, now trembling and white-faced with horror, ran blindly to her room. For some hours afterwards Elvira hammered dementedly on the door.

Early next morning Doria fled to her mother's house in a state of near-collapse. Within hours the whole village echoed with Elvira's claim to have surprised them *in flagrante delicto*. She threatened to drown 'the whore . . . as sure as there is a Christ and a Madonna', if ever she came near her husband again. Brandishing her large umbrella, she hurried to the Manfredis' house and repeated her accusations, even alleging that Fosca's child had been bribed to carry love notes between the guilty pair. Later that day she followed Doria through the streets and screamed curses overheard by the scandalised villagers, most of whom, knowing Puccini's reputation, believed the story. Elvira had a staunch ally in the local lawyer, who had long nursed some grievance against her husband, but the priest, while also more than half-convinced, refused to drive the girl from Torre.

Elvira had never been liked locally and was thought to have the evil eye, but most people assumed she must have had certain proof to provoke such a violent reaction. Doria's brother went about threatening to kill Puccini who was unable to endure the villagers' stony faces or Elvira's reproaches, and drove off to Milan. Soon afterwards he left for Paris. He hoped the Opéra-Comique's production of *Tosca* might distract him from his nightmare but told Sybil that he had 'often lovingly fingered' his revolver. If so, he made a surprisingly rapid recovery. 'A great success and a full house', he reported. 'The

King of Greece was there and I was presented to him. He was *charmant* . . . Now I go back to that hell of indecision . . .' He stayed a few days in Milan and took veronal to help him sleep, but finally decided that it was worth braving even Elvira's tongue to resume work. 'I'm very much concerned about my poor beloved Minnie,' he confessed sadly to Sybil.

The atmosphere at Torre had not cleared. Elvira was either sullen and silent or wore a semi-triumphant smile at having disgraced her 'rival', who rarely ventured out of doors and had locked herself away, refusing all food. Puccini sent her a hopeful note and assured her mother of the girl's complete innocence. 'I have always considered your daughter as a member of my family', he wrote. He also met Doria secretly with the object of comforting her. It was an appalling risk. Finding it impossible to concentrate on his music, he occasionally went out shooting and once came across Elvira, disguised in his clothes, obviously spying on him. She had by no means given up her accusations which were repeated in ample detail for the benefit of Tonio and Fosca. By now almost everyone in Torre seemed to be aligned behind her, while Doria was reduced to a pitiful state of semi-starvation and wept hysterically whenever the priest offered the solace of confession.

Puccini 'celebrated' his fiftieth birthday alone at Torre as Elvira was away in Lucca nursing her sick mother. She spoke often of leaving him but seemed in no hurry. 'I wouldn't mind staying here by myself', he wrote to Sybil on 4 January 1909. 'I could work and shoot—but if I go, where should I go to? I who have now grown accustomed to the comforts of my own house?' Three weeks later, Doria took several capsules of corrosive sublimate and died after five days of agony, leaving a pathetically illiterate note declaring her innocence. The villagers immediately rounded on the Puccinis, condemning them jointly for hounding a blameless girl to her death. Completely distraught, he joined Tosti and his wife in Rome, while Elvira made off to Milan with the intention of returning once the funeral hysteria had subsided.

A quite unexpected sequel added the final macabre touch. The Manfredis had previously been advised that there might be cause for action against Elvira for persecution. They filed suit, adding the complaint of defamation of character, when an autopsy conducted by Dr Rodolfo Giacchi, ironically one of the witnesses at Puccini's marriage ceremony, established Doria's virginity beyond all doubt. The effect was violent but wholly predictable. Elvira now faced a possible lynching if she dared show herself in the village, while Puccini automatically won sympathy as the victim of her insane jealousy. But he was still too sick at heart to return at once and stayed several more weeks in Rome, grateful for the Tostis' warm understanding.

The sensational newspaper reports of Doria's suicide and vindication had been acutely distressing to a man of his reserve. He grieved for the unfortunate girl and reproached himself for having at times made playful remarks which must have been magnified and distorted in his wife's sick mind, but he could not forgive her virulence. He paid a quick visit to Ricordi's lawyers and instructed them to arrange a separation. Undismayed, Elvira was now busily preparing to defend the Manfredis' action, declaring she had 'proofs' of the couple's guilty association during the months preceding that final midnight scene in the villa. Through mutual friends Puccini begged her in vain to think again. He was equally unsuccessful in urging Doria's brother to drop the lawsuit.

Back in Torre, his confused state of mind made all serious work impossible. He punted about on the lake, shot a few birds without enjoyment and rarely took his landaulette out of the garage. A sharp attack of influenza confined him to his bed for several days. He was nursed by two of his sisters but became impatient to visit Milan for a new production of *Manon Lescaut* at La Scala. It had a warm reception and was given eight performances that season, but he relapsed into despondency when Elvira again rejected his plea to withdraw her defence and throw herself on the mercy of the court. 'If she has the slightest heart, she must feel remorse', he told Sybil. 'My nights are horrible; I cry—and am in despair . . .

But she too deserves pity because the chief fault was not hers . . .' He could not withhold compassion from the unfortunate woman who had overlooked many of his past scrapes only to pounce so tragically on a wholly imaginary grievance.

Tonio sided with his mother but he was too highly-strung to remain cool. Exhausted by the wranglings, he suddenly broke off his engineering studies and left for Munich. Puccini begged him to return, declaring that he had not given up hope of a reconciliation. In this he was half-sincere, but probably concerned more by anxiety over Tonio and his own solitude than by any softening towards Elvira. Unquestionably he had wearied of his lonely workless days and nights at Torre, where reporters hammered on the door and then made for Gragnani's thatched summer house on the lakeside pier. The old fisherman was eager enough to feed them scraps of lewd gossip for a few lire.

Tonio's decision to uproot altogether and start a new life in Africa was no more than a melodramatic gesture, yet alarming enough to bring his parents together early that May for their first meeting in almost four months. Elvira looked thin and haggard but gave no sign of wishing to be reconciled. They parted in anger when she shrugged off his reminder that any defence in the coming lawsuit could only expose him to still more undeserved mud-slinging.

Guilt-ridden but irritated even more by her inflexibility, he travelled about to see performances of his own operas or any new production that took his fancy. He attended the Milan première of Strauss's *Elektra* which seemed to him a horror and inferior to *Salome*. With some half-hearted notion of attending the Covent Garden rehearsals of *Tosca* but, more likely, of unburdening his woes on Sybil, he spent a few days in London. However, without waiting for the opening night, he crossed the Channel to meet Gatti-Casazza, then in Paris to finalise arrangements for the first visit to Europe of any Metropolitan company. This was scheduled for the following year, with Caruso, Destinn, Scotti and Amato as the star performers, together with Gatti-Casazza's redheaded fiancée

Frances Alda. *Manon Lescaut* would share the honours of the Paris season with Verdi's *Aida*, *Otello* and *Falstaff*, and the inevitable double-bill, *Cav and Pag*.

Gatti-Casazza looked even more majestic in stylish Fifth Avenue clothes worn with a new touch of Wall Street distinction. He was brimming with confidence and brushed off the $200,000 deficit in his first Metropolitan season, explaining that the theatre had been expensively refurbished and a roof stage built for rehearsals. Caruso's illness had led to a falling-off in ticket sales, but a number of well-rehearsed quality productions had won back audiences and driven the rival Manhattan into near-bankruptcy. Toscanini had renewed his contract, which could not have given unalloyed pleasure to a hard-driven orchestra. According to Gatti-Casazza he had snapped at a musician during rehearsals of a Puccini opera, 'Only you are standing between me and the composer's intention.'

Puccini smilingly accepted the implied compliment which gratified him almost as much as Gatti-Casazza's flattering renewal of interest in *La Fanciulla*. They met almost daily and together attended the Russian Ballet's production of *Cléopâtre* with enchanting performances by Nijinsky, Karsavina and Pavlova. Ida Rubinstein's supple body gyrated voluptuously in the wild bacchanal but Puccini, with his new opera in his mind's eye, goggled even more at Bakst's Egyptian costumes and the vast architectural scene with its temple courtyard and a glimpse of the Nile discernible through columns.

They returned to the Châtelet for Chaliapin's *Ivan the Terrible* and next day spent several hours in the theatre where the Metropolitan artists would give their five-week season. It was still shabby and old-fashioned, but Diaghilev and Bakst had worked a transformation by bullying the carpenters, stage-hands and electricians. While Gatti-Casazza took experienced stock of the seating, traps, lighting, dressing-rooms and other essentials, Puccini prowled around the auditorium testing the acoustics.

This short but stimulating visit did wonders for his morale. He was impatient to return to *La Fanciulla* and imagined that

Elvira must soon take a more sensible view of the Affaire Doria. He already looked forward to resuming their well-ordered life which, in retrospect, seemed infinitely preferable to his recent isolation and misery. He missed his creature comforts but may also have reminded himself sentimentally that Elvira, however shrewish, socially limited and over-demanding, had given him a quarter of a century's devotion. Although he treasured Sybil's friendship and had no intention of giving up his extra-marital amours, his home life was clearly the solid and indispensable base of the triangle.

He returned almost amiably to Milan and with Tonio's willing help arranged a second meeting for 9 June. It was an unqualified disaster. Elvira again refused to place her defence in the hands of his lawyers and instead spoke glowingly of her own attorney's oratory which would surely vindicate her and humble the Manfredis. She ranted on so wildly about 'new evidence' of Doria's case history of hysteria that Puccini clapped hands to his ears and stamped out in a fury. Next day she wrote offering to forgive him if he would humbly admit his adultery, but still insisted on having her own name cleared in open court. This preposterous letter provoked him into replying, 'You are mad! Very well, do as you like. I am leaving . . . If you wish to return to me, I shall always be ready to take you back . . . I will not write to you again . . .'

Back in the villa, his widowed sister Nitteti looked after him for a few days until her children in Lucca needed her. Sitting in his silent study one night, he wrote self-pityingly to Sybil, 'Outside I hear the rain beating against the plants, it's cold, and I'm alone in this room. In the house there's only an old cook who—to make matters worse—cooked me a most horrible meal. I'm going to bed—what is there for me to do? I can't work . . .'

Elvira's situation was equally deplorable. With the case scheduled for 9 July, barely three weeks ahead, she began to panic and now implored him to try and soften the Manfredis. Once again he approached Doria's brother, who declared that he bore the Maestro himself no ill-will but swore to kill Elvira if the judges failed to punish her. By now she was too nervous to face the court and asked the attorney to excuse her absence on the grounds of illness. Nobody was deceived, least of all the judges who listened with obvious impatience to an eloquent though garbled statement of her alleged grievances. As Puccini and his lawyers had long feared, the defence had no possible chance of success, but the court went far beyond an expected fine and rebuke. Elvira was found guilty on each count, including the serious one of 'menace to life and limb', and sentenced to five months' imprisonment with a fine of 700 lire and payment of all costs.

Sick with anxiety, Puccini could not stay another day in Torre. He left for Bagni di Lucca, the beach resort where he had once played the piano in a café-dansant. He had reserved a luxurious suite in the Grand Hotel des Thermes and invited Elvira to join him, but she had to stay in Milan with Tonio, who had collapsed on hearing the court's decision. Puccini remained indoors for some days, seldom troubling to shave. His bushy crop of hair was now lifeless and spattered with the first grey patches, and an over-use of sleeping draughts had mottled his face. However, he finally braced himself to visit Tonio who, like his mother, welcomed the prospect of a few peaceful weeks at Bagni di Lucca while arrangements were made to appeal against the sentence.

Elvira was now more subdued but occasionally flashed into wrathful outbursts at her 'persecutors', once even threatening to jump from the window. Since their rooms happened to be on the first floor, this could not be taken too seriously. With rare self-discipline she managed to avoid any direct mention of Doria, and seemed pathetically grateful for Puccini's energetic efforts to hire new lawyers to argue the appeal. He also canvassed officials and others who might usefully pull strings, but as this was holiday time and most people were away at spas or the seaside with their families, he often had to drive to Montecatini and various beach resorts for meetings. In addition he visited Pisa to confer with the Manfredis' attorneys who, to his relief, seemed to be leaning towards a cash settlement.

The grounds for appeal had been skilfully explored. The libel charge was now admitted, but the judges would be asked to show leniency to a woman overwrought by her love and uncontrollable jealousy. In the meantime, Puccini reminded the Manfredis that she had already suffered much and was genuinely remorseful. Sweetened by the sum of 12,000 lire with which they erected a handsome monument to Doria and purchased a pleasant house for themselves near Lake Massaciúccoli, they agreed to abandon the lawsuit. It was then formally struck out by the Court of Appeal.

Puccini returned to Torre del Lago in September 1909 with his wife and son. 'In my home I have peace', he wrote thankfully to Sybil. 'Elvira is good and the three of us live happily together.' The anxious months, during which he had neglected his diet, had sent up his blood sugar, but this soon became normal after a course of injections and meals carefully supervised by Elvira. As she naturally hesitated to show herself in the village, although the local folk seemed tolerant and even felt some pity for her, Puccini had the kindly thought of taking her with him to Brussels for the première of *Butterfly*. Yet there was still a coldness between them which would not thaw for many years. Elvira was more careful to avoid scenes when he resumed work on *La Fanciulla* after almost eight months of inactivity, but her jealousy could still ignite from the smallest puff of suspicion.

He had to clear a heavy backlog of correspondence. There were business details which had been put aside and scores of messages from sympathetic friends who congratulated him on the ending of his long nightmare. He wrote to thank Lina Cavalieri and sent his good wishes for her début as Salomé in Massenet's *Hérodiade* which would open Hammerstein's fourth and final season before the Metropolitan bought him out. Elvira had good reason to resent his apparently continuing interest in the charmer, but she objected even more to his almost daily letters of comfort to Sybil Seligman, who was then under heavy strain. Her son Esmond, one of Eton's most gifted scholars, had suffered several epileptic fits, and her sister Mrs Walter Behrens was dying painfully of an incurable disease. Puccini wrote consolingly but, even for a self-centred man, seemed remarkably thoughtless in mentioning at such a time that 'Elvira has taken our friendship amiss. But this fancy of hers too will, I hope, disappear one day . . .'

The reconciliation was guarded on both sides. Although manacled by habit-forming years and an affection that had survived its severest test, they were still precariously near snapping point. The shock to Puccini's nervous system had been cushioned by returning to work and the comparative peace of Torre, but he had apparently found it difficult to resume sexual relations with even the pretence of ardour. While on a short visit to Fosca who had been taken ill, Elvira wrote, 'I miss you so much. Perhaps you miss me only for the comfort of your life. But I miss you in quite another way! Your Topizia.' This avowal of hot passion was either simulated or, if sincere, even more pathetic. Its effect, if any, was minimised in the same letter by a stinging rebuke for having forgotten his promise to make Fosca a monthly allowance for 'some little comforts without having to ask her husband.' A day or two later, she wrote to thank him effusively for the cash which had arrived by registered post.

After the nightmarish Manfredi tragedy such domestic pin-pricks seemed almost insignificant. By the end of the year he had almost completed the sketches for his opera and told Sybil he was 'working like a nigger and living like a hermit *without emotions and without anything else*'. But on 23 January, the first anniversary of Doria's death, he walked sadly to the cemetery and placed a bunch of flowers, 'to my poor little butterfly', on her grave. Every year thereafter, whenever he was in Italy, he repeated the solitary pilgrimage. He never forgot the tragic little servant and would pay a lasting tribute to her memory in the character of Liù, the slave girl who stabs herself to death in *Turandot*.

Chapter Eleven

By April 1910 Puccini had already orchestrated two hundred pages of the *Fanciulla* score. Some weeks later, with only Act Three outstanding, he travelled to Paris with Elvira and Tonio for rehearsals of the Metropolitan touring company's *Manon Lescaut*. He had looked forward to Lina Cavalieri repeating the title rôle, but Gatti-Casazza could not overlook her defection to Hammerstein. Lucrezia Bori, still in her early twenties and already a favourite at La Scala, was chosen to replace her. She had much of Cavalieri's sparkle but without her prima donna temperament. While singing in Paris she had been advised by Giulio Ricordi to learn a few arias from *Manon Lescaut* as 'three gentlemen' might wish to audition her. This terrifying trio—Puccini, Gatti-Casazza and Toscanini—arrived at her hotel and, as she recalled, 'looked at me from head to foot then from foot to head'. They approved her voice and decided to pair her with Caruso. 'I had new costumes made in Paris. They cost me a fortune... After the dress rehearsal Puccini came up, holding a cup of coffee. "Bori", he said, "everything was perfect. Only in the last act where Manon is starving and penniless, your costume is too clean". So he threw the coffee on my gown.' Even his perfectionism could not excuse such uncharacteristic boorishness, but tempers had worn wafer-thin long before opening night.

Otto Kahn had agreed to underwrite half the heavy costs of the season, but it soon became plain that only Caruso's name would ensure full houses. The French impresario, Gabriel Astruc, imprudently decided to increase prices for his appearances and even forced admirers to buy inclusive tickets covering non-Caruso operas. The public, already incensed, was not appeased by the Châtelet's gala palms, ferns and flowers or the smart new dresses for its beaky *ouvreuses*. The critics also sniped at Gatti-Casazza for having consistently excluded French composers and singers from the Metropolitan.

By now Puccini had almost overcome his disappointment at Lina Cavalieri's absence. 'The Manon is a new little artist who will do well' he assured Sybil, but the atmosphere at the Châtelet did not encourage over-optimism. Stagehands resented orders from 'foreigners', while the orchestra once infuriated Toscanini to the point of pulling out his watch and hurling it into the wings. He spent long hours on *Manon Lescaut*, putting forward his ideas for lightening the orchestration of a number of passages and also made suggestions which might help the company to overcome the theatre's doubtful acoustics. These modifications won hasty approval from Puccini, by now far too apprehensive to risk antagonising Toscanini. Anti-Italian prejudice had become apparent from the very opening of that troubled season. Only Caruso's voice saved *Aida* after a noisy demonstration in the second act organised by various French singers who had been turned down at auditions. Toscanini ignored the hisses and conducted with such verve that the orchestra excelled itself and won even his approval.

Manon Lescaut opened on 9 June to a large if far from hospitable audience. They soon yielded to charming interpretations from Bori, Caruso and Amato, although Massenet's publisher stormed out ostentatiously after the first act. Most critics praised the artists without sparing Puccini whose work was compared disparagingly with his French predecessor. Nevertheless, the second performance drew receipts of 65,000 francs, a record for that season. In an exuberant letter to Sybil, the composer declared, 'Those pigs—the gentlemen of the Press—were full of bile against me, and who cares a fig, if the public takes my side in this way?'

He also took comfort from Geraldine Farrar's success in *Tosca* at the Opéra-Comique, and was even more gratified by Gatti-Casazza's firm decision to present the world première of *La Fanciulla* in New York that December. He sounded genuinely optimistic and had already invited Destinn, Caruso and

Amato to sing the leading parts. Tito Ricordi would be in charge of the production and David Belasco had volunteered to lend his expertise to the elaborate staging and scenery. Toscanini would, of course, conduct.

Puccini left in high spirits, stopping only briefly in Milan to report all his news to Giulio Ricordi. During July he worked on the third act of his opera at 'horrible' Chiatri in torrid heat but could at least concentrate there without risk of interruption. By mid-August he celebrated the completed orchestration by ordering a new car. 'The *Girl* has come out, in my opinion, the best opera I have written', he wrote to Sybil from Viareggio where he had a daily swim and afterwards took his ease in the cafés with Ruffo and other friends.

He asked her to send him the correct inscription for dedicating *La Fanciulla* to Queen Alexandra, acting on a shrewd suggestion from Tosti, who thought London's touchy opera-goers might possibly resent losing the première to New York. Lady de Grey (now Marchioness of Ripon), requested to act as go-between, soon informed Sybil, 'The Queen says she will be very pleased to accept the dedication of Signor Puccini's new opera ... I am so delighted to think we are going to have a new opera by him, and am longing to hear it. Please remember me to him when you write.' Obviously touched by the gesture, the recently bereaved Queen sent him an elegant diamond and ruby pin with her good wishes. He was further cheered by a telegram from Toscanini reporting a most satisfactory first reading of the score on stage, followed by a cordial invitation from Gatti-Casazza to attend rehearsals at the Metropolitan in November. De luxe return passage for two would be provided at the management's expense.

In August he set off in his new 70 hp Itala, an exact replica of Queen Margherita's limousine, for a fortnight's tour of Switzerland. On returning to Torre, he immediately asked Sybil for news of Maeterlinck's *L'Oiseau Bleu*, then ending a long run at the Haymarket Theatre. He had thought of making a visit to size up its operatic potential but quickly lost interest in favour of something more cheerful. Sybil was now urged to canvass a Spanish friend of hers for possible play scripts; 'I'm looking for a contrast (to) sorrow—sorrow . . . I want to express moral sufferings without blood or strong drama.' The most promising choice seemed to be a light comedy *Anima Allegra* by the Quintero Brothers, but this had to be pigeonholed while he prepared for his American trip in a distinctly cold domestic atmosphere.

His strained rapprochement with Elvira had survived the testing last weeks on *Fanciulla*, yet her sulky fits of silence betrayed a lingering belief in his guilty association with Doria. He was too appreciative of his home comforts to risk a quarrel, but her uncertain temper and the memory of their last American trip did not encourage him to repeat that experience. He reminded her disingenuously of the turbulent Atlantic and the dangers of bronchitis in wintry New York, finally suggesting that she sacrifice her ticket to Tonio, who had begged for a chance to see America and promised to act as his father's secretary. She saw through their glib arguments but yielded after Puccini's solemn promise to take her to London in the spring for Covent Garden's opening of *Fanciulla*.

He sailed with Tonio and Tito Ricordi in *The Washington* a new 36,000-ton liner. Father and son occupied the opulent Imperial Suite, which had cost the Metropolitan £320. They revelled in the marble bathroom, the gilt bedsteads, sofas, silk curtains and furniture almost up to Savoy Hotel standards Meals were served in their private dining-room by an attentive squad of stewards, but the gadget-minded composer was even more impressed by the capacious wardrobes each fitted with indoor lighting. Poor Elvira had not only missed all this luxury but an unusually calm crossing. 'I shall not get over it,' she wrote snappishly soon after he landed. 'I am bored and always alone . . . You deprived me of . . . participating in your triumph . . . Now you are a great man and compared to you I am nothing but a pygmy.'

He may or may not have had a twinge of remorse when she

also reminded him pathetically, 'Take care of yourself and don't eat things that harm you', but he was soon too heavily engaged to brood on Torre del Lago. He diverted reporters with his broken English, ritually ending interviews with, 'Long live Italy! Long live America!' Tonio proved of little help, secretarially. He refused to sign the scores of photographs demanded by his father's fans, declaring primly that forgery offended his moral scruples. Instead, he enjoyed the round of parties and went on shopping and sight-seeing tours with a pretty ballet-dancer from the Metropolitan chorus. 'However, he is a good boy and one ought to let him live a little', Puccini commented to Elvira. His one attempt to warn him against reckless flirtations was met with an unanswerable, 'Like father, like son'.

Tonio's good looks and gaiety made a pleasant impression. That could certainly not be said of Tito Ricordi who had never forgiven the opera house for passing him over in favour of Gatti-Casazza. He scowled throughout Otto Kahn's party for the visitors, suddenly announcing in a loud voice, 'We did not come to America to drink tea and waste our time on official receptions, but to work and to rehearse.' He then hustled Puccini from the room, whispering, 'I wanted just for once to smack a billion dollars in the face.'

But he worked energetically enough at rehearsals and even swallowed his anger when Belasco reminded him that gold-miners of that period did not dress like cowboys and corrected other solecisms which Puccini and his librettists had introduced into some of their exuberant stage directions. The veteran showman was more than equal to the challenge of re-creating the blizzard on Cloudy Mountain and sending eight horses galloping across the stage. The scenic designers, who had spent weeks on their plaster trees and elaborate foliage cut from leather, accepted criticism from Belasco but resented Tito's autocratic manner. It took tact on the part of the management to avert more than one crisis.

Puccini showed surprisingly little pre-opening nervousness. 'I believe it will be a success and let's hope a big one', he

189

enthused to Elvira. 'Caruso is magnificent in his part, Destinn not bad but she needs more energy. Toscanini, the *zenith— kind, good, adorable* . . . I can't wait for the hour to see my little nuisance of a wife again (I am one, too, don't get offended!)'. Engelbert Humperdinck, whose own *Königskinder* would open at the end of the year with Geraldine Farrar as the goose-girl, was privileged to watch rehearsals, together with one or two influential reporters, who passed titbits of back-stage gossip on to their readers. All ticket prices had been doubled for the first performance but the advance publicity reached such fever pitch that 'scalpers' were able to dispose of seats at up to thirty times their face value.

The scenes outside the Metropolitan on the night of 10 December 1910 anticipated the ballyhoo for Hollywood's glossiest premières. Although it was bitingly cold, with thick snow on the sidewalks, crowds of sightseers made it difficult for ticket-holders to force their way through. Mounted police had to be summoned to keep the cars and carriages moving and a ticketless Otto Khan was turned away until someone identified him. The curtain went up almost an hour late, but spotting the Diamond Horseshoe boxholders and other cele-brities kept everyone in excellent humour.

Pleasantly relaxed, the audience cheered the scenery and hummed the waltz in Act One. They seemed fascinated by the showpiece poker game by oil-lamp in the second act and buzzed excitedly at the forest manhunt. And they applauded like cinemagoers when Minnie and her lover disappeared into A Brave Tomorrow to the miners' nostalgic warbling of 'Old Dog Tray'.

If some missed the magic and pathos of show-stopping arias like 'Che gelida manina' or 'E lucevan le stelle', they were far outnumbered by others who saw nothing incon-gruous in gold miners bellowing in Italian against a Fenimore Cooper setting. Caruso's artistry blinded his admirers to a bulging unathletic figure as the bandit chief, while Toscanini's virile interpretation carried the liveliness of the score over its mediocre passages. Those in the audience who had paid fancy prices in the expectation of seeing another *Butterfly* found some reward in Belasco's spectacular effects and his crowd scenes which drew almost as many encores as the duets.

Over fifty curtain calls greeted the opera, mounting to almost frenzied hysteria when Gatti-Casazza summoned Puccini to the stage and crowned him with a silver garland bearing the entwined national colours of Italy and the United States. The composer embraced Toscanini and whispered 'My heart is beating like the double-basses in the card scene.' After being fervently kissed by almost everyone in the company, he joined Caruso and Humperdinck at a reception in Mrs Cornelius Vanderbilt's mansion on Fifth Avenue.

The box-office netted him 120,000 lire personally, but he was even more gratified by the ecstatic reviews, although one small voice protested that the piece bore 'the same relation to music that melodrama bears to drama' and doubted whether it would have any permanent claim on the affection of serious operagoers. Richard Aldrich of the *New York Times* praised the production but missed 'the melodic lustre, outline, point and fluency' of Puccini's earlier works. He noticed the influence of Debussy's *Pelléas et Mélisande* while others had detected the subtle adaptation of Strauss's opulent harmonic idioms in *Salome*.

It was his most elaborately scored opera to date, with the savage choral scenes in Act Three anticipating some of the grandeurs of *Turandot*. There were echoes of the sensuous magic of *Bohème* and *Butterfly* and technical craftsmanship in plenty, but nothing could compensate for Minnie's essential lack of pathos or a score that was neither truly American nor Italian in flavour and, above all, lacked memorable arias.

Neverthelesss, the Metropolitan repeated the work eight more times that season, always to packed houses, while audiences in Chicago, Philadelphia and Boston welcomed performances staged by Tito Ricordi. With other productions scheduled for Covent Garden, Rome, Berlin and Vienna, Puccini had every reason for satisfaction when he ate in New York's Italian restaurants, gaily signing autographs for fellow-diners, or joined Caruso for coffee and liqueurs at his corner table in the dining-room at the Knickerbocker, where they would often talk animated 'shop' until the small hours with Gatti-Casazza, Frances Alda, Scotti and the Toscaninis. The conductor and his plump motherly wife, Carla, had smothered him with so much kindness, even helping him to pack for the homeward voyage, that he made them a present of a silver table candelabrum which, as he ruefully informed Elvira, had cost him $300.

He sailed home in the *Lusitania* with Tonio after a massed send-off which inspired a satirical sketch from a young reporter on the *Telegraph*; 'I heard a sound like somebody taking off a pair of wet galoshes in a hurry. That was Gatti-Casazza's double kiss, one for each cheek of Puccini ... A sound like Bossie the Brindle pulling her hind foot out of the mud; that was Amato's fervent salute. A sound like somebody stropping a razor rapidly; that was Scotti putting seven or eight quick ones over.'

With his son he spent a few days in London where Sybil Seligman attempted to interest him in a German play which she had hopefully started to translate. He was lukewarm about the subject but softened the blow by writing immediately on his return, 'It gave me *immense* pleasure to see you again and to find you exactly the same as ever—young, beautiful, good—and so kind!' She was also tactful in omitting to send him a stinging *Daily Mail* article in which the writer declared, 'Puccini never moves outside the old Italian shallowness of thought, but he strikes a personal tone at once trivial, sensual and cloying, remote from all the fine things of life, emotionally degraded ... His gift is a supreme slickness. He knows just what he wants and how to get it.'

Unaware of such bilious disapproval, rare indeed from London, he wrote warmly to Caruso, 'Tell me how *Fanciulla* is doing and if the crowds are flocking to it and if it is paying me well ... I salute you, O singer of many notes ...' But within a few weeks Caruso had to interrupt his New York season for throat surgery in Milan. He was therefore unavailable for the Covent Garden opening of *Fanciulla* which had been booked out within an hour of its announcement by the Press. Puccini was followed by photographers whenever he emerged from the Savoy to attend rehearsals, but he could not altogether conceal his disappointment at the *mise-en-scène* and the general performance level. Caruso's replacement, Amadeo Bassi, was hardly comparable and even Destinn, repeating her Minnie, could not salvage a production which conspicuously lacked both Belasco's master touch and the dynamism of a Toscanini. It would be given five times that season but the *Daily Telegraph* critic noted sourly that the composer and artists had taken many curtains, 'so ostensibly the opera is a public success.'

The première on 29 May 1911 was one of the highlights of a brilliant Coronation Season. The opera house had been sumptuously redecorated and a new £70,000 oak stage floor laid for the forthcoming visit by Diaghilev's ballet company. While London was agog to see Nijinsky and Karsavina, operagoers had their own banquets served by favourites like Melba, Tetrazzini, Destinn and McCormack. Every performance was acclaimed by audiences scintillating with diamonds and dress uniforms. After a gala performance of *Manon Lescaut* Puccini gave a supper party for Melba at the Savoy. Next morning Lady Ripon called at the hotel with huge bouquets for Elvira and himself and invited them to her beautiful country house on Kingston Hill where they were presented to the ex-King of Portugal among other notables.

He was far more delighted, however, by a chance meeting with his idol Marconi, who happened to be occupying the next chair in the Savoy's hair-dressing saloon. He was much amused by the inventor's irritable refusal to have a towel round his neck while his hair was being trimmed. They met later for lunch in the Grill where Marconi started a minor riot by insisting on having his meat cut for him in minute portions under the manager's personal supervision. But he talked amiably enough about sailing and made Puccini envious of his Rolls-Royce. A few months later he crashed it on the road from Pisa to Genoa after dining with the King and Queen of Italy at their hunting lodge. The accident cost him his right eye and Puccini was among the first to send a letter of sympathy with an affectionately inscribed photograph which would later have a place of honour in the study of his yacht *Elettra*.

The London visit provided a welcome tonic for Elvira whose morale benefited from a round of parties after the still-painful Doria scandal. Whenever Puccini was busily engaged at the opera house, Sybil would take her on shopping tours and presented her with scarves, dress materials and tasteful trinkets. From this time onwards there would be no hint of jealousy from Elvira, who showed genuine affection and concern when Sybil's son Esmond had another serious nervous breakdown which forced him to leave Eton. For the rest of his life he would become an almost helpless invalid and subject to epileptic fits.

In the coming months, while Puccini was preoccupied with various productions of *La Fanciulla*, Sybil hunted tirelessly for possible libretti, refusing to be discouraged by his pernickety objections and equally unpredictable impulses. He toyed briefly with her suggestion to adapt *Lorna Doone* and then raised her hopes by expressing enthusiasm for *Sumurun*, a mimed play which Max Reinhardt had successfully put on at the London Coliseum. He had not been interested enough to see it but continued to talk vaguely of having the piece translated, before announcing suddenly that 'the East does not tempt me very much'. His friends, the Angelis, also drew his attention to Beerbohm Tree's revival of *Trilby* which he promised to look at, but he was already flitting between such diverse ideas as Washington Irving's *Rip Van Winkle*, an opera based on the life of David Garrick, and once again the Ouida story *Two Little Wooden Shoes*, which his critic friend Pozza had mentioned to him while he was still engaged in scoring *Tosca*.

★　　★　　★　　★

This frantic scurrying for suitable subject matter had sprouted from a growing realisation that *La Fanciulla* had failed to gather the expected laurels. Unlike his three previous operas, each of which had survived disastrous openings to establish themselves as international successes, *La Fanciulla* had enjoyed one of the most glittering premières in operatic history but showed little box-office momentum once the initial publicity had subsided. Significantly, the Victor Company seemed in no hurry to make recordings even with artists like Caruso, Farrar and Scotti on call.

He had nursed high hopes for the Italian première at the Teatro Costanzi in Rome a fortnight after the Covent Garden production. Caruso was still absent and Bassi sang competently, with Amato in support, but even Toscanini's baton failed to strike any magic from the score. Although the spectacle and novelty of the setting again won applause, with praise for its original orchestration, few endorsed Pozza's customary eulogy in the *Corriere della Sera* that Puccini had 'never shown such a sure control of his genius and his skill'. Soon afterwards Buenos Aires welcomed the opera with Titta Ruffo singing Jack Rance, while other productions were being slotted in for Warsaw and Budapest.

In October Puccini visited Liverpool for a performance in English and afterwards sat through a civic luncheon given in his honour by the Lord Mayor. On his way home he stayed only one night in London as Sybil had gone off to Como with her family. He wrote to remind her of his desperate need for a new subject. 'Are you going on reading books for me? . . . Do you know of any grotesque novel or story or play, full of humour and buffoonery? I have a desire to laugh and to make other people laugh.'

Outwardly, he had no reason to be disgruntled. He had bought himself a new 15-metre yacht *Minnie*, with a 100 hp Volpi engine and an aerial propeller that pleased him in all respects except its unwillingness to propel! In addition to his Itala he had a small Fiat town car and a Sizaire runabout. Every new production of *La Fanciulla* was cordially received, but he took offence at any cool review which he would attribute to personal antagonism by the critic or incompetent artists. He did not spare his former idol Mugnone for his 'flabby' conducting at the San Carlo in December 1911, but the following April in Monte Carlo while supervising rehearsals, he was much impressed by Giovanni Martinelli who, though lacking Caruso's vocal subtlety, invested Dick Johnson with youth and a superb stage presence. Moreover, he could not fault the lavish production and was flattered by the deference shown him by the impresario Raoul Gunsbourg. After the excitement of over twenty curtain calls he caught the night express to attend rehearsals in Paris but quickly yielded to his familiar distaste for the capital. He shut himself away in his hotel suite, declining to receive all but a few old friends like Isidore de Lara, whose *Naïl* had been staged with indifferent success. *La Fanciulla* fared better, although with the usual divergence of opinion between French audiences and the critics.

Arriving back in Milan, he was briefly cheered to learn that some progress had been made on *Anima Allegra*, the Quinteros' comedy. Before leaving for Monte Carlo he had called on Giulio Ricordi, now sadly emaciated but still with a spark of his former creative zest. He had introduced a young playwright and music critic, Giuseppi Adami, as a likely librettist for the Spanish subject which he considered by far the most promising of all the ideas in Puccini's stockpot. The composer had quickly taken to Adami and at once outlined a verbal sketch of his own ideas for adapting the plot.

Adami produced a complete libretto after a month's hard non-stop toil but, like so many of his predecessors, soon discovered that he had a tiger by the tail. 'Yes, on the whole, I think it's good,' Puccini had declared. 'Now we can start from the beginning! But don't look so frightened—that's the way libretti are made! By re-making them.' He did not appreciate at the time that the nomination of Adami as collaborator was something of a last bequest from his publisher. With the clairvoyance of a dying man, Ricordi had anticipated

Puccini's desperate need of a talented librettist with far more staying power than Illica and others, who might pander to him for quick cash returns or the prospect of exploiting his name.

While in Munich early in June 1912, Puccini saw a newspaper report that Giulio Ricordi had been found dead in his study, slumped over a half-corrected sheet of music with a pencil still between his fingers. He was numbed at first by the loss of a man whom he had once described as 'the only person who inspires me with trust and to whom I can confide all that is going through my mind', but anxiety and self-preservation quickly followed. 'From now on everything is in the hands of *Savoia* (Tito)—we're in a nice fix!' he wrote to Sybil, 'But on the very first occasion that he tries any of his tricks, I shall leave the firm—you can be sure of that, I promise you!'

Ricordi's death had deprived him not only of a sympathetic guide, impresario and banker, but a second father, tolerant of his weaknesses yet resolute when others had yielded to flattery or self-interest. Neither Mrs Seligman nor Tito Ricordi could hope to replace him satisfactorily as a sheet anchor. Sybil had a musical instinct but plainly lacked an impresario's appraisal of popular taste. She would henceforth execute all Puccini's wayward whims without the salutary brake which Giulio Ricordi had applied for close on thirty years. To keep such a situation at safety levels would require both outstanding patience on the part of his successor and far more tolerance than the composer had shown in the past.

This was asking rather too much of two individualists whose egoes had never meshed. Puccini had long tended to ridicule an heir-apparent who gave himself too many airs and also cherished absurdly self-inflated ambitions as a librettist. At the same time his own vacillations could not fail to alienate such a forceful but tactless business operator. But he was still quite unprepared for an almost immediate declaration of war by Tito.

Chapter Twelve

Puccini was still grieving for Giulio Ricordi when he left for Viareggio with Elvira, Fosca and her children in mid-July 1912. He treated the youngsters to the local delicacy, *menta* (sugar sticks flavoured with mint), and often took them sailing in *Minnie*, but he soon grew bored. 'The family weigh on me', he grumbled to Sybil. 'My wife is—well, never mind! A pig of a life!' He asked her to check with Wilde's literary executor whether the rights were still available in *The Florentine Tragedy*, which Ricordi had once rejected as quite unsuitable for an opera. It was symptomatic of his confused state of mind that, so soon after urging her to find him a cheerful subject, he told Illica, 'I still want to make people weep; therein lies everything.' The librettist agreed to expand part of the Wilde material into a preliminary first act, but his draft once again failed to please Puccini, who abruptly abandoned the whole project.

He departed for Carlsbad with Alfredo Angeli, but the waters upset his digestion, and the weather remained stubbornly cold and rainy. However, he found solace with an attractive tourist who agreed to accompany him to Bayreuth. His sudden change of itinerary failed to excite Elvira's suspicions. For one thing she detested all Wagner's music and would certainly have refused an invitation to join him. But his enjoyable little excursion had its moments of embarrassment. During a performance of *Parsifal* he was recognised by a Milanese acquaintance who chanced to be sharing Cosima Wagner's box. In the interval she asked him to present Puccini, who explained hastily that he was registered at a quiet hotel as 'Archimede Rossi, merchant of Milan, with cousin', and wished to remain incognito. His countryman somehow convinced Frau Wagner that he had stupidly mistaken some tourist for the composer.

On his return he went on glum shooting sorties and was soon taking veronal for spells of insomnia. He affected indifference but worried over stories that Tito Ricordi was now parading Riccardo Zandonai, Mascagni's disciple and composer of Puccini's own discarded *Conchita*, as the most hopeful operatic prospect in years. As Tito now seldom troubled to answer his letters, it helped to confirm the disquieting impression that the firm had more or less written him off as a spent force.

This came at a time when a set of disgruntled critics had begun labelling him contemptuously as 'the Italian Massenet'. The campaign had opened with a searing article by Ildebrando Pizzetti, whose own compositions favoured the heroic subjects of d'Annunzio, his friend and patron. A fervent Verdian, he deplored Puccini's subordination of 'aesthetic values and high ideals' to artificial lyricism. His highbrow contemporary, Fausto Torrefranco, had been even more forthright in a book published that year which condemned Puccini as a mere melody-maker who had cynically sacrificed symphonic compositions in the great national tradition for commercial profit. He predicted solemnly that within a few decades hardly any of his work would be performed or even remembered. Others pooh-poohed his alleged claim (which he had never made) to be Verdi's successor, emphasising that he was totally lacking in the immortal Maestro's feeling for classical tragedy. They sneered more or less openly at his obsession with frail heroines and dismissed the death scenes as novelettish melodrama designed to squeeze a final tear from the vulgar bourgeoisie. Although deeply wounded, he would not be provoked into replying, but these attacks made it imperative to silence his critics and perhaps his own doubts about *La Fanciulla*.

A visit to Marseilles in November for a performance in French of that opera gave him an excuse to call on d'Annunzio, who had apparently forgotten their unfortunate last attempt at collaboration and seemed eager to start afresh. He was now living near Arcachon in the Landes, an area so humid and enervating that Puccini found some difficulty in breathing almost as soon as he entered the villa's grounds through a triple gate adorned by an imposing statue of St Dominic. The rented chalet-type house offered a desolate view of the sea beyond thorn-covered dunes, and Puccini surmised that only the poet's creditors could have driven him into this torpid provincial exile. In fact, shortly before his arrival, d'Annunzio had sent his valet to Sutton's in London to pawn a ring and a pair of diamond cufflinks given him by Eleonora Duse. With the local tradesmen now pressing him, he therefore forced himself, a passionate devotee of Wagner, to smother his dislike of Puccini's music for the chance of hard cash.

Dressed in a red hunting-jacket, tight buckskin breeches and Turkish slippers, he presided seignorially over an oval candlelit table sparkling with goblets continuously replenished from his cellar of Mouton Rothschild. They were waited on like sultans by a corps of demure but lissom hand-maidens, led by the host's latest acquisition Amélie, whom he introduced as 'ma petite Francaise' with a satyr's smile made even more hideous by alternating black and gold teeth.

He talked lightly of the latest Italian scandals and inquired about mutual friends, including Tosti and Sybil Seligman, but Puccini discerned the strain behind his drawled smalltalk. D'Annunzio explained that he was engaged on a deeply philosophical work *La Contemplazione della Morte* inspired by the recent loss of a poet friend. Reclining on a sofa while Amélie dabbed his temples with perfume, he recited melancholy passages from the manuscript before turning to the more immediate problem. He then flashed a dozen suggestions, the most promising of which seemed to be his film drama *La Crociata degli Innocenti* (The Children's Crusade). He blinked when the composer, already thinking in terms of a lyrical duet, suggested that a love affair between a couple of the youngsters might usefully be introduced, but promised to have his libretto ready within a very short time.

When a month had passed without so much as a syllable from Arcachon, Puccini sent him a telegram of reminder before departing for rehearsals of *La Fanciulla* at La Scala.

Martinelli repeated his spirited Dick Johnson and the piece was received well enough to justify another dozen performances. Most admirers had made charitable allowances for the possible effects of the Doria tragedy but plainly looked forward to his next opera.

So far, apart from d'Annunzio's promised scenario, nothing had emerged. He had now discarded the Quintero Brothers' subject as too Spanish and Bizet-like, although Adami desperately changed the locale to Flanders. He stoically accepted defeat after a gruelling year of re-drafting and would have to wait until 1921 before his libretto was set by another composer and enjoyed a reasonable success in Rome.

With so many critical puppies snapping at his heels, Puccini was touched by the devotion of 'Adamino', as he called him affectionately. Well-read and personable, with lively eyes behind his solemn-looking pince-nez, he was always welcome at Torre. He would gladly put aside his regular and more reliable work for talks in Via Verdi, never hesitating to rush off for meetings in Turin or Genoa if the composer happened to be passing through. At a hint from Puccini he re-read Heine's plays and diligently excavated Dickens for possible operatic nuggets. He came up with plenty of fool's gold, but proved invaluable as sifter, researcher and above-average librettist. He was perhaps too young and reverential in his attitude to a composer who disliked argument and needed the abrasive give-and-take of the Giacosa-Illica partnership rather more than bland acquiescence. But he was a useful sounding-board although, like Sybil Seligman, too apt to vibrate sympathetically to please the loved one.

Adami's rôle expanded automatically when d'Annunzio failed to produce a satisfactory libretto. 'He has given birth to a small shapeless monstrosity, unable to walk or live!', Puccini reported to Sybil. 'I am in despair! Is there nothing to be seen in London at the theatres? *Savoia* is more impossible than ever—I have found out that he is actually my enemy—or at least the enemy of my music!' He suggested alterations to d'Annunzio, who was unreceptive but appeared to show no personal animosity at being rebuffed. He continued to send Christmas greetings to Torre, usually accompanied by vintage wine from his cellars, but the wound festered. In his book of jottings *Libro segreto*, published years after the composer's death, he wrote tartly, 'Behold, Lake Massaciúccoli! Of waterfowl enough to feed the nation but miserably poor in inspiration!'

Puccini still hoped to extract a revised draft from him, but the winter months drifted by mournfully, relieved only by satisfactory royalties and batches of flattering press cuttings. He was delighted when Lucrezia Bori made a triumphant last-minute début at the Metropolitan in *Manon Lescaut*. It was also exhilarating to read that people had queued for standing room, from dawn onwards, for a Saturday matinée of *Tosca* conducted by Toscanini, with Caruso, Geraldine Farrar and Scotti taking the principal rôles.

Soon afterwards, in February 1913, the Galleria was hushed by reports of his death.* Telegrams poured into Torre del Lago, quickly followed by a horde of journalists and photographers. He was sitting down to dinner with some local friends when the first message of condolence arrived for Elvira. He gaily assured a reporter from the *Corriere della Sera* that his appetite was as healthy as ever and that he only regretted having to tip the postman for delivering so many telegrams, but the depressing incident revived all his morbid fears of old age and death. He left gloomily to see *La Fanciulla* mounted in Berlin. 'I have no libretto. I have no work. My publisher is my enemy,' he wrote to Elvira. He carped at the singers and could not make the German conductor understand his pidgin French, but the performance had a riotous welcome. After a banquet in his honour he was ringed by adoring women whom, he assured Elvira, he had resisted. 'Goodbye, dear Topizia,' he wrote affectionately, 'Kiss my Rolls-Roise!'

In this jaunty mood but still without an idea for a full-length work, he again thought of composing a trio of one-act operas, an idea which Giulio Ricordi had once so sternly

* A reporter had confused him with a man of similar name.

202

rejected. On reflection he had conceded that Gorky's tales were unsuitable, but still argued that Offenbach's *Tales of Hoffmann* indicated that such a structure could work, while *Cavalleria rusticana* had started a vogue for one-act operas which even Massenet had not disdained to follow. He now informed Adami that a short piece of Grand Guignol, *La Houppelande*, seemed to be drawing the crowds to the Marigny in Paris and might well fit into his triptych. He also urged Illica to reconnoitre for further subjects, but the hint failed to take root after so many previous miscarriages.

Early in May he hurried off to Paris with the combined intention of seeing *La Houppelande* and persuading d'Annunzio to return to 'The Crusade'. The poet found excuses to avoid a meeting but finally received him in his bachelor flat in the Rue de Bassano. He had just emerged from an aromatic bath with his sinewy monkeyish body encased in a woman's flowery kimono. It seemed appropriate to a sitting-room, redolent of joss sticks and cluttered with obscene-looking Buddhas of various sizes and colours. He extended two limp be-ringed fingers in greeting and observed with insolent detachment that Mascagni's version of his *Parisina*, which his visitor had scorned, would shortly open in Milan. The shaft went over Puccini's head. He spoke persuasively of including some 'noble subject', preferably heroic, in his triptych, hinting that a fellow-author would be Tristan Bernard, the playwright and parodist whom Sacha Guitry had saluted as 'the best-loved and fullest-bearded wit in Paris.'

Bernard was affable enough although disposed to talk only of motor cars, balloons and aeroplanes. His study walls were adorned with maxims such as 'Love affairs are like mushrooms. One doesn't know if they're the safe variety or poisonous until it's too late.' They often lunched together at his haunts on the boulevards, but talk was difficult with so many of the playwright's friends pecking for loans and other favours. He suggested off-handedly that one of his fairy-tales might make a good one-act comedy, but Puccini considered it too similar to *Hänsel and Gretel* and preferred Bernard's alternative idea of a satirical piece with an African setting. This concerned a cannibal, who had once been exhibited as a freak in a Paris sideshow, and later takes vengeance on some white explorers by having them roasted after a series of humiliations. Puccini must have been seduced by the Frenchman's witty tongue even to entertain such a theme for a comic opera, but the glamour of Bernard's name, coupled with d'Annunzio's, seemed to disarm him.

He enjoyed that summer month in Paris without rehearsals and the attention of jackal critics. He accepted few of the invitations which stacked his mantelpiece at the Westminster, but it was gratifying, though occasionally embarrassing, to receive so much adulation from the public. Whenever he went shopping and gave his name for deliveries, the staff would clamour for autographs and even form an impromptu guard of honour as he left. At the Café de Paris the manager invariably signalled the orchestra to play excerpts from *Butterfly*, which meant getting up and blushingly acknowledging the applause.

He saw *La Houppelande* and convinced himself of its operatic potential. The eternal triangle plot was sordid, but the Seine barges would make an excellent contrast to Bernard's African village and the mediaeval piece which d'Annunzio had half-promised. In a cordial letter to Tito Ricordi, asking him to secure the rights of Didier Gold's melodrama, Puccini mentioned having seen a production of Stravinsky's *Le Sacré du Printemps*; 'The choreography is ridiculous, the music sheer cacophony. There is some originality, however, and a certain amount of talent. But taken altogether, it might be the creation of a madman.' Nevertheless, Stravinsky's discords are audible in passages of both *Il Tabarro* and *Turandot*.*

His overheated enthusiasm for *La Houppelande* sparked off a quite remarkable error of judgment. As Adami was then busily writing a play of his own, while still researching

* Stravinsky considered *La Bohème* by far the best of Puccini's work but dismissed *Butterfly* as 'treacly violin music'. Richard Strauss was even less charitable, once declaring that he could not 'tell them apart'.

Dickens and other possible sources of full-length operas, the composer had impulsively invited an old friend of his to adapt Didier Gold's piece. Ferdinando Martini was a writer of some distinction and also a career diplomat but, at seventy, he could not be expected to quicken his stately tempo or adapt his meticulous prose to the language of French bargees. Although out of his depth on the waterfront, he persevered while Puccini, drained by a hot summer and Fosca's shrill infants, left gratefully enough for Vienna in October to attend the opening of *La Fanciulla* at the Hofoper.

He was soon trapped in the usual hospitable web, but that short visit took a most unexpected turn. One evening he had amused himself by looking into the Karl Theater. Hearing that he was out front, the directors invited him to refreshments in their private room. To his astonishment one of them suggested that he might consider writing a number of tunes for an operetta. They offered 200,000 kronen (about £8,000) and fifty per cent of the royalties. His immediate reaction was to refuse, but the invitation intrigued him enough to promise considering a draft scenario.

As Martini had now bowed out of *Il Tabarro* (the re-titled *La Houppelande*), Adami took over. He produced a sound draft in little over a fortnight, but Puccini was unwilling to set it until the other two subjects of his 'Trittico' had materialised. So far the outlook was none too promising. D'Annunzio seemed far more interested in an opera which Puccini's 'rival', Zandonai, had adapted from his play *Francesca da Rimini*, with Tito Ricordi as part-author of the libretto. It would open in Turin in mid-February. Tristan Bernard, possibly taking his cue from d'Annunzio who may well have warned him of the composer's capriciousness, was equally unproductive.

With only one-third of his triptych in hand, Puccini found himself warming briefly to the Viennese offer. But the suggested plot was too hackneyed, and he had already questioned the wisdom of writing musical numbers interspersed between dialogue. Frustrated, he had again dusted off Ouida's *Two*

Little Wooden Shoes, a subject pigeonholed, on and off, for the past fifteen years.

It appears that one night in February 1913 he and Adami were dining at Torre del Lago, where they had been discussing *Il Tabarro* over some excellent claret sent by d'Annunzio, possibly as a peace-offering. Puccini had walked out on the terrace and, gazing across the misty lake, suddenly recalled the eccentric English novelist whom the poet used to visit. For Adami's benefit he outlined the touching story of the simple Flemish girl who walks all the way to Paris in her sabots to discover that her artist-lover has betrayed her for the delights of *La Dolce Vita*. Her death scene by drowning, as narrated by Puccini, moved the gentle Adami, who could already hear *Butterfly* music. He borrowed a translation and agreed without hesitation to prepare a first draft.

While he scribbled away, Sybil was trying to clarify the copyright position with Ouida's London publishers. Puccini had meanwhile discovered that the novelist's Italian creditors might be troublesome. He therefore decided to pay her executor, a Viareggio lawyer, 1,000 lire option money, announcing in the *Corriere della Sera* that he had 'precedence over all others' in the Ouida novel which would be the subject of his next opera. This had a very mixed reaction. Mascagni promptly declared that he was already working on the same theme, but a Viennese publisher at once approached Puccini with an offer of 400,000 kroner (£16,000), plus a forty per cent royalty. Although flattered, he was still friendly enough with Tito Ricordi to avoid this entanglement and sent him a cordial Easter greeting together with an enthusiastic report on Adami's draft libretto.

The truce did not last. Puccini went to Vienna for a production of *Tosca*, but Tito was too busy rehearsing the next performance of *Francesca da Rimini* at San Carlo to accompany him. As his representative he appointed Carlo Clausetti, who ran the firm's branch in Naples after his father's publishing house had been absorbed by the Ricordis. He was amiable enough but Puccini, already aggrieved by the snub, became incensed when Clausetti received a telegram from Tito, five days before the opening of *Tosca*, recalling him to Naples. Puccini protested angrily but Tito wired back, 'I order Clausetti to leave at once.'

Tosca survived this last-minute crisis, thanks to an all-conquering début in the leading rôle by Maria Jeritza, a young Moravian soprano who had charmed Germany and was already idolised by Hofoper audiences. This stately golden-haired beauty, with a physique and breath control developed by swimming and rowing, shared Puccini's passion for motor-boats but could never persuade him to go riding with her. He had absolutely no feeling for horses and used to laugh at d'Annunzio's weakness for sending out hundreds of pictures of himself taking fences. Jeritza found him charming but, like Melba, disliked his chain-smoking. However, she was still too over-awed by him and grateful for his consideration at rehearsals to object when he puffed cigarettes in her presence, making the excuse that while she ate vast quantities of potatoes and sweets without putting on weight, he had to smoke to maintain a strict diet.

She could learn any opera in eight days, memorising her own parts as well as her partners', and never needed the services of a prompter. But this did not exempt her from Puccini's unyielding demands for perfection. As she recalled, 'He would never take no for an answer. If a phrase had to be taken in one breath, he would keep me working until he got what he wanted . . . He helped me technically. He could also insult you in the most gentlemanly way. We went over the music step by step, phrase by phrase. He moulded me. I was his *creation*. Sometimes he would make me so angry that I wanted to cry. Then he would get angry. "Jeritza", he would say, "if I ever wake you at three in the morning and ask you to sing a high C, you *will* sing a high C!" ' Both deeply regretted that being five foot seven she was too tall for his geisha. 'Just because I am a few inches too high', she wrote sorrowfully in her memoirs, 'I am prevented from attempting to portray one of the most touching and expressive heroines to be found in a Puccini score!'

Her sultry splendour as Tosca was the season's sensation. Puccini would never again hear anyone else in the rôle without sighing for her dramatic voltage and astonishing vocal nuances. On his piano at Torre del Lago her framed portrait now took precedence over that of Lina Cavalieri, who had recently married the handsome French tenor Lucien Muratore. Henceforth his rapport with Jeritza made him impervious to other singers who had formerly commanded his admiration. He would speak contemptuously of Melba as 'the centenarian' (she was three years his junior!) and once assured Sybil, 'I'm sorry that she is ill, but I think that Mimì will be pleased to be *unsung* by her.' He consistently underrated Geraldine Farrar and declared sourly, years before she retired, 'she has no voice left'. He could dismiss Selma Kurz, then in her forties, as 'rather too old but not yet *Melba*'. His first admiration for Destinn's Minnie also faded as soon as *La Fanciulla* became subject to the law of diminishing box-office returns. He would even shrug off Rosina Storchio, his once-adored first Butterfly, as 'too brittle and kittenish'.

Tosca brought Jeritza world fame and an offer from the Metropolitan which she could not take up until after the war. Puccini had quickly assessed her star quality, but in other respects his judgment was gravely at fault during that last excitable pre-war season in Vienna. Nettled by Tito Ricordi's behaviour, he saw his chance of simultaneously snubbing him and restoring his own prestige when the Karl Theater impresarios repeated their invitation. This time they promised a more acceptable libretto and engaged Alfred Willner, who had part-authored scripts for Lehár and written much light comedy. Puccini agreed in principle and left for home, heartened by this new project and with the added balm of having been made a Grand Officer of the Order of Franz Josef by the Emperor. The decoration was particularly welcome since most Austrian and German critics, ignoring his army of admirers, had so often dismissed him as a *Salonmusiker* by comparison with Strauss and even Lehar.

He now bought himself yet another Lancia which he drove at high speed to Rome where Paolo Tosti had finally come to rest after so many comfortable years of 'exile'. His beard still wagged mischievously as he held court at the Caffé Greco, but the sparkling practical joker of Pagani's was now in his anecdotage and pathetically grateful for an audience. Puccini had hoped for shrewd advice but returned sadly to Milan with little more than affectionate chit-chat from the frail septuagenarian, who already had the crackle of dead leaves about him.

Adami was far more helpful, although *Il Tabarro* had been shelved in the absence of two more panels for the triptych, while Ouida's sabots had sunk into a legal quagmire, and he needed all his dedication and resilience to switch to Puccini's new Austrian venture. He conceded politely that Willner's first draft for *La Rondine* had possibilities, but seemed surprised that Puccini had swallowed such a Viennese éclair of sentimentality, laced with cheap cynicism, at a gulp. The so-called 'plot' whirled in waltz-time round a rich banker's mistress, who leaves him for a poor but romantic lover before finally sacrificing all for a life of luxurious anguish. This pot-pourri, obviously derived from *Traviata*, with sweepings from both *Manon* and *Bohème*, even included among its clichés a comic maid from *Fledermaus*, masquerading as her mistress.

After agreement had been reached on various points, Puccini readily consenting to the première being staged in Vienna, the Austrian impresarios and writers arrived in Milan, with their wives, in July. Puccini now seemed happy enough with the revised libretto which Willner read out to him. 'It will be finished in the spring,' he was soon reporting chirpily to Sybil. 'It's a light sentimental opera with touches of comedy, but it's agreeable, limpid, easy to sing, with a little waltz music and lively and fetching tunes . . . So many sweet and kind thoughts to you—the only war I've had has been in my home; but things are going better now.'

That letter, written on 14 September 1914, when Sybil's

brother-in-law Herbert Seligman was already in France with the first British Expeditionary Force, and Vincent almost of military age, discloses Puccini's remarkably self-centred attitude to a war which some of his countrymen already took far more seriously. It would cost him the friendship and respect of Toscanini, whom he had once saluted as 'kind, good, adorable'.

Vivacious Lina Cavalieri, 'the most beautiful woman in the world', sang Manon during Puccini's first visit to New York, 1907. Their infatuation was an open secret. Gina Lollobrigida starred in the film version of Cavalieri's life and loves.

Tito Ricordi at wheel of the cabin cruiser *Cio-Cio-San*. In background a smiling Puccini, who often clashed with Giulio's autocratic successor.

M. Puccini. M. Victorien Sardou. M. Albert Carré. M. André-Messager.
M. Ricordi. M. Paul Ferrier.

(top) A *Tosca* rehearsal at the Opera-Comique. (l. to r.), Puccini, Tito Ricordi, Sardou, Albert Carré (gen. manager), Paul Ferrier (translator) and André Messager, conducting.

(below) At the Metropolitan for *La Fanciulla del West*, December 1910. Gatti-Casazza, Belasco, Toscanini with the composer.

(top) Relaxing on terrace at Torre del Lago with his wife and son, Antonio.
(below) A spin on Lake Massaciúccoli. In New York Puccini once autographed a few bars of Musetta's Waltz for $500, using it as down payment on a speedboat, shipped out to Italy.

10.2.24

Cara Sybil

Vi accludo un Telegramma
arrivato ora – Ho sentito
del viaggio poco felice –
adesso sarete riposata... ma
il sole un l'avete trovato.
anche qui piove –
I pochi giorni che siete stato
fra noi sono stati simpaticis-
simi – Un'altra volta
vi fermerete di più – Lo spero.
Ho seguito la mia vita monotona
di lavoro – Eloina vi
manda tanti cari saluti
e anche il vostro aff. G. Puccini

One of Puccini's many affectionate letters to Sybil Seligman. Dated 10 February 1924, ill and desperate to finish *Turandot*, he writes, 'I continue my monotonous life, working. . .'

Part of the celebrated aria, 'E lucevan le stelle'. A specimen page from Puccini's manuscript of the *Tosca* score.

Prima donna Maria Jeritza was Puccini's favourite Tosca. She triumphed in that role in every leading opera house, but Puccini did not live to witness her interpretation of the Princess in *Turandot*.

One of Puccini's last photographs, posed in his garden at Viareggio. He had been driven from Torre del Lago by the noise and fumes of a peat factory but kept his old villa for occasional visits. It now houses his tomb and a museum.

Chapter Thirteen

Others were closer to Puccini than Arturo Toscanini, but their volatile relationship helps to focus the composer's last years rather more sharply than his dealings with over-affectionate intimates like Sybil Seligman and Adami. The Maestro was in a unique position to assess his faults and virtues without sentimentality or the smallest taint of self-interest. He felt free at all times, both as friend and meticulous interpreter, to offer either praise or honest criticism.*

His disparaging view of the *Butterfly* score had long been an open secret, but Puccini took bitter offence when Toscanini, after listening impatiently to his outline of *Il Tabarro*, dismissed it as 'tasteless Grand Guignol' and quite unworthy of his talent. The squabbles with Tito Ricordi and his abortive pursuit of suitable libretti had made him almost paranoically testy, but he seemed genial enough when he drove over to Viareggio with Elvira and his son almost every day during July 1914. Fosca had rented a house in Via Colombo for the season and her daughters sported on the beach with Toscanini's three children. Puccini, replacing his motoring cap and goggles with a fez, took them for gay picnics in the pinewoods, but their special delight was being piped aboard the *Minnie* by the composer who, sporting full yachting regalia, insisted on being addressed as Lieutenant Pinkerton and having tea ceremoniously served by his young 'geishas'.

---

* He once declared, 'In many Puccini operas the words and the notes are not inextricable. You could change the words, and any other set would do.' He could also accept criticism. He had often scoffed at the opening theme of Mozart's G Minor Symphony as 'tweet, tweet' until Puccini, returning from a visit to Vienna, spoke enthusiastically of how Hans von Bülow's robust conducting had transformed the music. Years later, Toscanini recalled humbly, 'At last I understood. That was the way for me.'

Toscanini had joined in the fun but became pricklier and perceptibly more anxious as the war clouds gathered. Puccini, who had never had more than a nodding acquaintance with domestic issues, still less international affairs, remained unmoved by the prospect of a holocaust. He would usually doze over an unread newspaper once he had snipped out some alluring advertisement for sailing paraphernalia or an 'everlasting' match guaranteed to stay alight in the wind when he needed to smoke at the wheel. With his habitual acceptance of the *status quo*, he had lazily aligned himself with the royalists, the Vatican and the bankers whose open sympathy with the Central Powers was paralleled by their insistence on Italian neutrality. Toscanini had no strong political convictions but would never forget that his father had marched with Garibaldi. He found it difficult to stomach either Puccini's selfish fears of losing his royalties or his scoffing dismissal of reports that the Germans had raped Belgian nuns and cut off babies' hands.

Although three of his most successful operas—*Manon Lescaut*, *La Bohème* and *Tosca*—derived from French sources, his francophobia had been exacerbated by every visit to the capital. But it was tactless in the extreme to remark at a party of gay holidaymakers, 'As far as I'm concerned, the Germans can't capture Paris too soon.' This was repeated maliciously to Toscanini, who threatened to slap Puccini's face in public at the first opportunity. In the evenings he would pace his terrace, snapping at mutual friends who pleaded with him to forgive the composer. He was still touchy when he sailed back to the United States in October with Gatti-Casazza, Caruso and other members of the Metropolitan company who had been vacationing or singing in Europe. Puccini had intended seeing them off from Naples but shrank from an unpleasant scene with Toscanini. Their departure deepened his sense of isolation. While unctuously assuring Sybil that 'England is certain to come out well—she is so wise and so strong', he could not help mentioning that 'for us poor devils, it's a great blessing not to be involved in the conflict'.

212

He seemed altogether more concerned with his press cuttings than the gloomy reports of wounded French troops streaming back from the Marne. He sneered at d'Annunzio's flamboyant efforts to raise a battalion of Italian volunteers in France, but was sharply reminded of pro-Allied sentiment when a band of militant young 'Futurists' interrupted a performance of one of his operas in Rome and burned the Austrian flag on the stage. It registered their disgust with his recent decoration from the Emperor and the operetta he was said to be composing for Vienna. Others were quick to point approvingly to Leoncavallo, who had once glorified the early Hohenzollerns in his opera *Der Roland von Berlin* (1904), but now denounced his old patron, the Kaiser. As a result, his works were banned immediately throughout Austria and Germany.

By contrast, Puccini's ambivalent stance did him little credit. A joint condemnation by leading British, French and Italian composers of the invasion of Belgium was answered by a Berlin newspaper which had mistakenly included his name in the list. Instead of simply correcting the error or ignoring it altogether, he had most unwisely chosen to affirm his friendship for *all* countries who performed his operas, stressing his duty as a good Italian to remain 'impartial and neutral'. It drew a stinging open letter in *L'Action Francaise* from Léon Daudet accusing him of German sympathies. The Opéra-Comique at once banned all his operas, but he remained unrepentant, considering himself the innocent victim of French chauvinism. 'Oh, how grateful I am to the English for being so utterly different from those *pigs*—your neighbours!' he told Sybil, but many of his countrymen echoed Daudet's tirade as Italian sentiment veered swiftly towards the Allies. Before the end of May d'Annunzio reported exultantly to his friend Maurice Barrès, 'They are singing the Marseillaise this evening around Trajan's Column. Until now we had two fatherlands, but this evening we have only one, extending from French Flanders to the sea of Sicily,'

Puccini's reaction was distinctly more muted. 'May God

protect us and may the star of Italy shine on the final victory!', he wrote piously to Sybil. By now *La Rondine* was well advanced although at one time he had almost given it up. 'It's a solemn piece of muck', he told Adami in November. 'I curse the day when I made a contract with Vienna.' Fortunately the Austrian impresarios accepted Adami's offer to replace the original spoken dialogue with lyrical verses which helped to extricate the preposterous plot from its tight corset of operetta. Adami would, however, still be subject to merciless pressure from the composer. He wrote sixteen acts in all for *La Rondine*, but was at least spared further work on *Two Little Wooden Shoes* after a series of near-farcical negotiations.

By March 1915 Ouida's creditors had impatiently organised a public auction of the copyright in the hope of stimulating competition between the rival composers. Mascagni was represented at the sale in Viareggio, but Puccini came over in person from Torre del Lago. The local tradesmen made early bids to boost the price, but Mascagni's agent had remained oddly apathetic while Puccini, scenting something familiar about a suave young bidder in the crowd, also hung back. This stranger caused consternation by announcing that he would take no further part in the auction. However, he purred soothingly, Casa Ricordi had empowered him to make an *ex gratia* payment of 4,000 lire and thus avoid unnecessary copyright arguments. His offer was hastily accepted. He then took Puccini aside and solemnly handed him the documents with Tito Ricordi's compliments!

It was a superbly arrogant gesture on the part of 'Savoia' who must have relished putting the composer firmly in his place although Puccini, for once curiously thick-skinned, seemed grateful enough for a possible subject to follow *La Rondine* (The Swallow). By the end of October, while still assuring 'Adamino' of his interest in Ouida's novel, he hinted that it might be more practical to resume work on *Il Tabarro*. Within a few months the wooden shoes had finally clattered off into the limbo of Puccini rejects.

★   ★   ★   ★

La Rondine, conceived in pique and delivered amid wartime frustrations, achieved a minor miracle in surviving at all. In normal circumstances the fluffy plot and basically uncongenial genre would no doubt have led Puccini to abandon this project, like so many others in the past, but he now found himself with little choice. Sybil Seligman was too busy with her war work to nose out alternative libretti, while the faithful Adami, who could always be relied upon to translate or adapt, lacked creative flair.

Dwindling receipts from countries still giving opera (*La Fanciulla* had been dropped from the Metropolitan repertory after only four seasons and would not surface during his lifetime), coupled with the banning of his work by enemy impresarios who had already frozen royalties due to him, had muffled his misgivings over *La Rondine*. However, he was determined not to be hamstrung by the original arrangement to stage the première in Vienna. In September 1915 he had a secret meeting in Interlaken with Heinrich Berté of the Karl Theater who finally waived this stipulation and agreed to hand over all performing rights with the exception of Austria, Germany, Scandinavia and the United States.

It was a valuable concession but failed to mollify Tito Ricordi whose firm had invariably insisted on world rights in the works of their composers. The loss of the American market, in particular, outraged all his business instincts. Already huffed at being by-passed in the Viennese negotiations, quite apart from Puccini's ludicrous somersaults over the Ouida novel, he could feel little excitement for an Austrian operetta which had practically no chance of being staged in wartime Europe with Covent Garden shuttered and most of the leading Italian opera houses uncertain of their future. (La Scala closed down in 1917 after giving eight performances of *Tosca* in its last wartime season). Tito therefore reserved judgment, but with a strong hint of condescension, until the score was further advanced.

Puccini refused to be discouraged although now working under extreme domestic pressure. He had offered to find his son a safe Ministry job, but Tonio preferred to enlist and was soon serving at the Front as a despatch rider. This naturally made Elvira anxious and affected a temper already on edge through losing her servants. 'We go for lunch and dinner to Viareggio and sleep at Torre', Puccini moaned to Adami. 'My melancholy is immense, unspeakable, frightening!' The war had deprived him of his major domo, Gnicche, who had been called up for military service, and there was little satisfaction in sailing or water-fowling without him and other congenial spirits. Once or twice he escaped to the wild Maremma for snipe-shooting but nothing could replace the stimulus of supervising productions of his operas. He seemed to be mouldering away in Torre. 'I am here by myself', he wrote to Sybil in April 1916. 'I am quite well, though I am getting older. How I long to travel! When will this accursed war be over? It seems like a suspension of life!'

He visited Rome once or twice to call on the Tostis, whom he found 'as sweet and kind as ever', but avoided Milan where Tito Ricordi was either unavailable or very pointedly shunted him into Clausetti's office. In the Galleria and old haunts like the Ristorante Cova he saw few recognisable faces and rarely anyone disposed to gossip about happier times. Many now wore crêpe armbands for sons or brothers and others croaked despairingly of an imminent Austrian advance from the north.

Toscanini's son Walter, a captain of artillery, sometimes enjoyed a reunion with Tonio when they were both home on leave, but their sires remained bitterly estranged. The conductor had returned from New York, giving up a salary of $42,000 a season, rather than work with Gatti-Casazza, whose penny-pinching and narrow-minded chauvinism had become intolerable.* He began organising concerts for War Relief and at his first open-air production in Milan led an hysterical audience of 40,000 in the singing of Garibaldi hymns. He also conducted military bands at the Front and was awarded a

---

* During his seven seasons at the Metropolitan, Toscanini had as always given affectionate dedication to Verdi's later works, but Puccini's operas easily dominated all contemporary composers.

silver medal by the government for bravery under fire, but it took even more courage to include Wagner and Beethoven's Ninth in his programmes. Working so often without payment, he had to sell his seventeenth-century mansion in Via Durini when his savings vanished. One night, towards the end of the war, he unpacked his cello and made plans to take a modest position in some orchestra. He could therefore feel little warmth for a composer who never offered benefit performances of his operas and preferred to scribble waltz music for his Austrian friends.

Puccini had blubbered when Tosti died in December 1916, but he saw no reason to follow the example of Isidore de Lara, who organised an In Memoriam Matinée of Tosti's music at the Steinway Hall in London, with Sybil Seligman among the patrons. The entire proceeds of £1,500 were handed over to the Italian Red Cross. Puccini's self-pity immunised him to such sentimental gestures. Although Sybil was suffering from painful sciatica and had the additional anxiety of looking after an incurably epileptic son while Vincent was fighting in Salonika, he kept imploring her to come to Italy. 'How gladly would I tell you all my griefs and troubles . . . Elvira is always in such black spirits that I feel a longing to get away . . .'

She had every cause for despondency. His amours, so conveniently arranged in pre-war days during visits abroad or to provincial theatres, were now closer to home and inevitably started gossip. After one quarrel he had attempted to justify himself in a letter from Milan. 'You invent women in order to give free play to your policeman's instinct . . . You have never looked at these matters as do other women who are more reasonable . . . All artists cultivate these little gardens in order to delude themselves into thinking that they are not finished and old and torn by strife . . . Be calm. Wait for me. I shall always be your Topizio.'

Claustrophobia and restlessness drove him to cultivate one of these 'little gardens' just across the Swiss border. His visits to the wife of a German officer became so frequent that the frontier guards, unaware of his identity, suspected him of

217

espionage. After the Italian Ambassador had hinted privately that these trips might become an embarrassment, he discontinued the liaison until the woman's husband was killed on the Western Front. She then settled in Bologna and soon took a handsome young Italian officer as her lover. Puccini was too vain and sensitive to ridicule to share her favours but the episode, rare in his experience, had reminded him cruelly of the passing years. He was regularly dyeing the white patches in his hair and had developed a morbid fear of going blind. He now wore glasses while composing and used manuscript paper with widely-spaced staves. Before the end of the war he would be writing plaintively to Sybil, 'I'm nearly sixty, dear friend! How unjust it is that one should grow old—it makes me simply furious, confound it! And to think that I won't surrender and that there are times when I believe I'm the man I used to be!'

His liaison with the German woman would prove an embarrassment for many years. She continued to pester him for loans which he advanced rather than risk scandalous publicity and ugly scenes with Elvira. He finally extricated himself when 'La Tedesca' requested a further 10,000 lire to start an hotel in Bologna. As he had no faith in her business ability and little hope of seeing his money back, he decided to cut his losses by sending her 5,000 lire *as a gift*, on the clear understanding that there would be no more demands on his purse or any further communication.

With *La Rondine*, his difficulties were less easily resolved. By Easter 1916 he had completed the score and was already busily orchestrating *Il Tabarro*, while scouting for two more panels to complete his triptych. Tito Ricordi had left him in no doubt that he thought *La Rondine* 'bad Lehár'. According to Puccini, he had offered him this opera '100 times' before taking it to Sonzogno, the firm which had once frustrated all his early hopes. Tito's contemptuous indifference had been a factor, but his own eagerness for a world *prima* after seven long years of frustration, had no doubt triggered off this extraordinary act of defiance. Nevertheless, while gratified by Sonzogno's promise to stage *La Rondine* at Monte Carlo, he hedged his bets by giving Casa Ricordi the first option on all his future work.

Unabashed, Tito changed his tactics. Although offended by Puccini's defection to a rival publisher, he had few regrets over losing the Viennese piece. Instead he quickly agreed terms with Puccini for *Il Tabarro* and also placated him by placing the firm's considerable technical resources at his disposal, including the services of Maestro Raffaele Tenaglia, the only member of the staff who could decipher his pencilled scores and prepare them for publication.

Puccini's star suddenly rose like a comet. By early 1917 the first of the long-missing companion pieces for *Il Tabarro* had appeared. As Adami had few ideas of his own, he had unselfishly recommended one of his friends, Giovacchino Forzano, a former baritone and journalist who had something of Illica's adroitness for expanding an anecdote or merely a few lines from a novel into an effective theatre sketch. During his very first visit to Torre del Lago he recalled a one-act play now gathering dust in his desk. The simplicity and pathos of the plot made instant appeal to Puccini. A girl enters a convent to expiate her guilt for a sinful love affair. Seven years later, 'Suor Angelica', learning that her abandoned baby son has died, poisons herself with herbs from the convent garden. On her deathbed she is comforted by a vision of the Madonna placing an infant babe in her arms.

The libretto, written in a few weeks, was approved with uncharacteristic speed by Puccini, who lost no time in familiarising himself with the atmosphere by visiting the convent of Vicopelago near Lucca, where his sister Iginia was Mother Superior. He brought gifts of a new altar cloth and food hampers, but the gentle nuns were even more charmed by the exquisite melodies which he played over to them on the piano while his sister turned the pages. He spoke later of his embarrassment in recounting Suor Angelica's sinful past and suicide, but the shocked silence had ended with murmurs of sympathy as he described the closing scene; 'I saw many eyes that looked at me through tears. And when I came to the aria *Madonna, Madonna, salvami per amor di mio figlio*! all the little nuns cried, with voices full of pity but firm in their decision, "Yes, yes, poor thing!".' Puccini's old friend, Father Panichelli, was similarly affected and again proved helpful by furnishing the words of the hymn sung in praise of the Madonna.

By a quirky coincidence, Forzano had recently adapted Ouida's *Two Little Wooden Shoes* for a Mascagni opera which opened at the Costanzi in Rome in April 1917. Entitled *La Lodoletta*, it had a pleasant enough reception but gave Puccini no heartburning regrets, then or later, and even artists like Caruso, Geraldine Farrar and Gigli failed to establish it in the Metropolitan repertory. Forzano was now in constant demand as a librettist, but his surprisingly smooth passage with *Suor Angelica* had encouraged him to embark almost at once on another one-act play for Puccini, this time a droll comedy inspired by an anecdote of fourteenth-century Florence in the thirteenth Canto of Dante's 'Inferno'. Puccini was so amused by Gianni Schicchi, the engaging rascal who impersonates a dead man before ingeniously turning the tables on some scheming relatives, that he commissioned the libretto without hesitation, even putting aside *Suor Angelica* to start composing the first scene of the comedy. The libretto of *Gianni Schicchi* was almost ready by the time he arrived back from Monte Carlo after an overwhelming first night.

La Rondine was staged at the ornate Casino Theatre on 27 March 1917. Raoul Gunsbourg, with pleasant memories of many Puccini successes, had mounted it with money and taste. Puccini spent many hours rehearsing the beautiful Gilda Dalla Rizza as Magda, with Tito Schipa singing her lack-lustre lover Ruggero. The audience of gamblers, war-bored sophisticates and profiteers seemed almost hand-picked for this tuneful and sentimental confection. They may not have appreciated its contrapuntal nimbleness, but the waltzes and lilting duets were enchanting.

Flanked in his box by Elvira and Fosca, Puccini bowed smilingly as the final curtain came down to thunderous applause. The local papers lauded his opera's 'rich inspiration' which helped to silence any lingering self-criticism. From his suite at the Hotel de Paris, crammed with bouquets, he sent Sybil copies of the fulsome reviews but commented that Tito Ricordi had failed to send him a telegram of good wishes, adding darkly, 'and now he will be sorry, because the *Rondine* is an opera full of life and melody.' Even in his hour of jubilation he could not avoid dilating on his diabetic troubles and certain mysterious shooting pains in an arm. As always, he deplored the war and its particular unpleasantness for himself. 'My God! It is as horrible as it is endless! I cannot stand it much longer.'

He took affectionate leave of Dalla Rizza who went off to Buenos Aires to repeat her Magda. Back in Italy he received news of another blast from his old enemy Léon Daudet, who attacked him for shamelessly 'trafficking with the enemy.' In an impassioned letter of defence he protested vigorously that he had removed the property from the Viennese and given it to an Italian publisher. As a somewhat belated sop to French public opinion he then asked the Comique to hand over a year's royalties from his operas to a fund for disabled soldiers.

His sensitivity to criticism was matched by an insatiable appetite for compliments. He almost pranced on hearing that Dick Johnson's aria from *La Fanciulla*, 'Ch'ella mi creda libero', had been adopted as a marching song by the Italian infantry. He was even more delighted by a report from the San Remo hospital that a shell-shocked soldier had recovered his speech and burst into song while strumming excerpts from the third act of *Bohème* on his guitar. Such newsy titbits nourished his ego and comforted him for having to give up his cars for lack of petrol and being forced to use a motor-cycle for travelling into Viareggio. He managed to secure a permit for his motorboat and even laid hands on some cartridges for his shotgun which helped to supplement the slender meat ration. 'One spends a fortune—everything is three or four times as dear', he informed Sybil, who must have smiled when she received his next letter reporting that Sonzogno had paid him 250,000 lire for *La Rondine*.

Leoncavallo was in far worse shape, physically and financially. Unlike Mascagni who remained hostile towards Puccini, he had lost his sting and often came over from Viareggio to reminisce nostalgically over a bottle of wine. Although they were of similar age, he looked pathetically fragile with his watery bloodshot eyes and a pendulous but shrunken frame wobbling on short legs. Only the Kaiser Wilhelm moustaches, still defiantly waxed, recalled the old showman who had once toured the world conducting his operas for princely fees. He now lived very modestly on his royalties from *I Pagliacci* but manifested no envy of his friend's cars and boats. Puccini went to his funeral some months after the war and remarked sadly, 'He had the head of a lion (*leone*), the body of a horse (*cavallo*), and the honest heart of a boy.'

Although still inclined to self-pity, particularly when Elvira's temper grew frayed either through boredom or her anxiety over Tonio, he had become a little more tolerant, not only towards her but others whom he would normally have disdained. He once paid an impulsive visit to Pisa for a performance of *Butterfly* by a very scratch wartime company. The nervous and unknown Pinkerton, hearing of the celebrated composer's presence, made a very shaky entrance and almost dried up in the love duet. Puccini hurried backstage during the interval and urged him not to worry about his lapse. '*Una stecca non è la fine del mondo*' (one flat note is not the end of the world), he declared cheerfully. The young tenor went on to give a very creditable performance.

But he was far more exacting over productions of *La Rondine* which, he sensed, depended heavily on a sparkling Magna partnered by a tenor who could somehow animate Ruggero with song and waltz. At the first Italian performance scheduled for Bologna on 5 June, he was satisfied with Magda but could not see the portly Gigli in the main tenor rôle. They went over the score together several times before Puccini rejected him as 'too fat to look romantic'. He was replaced by the more svelte but otherwise unremarkable Aureliano Pertile. The piece fell flat and another production at the Dal Verme in Milan, with an entirely different cast, suffered a critical drubbing although the audience gave Puccini a personal ovation. The following February, when it was decided to mount the opera at the Costanzi, he again auditioned Gigli and this time gave him the rôle. 'But what about my stomach, Maestro?' the tenor asked teasingly. 'The people won't notice the figure when they're heard the voice,' Puccini assured him with a chuckle. Gigli fulfilled his expectations but could not save a libretto which waltzed unsteadily between serious opera and sentimental operetta, only finding itself too late in the pathos of the last scene.

As few other Italian opera houses showed much longing for *La Rondine* and the Metropolitan was making only non-committal noises, Puccini decided to revise the score. He added a romanza for Ruggero in the first act, transposed some of the music in the other acts, and seriously talked over with Adami the possibility of changing the whole action into a contemporary setting with modern dress. 'But the subject is the great enemy,' he now admitted gloomily to Sonzogno. These revisions had to be shelved while he completed the two half-finished panels of his *Il Trittico*. By May 1918 he was ready to discuss arrangements for a world première at the Metropolitan. He would receive a fee of $7,000 and the same royalty of $400 a performance as all his other operas (with the exception of *Manon Lescaut*, which was rated at $50 less by the management!).

For the summer months he retreated to Viareggio where Tito Ricordi arrived in mid-June to talk over details for the New York production in December, to be followed by the first Italian performance at the Teatro Costanzi in Rome. Since they had not yet forgiven each other for *La Rondine* the meeting remained at a level of frosty politeness. Before the end of the month Puccini was badgering poor Sybil, now half-crippled by sciatica, to interest Boosey or some other suitable English publisher in *La Rondine* and other future operas as he was disenchanted with 'that queer, capricious fellow' (Tito). However, although hinting that a good offer would still be worth considering, he announced soon afterwards that they had made their peace.

Viareggio was only tolerable when Fosca arrived with her pretty daughter Franca, but the crowded beach ('the sight of all this flesh in the sea disgusts me', he told Sybil) either drove him indoors or hurtling back to Torre on his motor-bicycle. He did not share her view that the war was coming to an end; 'I say the contrary . . .' However, he promised to take the train straight to London if events justified her optimism.

He was cheered by the arrival from America of Roberto Moranzoni, who was to conduct *Il Trittico* at the Metropolitan. They spent several days going over the scores and Puccini's sketches for the sets, together with his hieroglyphic stage directions. Soon afterwards Gatti-Casazza wired to announce that the first reading on stage had been well received. He regretted that Puccini would not be present on the opening night but sympathised with his difficulties; shipping was scarce, mines still sprouted in the Atlantic and there was an endless queue for visas. In any event he was reluctant to miss rehearsals for the Rome production, his long-awaited chance to re-establish himself with the Italian public.

Il Trittico opened at the Metropolitan on 14 December with all the razzle-dazzle of a world première. Although some grumbled at being charged an extra dollar for orchestra stalls, Geraldine Farrar was rapturously welcomed back after a recent throat operation. Her voice had plainly suffered, but her success in motion pictures and a tendency to overact flashy rôles like Carmen proved even more formidable handicaps to her interpretation of Puccini's gentle nun. Claudia Muzio made a better show in *Il Tabarro*, but *Gianni Schicchi* was plainly the hit of the evening. Giuseppe de Luca played the wily rascal with exactly the right touch of bravura, while Florence Easton's sugary aria, 'O mio babbino caro', started such a clamour for encores that the management had to relax its house rule.

The consensus of critical opinion indicated that only the comedy had any real meat in this three-course snack. One or two reviewers spoke kindly about *Il Tabarro* although disliking its sordid brutality, but scarcely a word was said in favour of *Suor Angelica's* mystical sentimentality or the novelty of an all-woman cast who left an inevitable impression of vocal monotony.

Puccini would always consider the nun the most appealing of all his heroine, second only to Butterfly. New York's lukewarm reviews, for which he held the miscast Farrar responsible, had hardened his determination to win Rome's favour. He seemed convinced that Gilda Dalla Rizza was a natural choice for Suor Angelica but still took the precaution of coaching her, hour after hour, until both were almost collapsing from exhaustion. During rehearsals he often had to be fortified with camphor injections.

The curtain went up at the Costanzi on 11 January 1919 in a gala atmosphere, with the King and Queen of Italy in the Royal Box and a fashionably élite audience which included a strong invasion from Milan, among them Toscanini. New York's mixed reception accounted for much of Puccini's pre-opening nervousness, and he could not help recalling that *Tosca* had been savaged at its première in that very theatre. He was reassured by the applause for his opening piece *Il Tabarro*, particularly such novel touches as the snatches of hurdy-gurdy waltz music, but his spirits sagged a little at the formally polite reception for *Suor Angelica*. Once again *Gianni Schicchi* ended to roars of laughter and applause. It received so many curtain calls that Puccini joined the principals on stage. According to 'Edouardo di Giovanni' (Edward Johnson, later General Manager of the Metropolitan Opera) who sang both tenor rôles that night, the composer feigned reluctance and asked to be 'dragged' from his box!

In the lobby he glimpsed Toscanini who ignored his nod of recognition and strode off unsmilingly. While waiting for a cab, he was greeted by the critic Vasco who singled out *Il Tabarro* for approval. 'Well, I don't like it a bit', snapped Toscanini. The remark, soon relayed to Puccini, convinced him of the Maestro's implacable enmity, but his solitary croak was almost inaudible in the chorus of praise. Following numerous receptions a banquet was given in the composer's honour at the Grand Hotel by Prince Prospero Colonna, Mayor of Rome, who flatteringly invited him to write a song celebrating Italy's victorious arms. This piece entitled *Inno a Roma* was quickly composed for chorus and orchestra and enjoyed an open-air performance some months later. Published by Sonzogno, it would be salvaged as an official Fascist hymn under Mussolini's régime.

The success of his brilliant knockabout comedy stimulated some of Puccini's bohemian cronies from Torre to unite with other kindred spirits in Viareggio to form a Gianni Schicchi Club, dedicated to reunions in fancy dress and general buffoonery. Soon afterwards they had an opportunity to tease their President for allowing himself to be hoaxed by a charming practical joker. He was sunning himself one day with Titta Ruffo outside a café in Viareggio when an attractive, sunbronzed young woman sat down at their table and introduced herself as 'Pellerosa' (Redskin) the daughter of an Iroquois chief and now hopeful of starting in opera, perhaps in the chorus. Over drinks she prattled on about Red Indian life and flirted with both men, demurely pleading that the world-famous composer or his friend might use their considerable influence. They exchanged amused glances and were already congratulating themselves on an easy conquest when Puccini recalled having recently seen her photograph in a newspaper or some theatre programme. She then identified herself as Rosa Ponselle, American-born but of Italian origin, and currently on a holiday visit to relatives. With her sister Carmela, she had begun her theatrical career in vaudeville as a song-and-dance act before studying opera. On 15 November 1918 she had made her Metropolitan début opposite Caruso in *La Forza del destino* and later established herself as one of the greatest of all Giocondas. Puccini laughed uproariously and presented her with a signed photograph, but his attempts to add her scalp to his collection went unrewarded.

He had returned to Torre in glowing spirits after the première in Rome. The triptych would be repeated several times that season at the Costanzi, and arrangements had also been finalised to present it in Buenos Aires. There was already talk of a production at Covent Garden which would re-open in May after being used as a furniture repository for five years. Melba was back but Sir Thomas Beecham, no devotee of Italian opera except for his adored Verdi, had been appointed artistic director. Puccini mourned the passing of his admiring friend Lady Ripon, but had every confidence that Sybil would protect his interests with Higgins, now general manager.

At home, however, he was under combined threat from jealous rivals and ill-disposed critics. An article in the influential Milan newspaper *Il Secolo*, signed by a close friend of Toscanini's, viciously disparaged his triptych. Recalling his frosty meeting with the Maestro in the Costanzi foyer, Puccini at once put two and two together, not without justification. The article would be echoed with approval some years later by Toscanini, who wrote '*Suor Angelica*—no good! *Il Tabarro* also no good. But *Gianni Schicchi*—a little masterpiece'. In these circumstances it was difficult to credit the rumour that he had accepted an invitation from Beecham to conduct *Il Trittico* at Covent Garden, but Puccini reacted explosively. 'If you see Higgins or any of the others tell them that I don't want this *pig*', he told Sybil. 'If he comes to London, *I shan't come*, which would be a great disappointment to me . . . I have no need of *Gods* because my operas go all over the world—they have sufficiently strong legs to walk by themselves . . .'

Such bluster, nudging on hysteria, concealed obvious over-anxiety. Toscanini had in fact made no move to conduct at Covent Garden while Higgins, despite Sybil's prompting, was anything but convinced that *Il Trittico*, still less *La Rondine*,

227

would be suitable for his first post-war season. He preferred to rely on well-tried favourites like *La Bohème* the opening attraction, with Melba's Mimì an infallible guarantee at the box-office. This pleased Puccini but without blunting the shock of Covent Garden's offhand decision to postpone *Il Trittico* until the following year. He could no longer protest to Tito Ricordi, who had been ousted from the firm by his fellow-directors after a costly series of misjudgments, including his reckless sponsorship of some of Puccini's younger and far less gifted rivals. His joint successors were Renzo Valcarenghi and Carlo Clausetti. The latter would become a staunch ally but, for the present, Puccini angrily condemned him to Sybil as 'that false friend and lickspittle of Toscanini.'

Although *Il Trittico* had been shelved, he refused to forgo his long-anticipated visit to London. Early in June he arrived for an emotional reunion with the Seligmans, who gave several dinner-parties in his honour at their Georgian house in South Street. It was all grace and charm, reflecting the taste of its owners, notably in the library stocked with fine first editions and scores in tawny leather and gilt bindings. Sybil looked frail and years older but had lost none of her vivacity. She persuaded Puccini to share her box at Covent Garden, but he showed little interest even in productions of his own operas. He seemed shocked by the theatre's run-down state and continually expressed horror of the orchestra, singers and scenery. Most of all he missed the glitter of Edwardian gala nights. There were now as many lounge suits as boiled shirts in the stalls. He sympathised fully with Melba's disdain for 'men sitting in the stalls in shabby tweed coats' and took her to lunch to reminisce about past elegance and such lamented mutual friends as Alfred de Rothschild, who had died the previous year. At the Ivy Restaurant they were personally served by the manager Mario Gallati, whom the composer recognised as his one-time waiter at the Caffé Reale in the Galleria. Mario noticed that Puccini pecked at his food without enjoyment. ('It was obviously an effort for him to get up from the table and he seemed suddenly to have aged.')

The white patches in his hair showed plainly through the dye. He looked thinner and his step less springy, but although he deplored postwar London's concrete, now rapidly replacing the mellowness of Portland stone, its shops were still a welcome tonic as he set out to replenish his wardrobe under Sybil's guidance. Vincent Seligman recalls that she would return home exhausted from a two-hour tour of Bond Street, followed by a raid on the Burlington Arcade hosiers. Puccini uninhibitedly bought himself Old Etonian, Harrovian and several regimental ties, ignoring Sybil's warning that it would not be etiquette to wear any of them in London. Next day, however, he lunched with her in the Savoy Grill proudly sporting a Rifle Brigade tie with a new blue suit speedily cut for him in Savile Row.

He made the round of London theatres, especially enjoying the long-running musical comedy *Chu Chin Chow*, and he also saw Beerbohm Tree's adaptation of *Oliver Twist* at His Majesty's, seeming impressed with the operatic potential of Nancy.

Stopping off for a few days in Paris, he ran into Tito Ricordi 'the Prince of Savoy without a crown', as he reported acidly to Sybil. But they had parted on affectionate terms, Puccini generously promising to help his old enemy establish himself in the cinema business or one of the many other fields he was feverishly prospecting.

The interregnum at Ricordi's, while the new directors were cautiously digging in, gave Puccini an excuse to promote his own affairs. He took some comfort when Chicago arranged a production of *Il Trittico* for December, to be followed in the summer by the London opening, (he had now vetoed Mugnone as well as Toscanini!) He also busied himself with revising *La Rondine*, urging Sybil to try and interest C. B. Cochran since Covent Garden seemed even more apathetic than the Metropolitan, and he was cheered by tentative approaches from Vienna for productions of both *La Rondine* and *Il Trittico* at the Volksoper, though nothing definite could be promised before October 1920, which meant an exasperatingly long wait. The scheduled winter plans for *La Rondine* in Florence and Palermo were not much of a consolation.

As always after an enjoyable London visit, he soon lapsed into gloom, intensified by the daily alarms of national unrest, strikes, currency devaluation and galloping inflation. 'I'm just off to Viareggio in the car,' he informed Sybil. 'I hope they won't take it away from me, because there are riots there owing to the high cost of living, and it appears that it's half Bolshevik.' Like most of his countrymen he was both sceptical and somewhat apprehensive of Mussolini's *Fasci di Combattimento*, a militia of ex-soldiers pledged to tax war profits, split up the large estates and increase death duties. Toscanini, soon to become an embittered opponent of the Fascist régime, had impetuously joined this new 'Bolshevik' party which failed to win a seat in the first post-war elections. Puccini learned, no doubt with satisfaction, that the conductor's candidacy had cost him his deposit of 30,000 lire.

Without a new operatic subject to engage him, he spent a fretful summer cursing the noisy and malodorous peat factory which a wartime administration had set up in Torre del Lago but showed no haste in dismantling. He talked wildly of leaving the country for long trips to Turkey and the Far East, but found sanctuary much nearer home in the primitive Maremma overlooking the sea opposite Corsica. Perched above a once-malarial plain and dominated by the highest peak in Tuscany, its desolation more than justified Pia's lament in Dante's 'Inferno': '*Siena me fe, disfece me Maremma*' (Siena made me, Maremma unmade me). It was scarcely the most hospitable refuge for a man prone to melancholia but offered a guarantee of solitude. His shooting lodge, the Torre della Tagliata, was two miles from the nearest house and virtually inaccessible by road. To ensure deliveries of fresh bread, he provided the local railway official with stout canvas bags which could be dropped from passing trains. Ignoring the difficulty of obtaining other food supplies and fresh drinking water, he planned to occupy it early in the new year after making extensive structural alterations.

He went off for a week's relaxation at Bagni di Lucca where Adami soon joined him and presented fellow-Venetian Renato Simoni, a former critic of the *Corriere della Sera*, who had written libretti for Giordano among others. Extremely well-read, he had such an obvious truffle nose for subjects that Puccini gave him the most flattering consideration. Within a day or two he engaged the couple to develop the character of Dickens' Nancy, who had become even more attractive as an operatic heroine in the almost total absence of alternatives. However, he still continued to canvass all his friends, including Sybil and Professor Carlo Paladini (an intimate since their boyhood days in Lucca), for other possibilities.

Gatti-Casazza, whose Metropolitan season had opened in triumph with *Tosca* sung by Caruso, Geraldine Farrar and Scotti, was the first to respond. Before the end of the year he sent a copy of Belasco's new play *The Son-Daughter* pointing out that Ricordi's American agent had already bought an option. Puccini may have been intrigued by its Chinese setting but made no move to have the play adapted. He was perhaps too disenchanted with the comparative failure of *La Fanciulla* to tap Belasco again, and the Dickens subject, which he had already decided to call *Fanny*, had taken a firm grip on him. Furthermore, he could not have been too impressed by Geraldine Farrar's warm recommendation of *The Son-Daughter*, doubtless with herself in mind for the leading soprano rôle!

He was now self-intoxicated with extravagant hopes of his new team of librettists. 'Tell Simoni that I shall expect him at Torre della Tagliata', he wrote gaily to Adami in November 1919. 'There will be everything that you two can desire! You will find Bordeaux of 1904 and grapes from Lecce, tobacco from Brazil and Abdullah cigarettes. Boats, motor-launches, motor-bicycles, every kind of tackle for fishing, everything you want for fowling. Goodbye, dear Adamino; if I get a good new subject, I think I shall do you honour . . .'

This bonhomie persisted throughout December when he celebrated his own and Tonio's birthday at Torre del Lago. The jollity was only marred by an absurd contretemps, caused by his own petty vindictiveness. In sentimental mood he had decided to revive his prewar Christmas custom of sending his friends gifts of *pannetone*, the fruity sponge cake much enjoyed by northerners. Death had sadly thinned the number of recipients; Tosti, Angeli, Boito, Illica and Leoncavallo . . . He replaced them with others but had carelessly failed to remove one hated name from the list sent to a baker in Milan. Furious at his error, he wired pompously: '*Pannetone Sent By Mistake. Puccini.*' Back came a telegram: '*Pannetone Eaten By Mistake. Toscanini.*'

Chapter Fourteen

Sybil had eagerly resumed the rôle of lady bountiful and was soon sending Puccini ties, socks, pipes, Turkish cigarettes and the usual prescriptions for new elixirs or cough mixtures. She did not forget Elvira, while Fosca's pretty daughter Franca, a special favourite of the Seligmans, received scarves and lingerie. Sybil had lost none of her zest for advancing Puccini's interests. Seldom of much value in discovering libretti in the past, she now became his indispensable 'lobby correspondent' at Covent Garden. Her letters from Higgins, at first formally addressed to 'Dear Mrs Seligman', soon warmed to 'Chère amie', a rare gesture by the aloof lawyer-impresario. His first note thanks her 'for coming to have a straight talk today. I am sure it will do good.' He also ask her to telegraph Puccini for his views on Mario Sammarco (the baritone who had often sung Scarpia and Sharpless) as a candidate for Gianni Schicchi. 'Is he still in good form or an extinct volcano?' asked Higgins. Puccini replied brusquely, 'He's *finished*.'*

Higgins and Casa Ricordi continually accused each other of hedging, and negotiations might have broken down altogether without Sybil's soothing touch. Puccini's strong prejudices did not help the harassed Covent Garden management. With top-class singers like Destinn, Melba and Martinelli unavailable, he rarely saw eye to eye over alternatives with Beecham, whom he privately called 'the Purge'. But he seemed to lose all interest in casting once Higgins had agreed to engage Gilda Dalla Rizza to sing Suor Angelica, also slotting her in for Lauretta in *Gianni Schicchi*.

* He had been equally uncharitable when Jeritza's countryman Leo Slezak, a huge labrador of a man who had followed his Metropolitan début in *Otello* with other successful rôles all over the world, expressed a desire to sing Rodolfo in the first post-war production of *Bohème* in Vienna. Puccini snorted, 'It will be like an elephant wooing a weasel.' (Quoted by Mosco Carner).

On his way to Rome for a second production of *Il Trittico*, Puccini lunched in Milan with his young librettists whose feathers were still a little ruffled by his rejection of their labours on *Fanny*. He soon charmed them with compliments and reiterated his pressing need of a suitable subject on which they might collaborate more fruitfully. Mention was made of Carlo Gozzi the eighteenth-century Venetian dramatist, whose *Turandotte* had already inspired several composers including Puccini's former teacher at the Conservatoire, Bazzini, and more recently Ferruccio Busoni. The operatic possibilities of this Persian fable about an autocratic princess who kills off her suitors by setting them three insoluble riddles, soon shuttled across the table. Simoni recalled having a translation of Schiller's adaptation of the play on his bookshelf and quickly telephoned for it to be brought to the restaurant. Puccini read it through on the train and, immediately after returning to Torre, urged Simoni and Adami to prepare a draft treatment. They worked so fast that he had already approved their first act before leaving for London early in June to attend rehearsals of *Il Trittico*.

Pleased as he was to learn that the season had again opened with *La Bohème*, he was none too sorry to have missed the soprano Kousnezova, who had escaped from the Bolsheviks in boy's clothes aboard a Swedish ship. She proved rather less successful in her interpretation of Mimì. Beecham was also below his best, but later sank his pride by inviting the composer to go over the score with him. Puccini again became uneasy over the run-down scenery and general shabbiness which had not improved since his last visit. Conditions were so cramped that the orchestra had to rehearse in the foyer. John Barbirolli, leading the cellos, would often recall his nervousness when Puccini stood behind him. 'I was too damned shy to speak to the great man and have regretted it ever since', he once declared. No doubt the composer would have reacted to a greeting in Italian after trying to make himself understood in broken English and usually lapsing into French. Accosted by a reporter as he was leaving the British

Museum one day, he sighed, 'If only I could speak English, my happiness would be complete. I shall have to start learning ... There is such beautiful noise in London, it is so restful and your people here work so seriously. They have not the nervousness of the Latin races.'

That season seemed to be all Puccini, with only one Verdi opera *La Traviata* on offer, but he was spared some poorish performances. Dalla Rizza's geisha had been pinioned by *The Times* critic as 'a vocal butterfly who hovered over the notes, swayed from one side to the other, and never seemed securely poised'. Puccini began to grieve for the missing Caruso and even 'the centenarian' (Melba), who detested Beecham enough to opt out of the season rather than submit to his direction. Others like Charles Ricketts, the scenic designer, thought the management 'incapable of even sweeping a crossing properly', a view with which Puccini soon concurred. More than once during rehearsals of *Il Trittico* he stamped angrily out of the theatre and had to be coaxed back by Sybil. Toscanini might have squeezed a little magic from the mediocre orchestra, but Gaetano Bavagnoli seemed far more at home in Rome, and Gilda Dalla Rizza had also failed to transplant.

The three pieces opened on 18 June 1920, this time with a full panoply of tiaras and stuffed shirts in honour of King George and Queen Mary. Nervously biting his nails, Puccini spent most of his time in the wings during *Il Tabarro*, occasionally creeping into the Seligmans' box for reassurance. After several rather half-hearted calls for *Suor Angelica*, he was summoned to the Royal Box for a congratulatory word. *Gianni Schicchi* again won the only true ovation. Next morning a critic proclaimed it 'a gem, a masterpiece of comic opera', without however sparing 'the anaemic and affected sentimentality of *Suor Angelica*.'

The Times reviewer once more mauled Dalla Rizza; 'She has so little variety of tone at her command, and so often engages one's attention in wondering which note she really means to sing, that her performance did not help matters much.' His final judgment of the three ill-assorted panels was

235

veiled in irony; 'They could scarcely be anything but a success at the present moment when their composer is so much the darling of the operagoing public that half at least of the present season has been devoted to a repetition of four of his earlier works. What would Covent Garden be without Puccini? It was a unique chance to offer him the personal tribute of thanks . . .'

The savage dismissal of *Suor Angelica* was painful, but his spirits revived a day or two later on hearing that the Berlin Staatsoper had relayed a performance of *Madama Butterfly*, the first time a complete opera had been broadcast. He was quickly deflated by Higgins and Beecham who, after only two performances, seemed disinclined to commit themselves to repeats of *Il Trittico* which ran for almost four hours with Covent Garden's lengthy intervals. Both hinted ominously that *Suor Angelica* might have to be dropped until a suitable replacement could be found for Dalla Rizza, who had departed in some haste.

Puccini wrote from Torre thanking Sybil; 'you were a real angel of goodness, of tact, of kindness and courtesy', and deploring the state of his own country by contrast with 'the orderliness and prosperity of London'. He became even gloomier after reading two further and most disappointing acts for *Turandot* and begged the librettists to join him in Bagni di Lucca for an urgent conference. By the time they arrived he had made numerous notes for revising Act One and sketched out ideas for his *piccola donna*, the slave-girl Liù, a far more sympathetic character than either Turandot's confidante or the slave Zuleima in the original play. He already visualised her as a tragic figure who would sacrifice herself for love of Calaf and thus make an effective dramatic contrast to the cruel princess.

He had also developed the acquaintance of Baron Fassini, a former consular official in China, who enlightened him on local colour and happened to possess an ancient music box which played the ceremonial tunes later adapted and incorporated in Act One. As always, he studied books and paintings to familiarise himself with the period and urged the ever-willing Sybil to examine the British Museum's collection of contemporary Chinese scores.

Inevitably, he became impatient with the librettists who were not working fast enough for his liking, but he was even more irritated by Covent Garden's ruthless decision to separate his 'triplets'. Slyly pleading difficulty in replacing Gilda Dalla Rizza, Higgins had first abandoned *Suor Angelica* and then dropped *Il Tabarro* after a few unsatisfactory performances. Puccini had reluctantly allowed his 'beloved little nun' to be sidetracked, but he accused Covent Garden of cynical treachery, compounded by weakness on Casa Ricordi's part, when even *Gianni Schicchi* was disengaged from the others and used as a makeweight for the Russian Ballet.

Still smarting, he visited Vienna in October. The unseasonably cold weather chilled him almost as much as a poor production of *La Rondine*. This swallow, so dismally unhappy in various migrations, fared no better in its native skies. Felix Weingartner spiritedly conducted a listless orchestra at the Volksoper but, although the composer was mobbed before and after the performance, few seemed to differ from Tito Ricordi's dismissal of this piece as 'bad Lehár'.

Puccini found a very different atmosphere in the former Imperial Opera House where *Tosca* was being staged. He could not fault the *mise-en-scène* or the vibrant Jeritza whom he extolled to Sybil as 'perhaps the most original artist that I have ever known'. Over the years she had gained in confidence and startled him by taking a very independent line on dress and other details. She discarded the traditional black wig and wore a bandeau and lace shawl over her blonde head, although he argued that Tosca's scoop bonnet was historically correct. She also rejected the usual white dress for a Directoire gown of sky-blue satin in the First Act, but the most startling change, which would become standard practice for most sopranos, was literally accidental. During a rehearsal for Act Two, when she was about to collapse grief-stricken on a sofa, the baritone bumped into her. She slipped to the floor but, instead of picking herself up, sang 'Vissi d'arte' on her stomach. Puccini clapped delightedly and exclaimed, 'That's exactly how it should be sung. It was from God!' Thereafter Jeritza sang it in that posture, taking infinite pains to make her fall more realistic.*

After introducing various changes of tempo and expression to suit her style, Puccini autographed her score, 'To the great interpreter of Tosca, in grateful remembrance.' Demanding still more effort, he once clasped her hands and whispered tenderly, 'Carissima mia, you have to walk in clouds of melody.' Their rapport grew even more closer during rehearsals of Il Trittico (in German), which raised his morale sky-high. Jeritza, whose range and weight of voice, quite apart from her magnificent stage presence, already seemed to him ideal qualifications for Princess Turandot, dominated Il Tabarro but she could not outshine Lotte Lehmann's Suor Angelica. He enthused to Sybil over Lehmann's sensitive acting with 'a voice as sweet as honey', and urged Higgins to snap up these two remarkable singers, hinting that they wished to repeat their rôles in London. Higgins expressed polite interest in Jeritza but would not commit himself to re-staging Il Trittico while Covent Garden's whole future remained uncertain.

In Vienna the operatic scene was very different. After a flying visit by Adami, the Imperial Opera House had promised to stage La Rondine the following year, subject to agreed changes in the libretto. Puccini sighed to Sybil, not perhaps without satisfaction, that he was being fêted 'in a dreadful, atrocious, indescribable manner.' He later spoke of having 'signed postcards for all the Fräuleins Mitzi, Fritzi and Schitzi who munch pastries while they snivel over my music', but had to admit that the Viennese remained unequalled for gaiety and courtesy. To repay such overwhelming hospitality he gave a reception at the Hotel Bristol and welcomed Lehár with a warm embrace. According to Richard Specht, a future

---

* Scotti, as Scarpia, often partnered her but complained at being left to stand against the back wall until she chose to come upright again!

biographer who saw him there for the first and only time, her fingernails were badly bitten and he spoke very huskily in halting French as his German was still limited and few could understand his Tuscan-accented Italian.

Recently he had been afflicted by sore throats and complained more often of tiredness. He had begun to think half-seriously of visiting a doctor in Chicago for rejuvenating injections. His distinguished looks and an aura of celebrity still made him sexually magnetic, but his conquests were inevitably fewer and sometimes needed an emollient touch. While in Vienna he became attracted to a young soprano whose career he guilefully promised to advance. For months afterwards he was still pulling strings with various managements but his efforts to interest the Metropolitan earned him a snub from Gatti-Casazza, who wrote back severely, 'She belongs to that category of artist that is not lacking in America and which we are obliged to favour for obvious reasons of local politics.'

His exhilarating visit to Vienna was followed by a bout of acute depression. He gloomed over a rumour that Giordano was also contemplating an opera on Gozzi's play. Although unfounded, it caused him to lose patience with his librettists. 'If they wait much longer,' he told Sybil, 'I shall have to get them to put pen, paper and inkpot in my tomb!' His letters to Adami reveal a mounting despair. 'I have carried about with me in all my journeys a large bundle of melancholy. I have no reason for it, but so I am made . . . I am afraid that *Turandot* will never be finished . . . If I touch the piano my hands get covered with dust. My desk is piled high with letters—there isn't a trace of music. Music? Useless if I have no libretto . . . If only I could be a purely symphonic writer. I should then at least cheat time . . . and my public. But that was not for *me* . . . Almighty God touched me with his little finger and said; 'Write for the theatre—mind, only for the theatre'. And I have obeyed the supreme command . . .'

239

He protested petulantly that Adami kept neglecting him for 'films, plays, poetry, articles' (one of his plays *Parigi*, happened to be enjoying a long run at Milan's Olympia Theatre). This was unreasonable. His collaboration with Giacosa and Illica had often been at long range and dependent on their other commitments. This younger and less celebrated team treated him with deference and would meekly agree to visit him for discussions, often at very short notice.

On 22 December 1920, his sixty-second birthday, they arrived at the Torre della Tagliata with the first act of *Turandot* which they read over for his approval. He groaned, 'This isn't an act, it's a conference. How can I possibly put a conference to music?' He was particularly sharp with Simoni whose appetite for local colour tended to clog the action. They left glumly, promising to make the necessary revisions.

Their slow progress on *Turandot* was not the only reason for his irascibility. He was still tinkering with the score of *La Rondine* and also fulminating at both Covent Garden and Casa Ricordi for dismembering *Il Trittico* which, he reminded Sybil, continued to delight German and Swedish audiences in its entirety, with *Suor Angelica* 'leading the way in popularity'. He had already tired of the Maremma hunting lodge, and placed it in the hands of an agent without, however, finding a buyer. Worse, the peat factory's siren blasts and smells had finally driven him from his beloved village. Early in 1921 he purchased a site on the northern edge of Viareggio facing the pine forests and a mile or so from the spot where Shelley's body had been washed up. An architect was commissioned to design a spacious bungalow-type villa which would hopefully be ready for occupation by the summer. He intended to maintain his house in Torre del Lago but only for short visits and shooting trips.

The too-sluggish builders were persecuted, but his obsession with the house at least took the pressure off Adami and Simoni. Without too many interruptions they were able to deliver a much more satisfactory first act on which he worked for up to ten or twelve hours a day. Early in March, between stretches of intensive composition, he decided to join Sybil in Monte Carlo for a little rest and frivolity, but she was suddenly almost crippled by an attack of sciatica and had to leave for London in the care of a doctor.

Puccini's own health and morale had deteriorated. 'I've had a pain in my mouth', he wrote to her a few days later. 'I'm very, very down . . . I feel as though, from now on, I were finished . . . I am old—this is literally the truth—it's a very sad thing, especially for an artist.' Elvira had also been ill but he sympathised with her rasping cough and discouraged Titta Ruffo from poking too much fun or making wounding remarks at her expense. In April while attending rehearsals of *Manon Lescaut* in Rome, he surprised her with an invitation to join him; 'Come quickly and I will start to live again.' This absence of tension, after so much bickering in the past, was apparent to the Seligmans when they arrived that August in Viareggio. Vincent recalled, 'Elvira was still a confirmed pessimist and complained . . . at the high price of food, at the weather, at the strikes, at everything . . . except her husband and her family; yet age, which had destroyed her looks, had given her a new sweetness and a new serenity . . .' A month or so earlier, when Mascagni was rumoured to have been nominated for the Senate, she vowed hysterically to renounce her Italian citizenship and emigrate with her husband if his rival were elected. In fact both composers had been mentioned as probable candidates but nothing more would be heard of that proposal for two years.

According to Vincent, Puccini had never been more 'tender, gentle, affectionate, gay'. He showed them proudly over the villa, where he had already installed a Steinway grand (a gift from the makers) in the studio which led to his bedroom by a staircase. Here, one afternoon, he enchanted them by running through the first act of *Turandot*. Sybil toured each room, making tasteful suggestions for improving the décor and the disposition of the furniture, some of it rather too ramshackle for her taste. During that month, made still more enjoyable by the arrival of Fosca and her high-spirited children, he had long talks with Sybil while they walked, hand-in-hand, on the sandy beach.

He seemed reasonably sanguine about *Turandot* but his more immediate anxiety was to see *La Rondine* staged in England. With Covent Garden closed, apart from an eight-week season by the Carl Rosa Company, he urged Sybil to engage an agent in the hope of stimulating other impresarios. She did so but privately asked Higgins to assess its chances of a short season at some London theatre or perhaps on tour. He was anything but hopeful. In his view the only chance of covering the heavy costs of production would be to broaden the opera's appeal by introducing comic *spoken* dialogue and perhaps writing in 'a part for a low comedian'. These suggestions drew a splutter of indignation from Puccini. He fared no better with Gatti-Casazza to whom he wrote, 'Modesty apart, for me it is perhaps my best music', pleading that with good singers and finesse in production, 'it cannot fail.' But the Metropolitan was far less concerned with rescuing Puccini's bedraggled swallow than the urgent problem of replacing box-office favourites like Caruso and Geraldine Farrar.

The tenor's death in Naples on 2 August 1921 depressed Puccini. 'Poor Caruso! What a sad destiny! It has made me dreadfully unhappy,' he wrote to a grieving Sybil. He had not only lost a good friend but a peerless interpreter of des Grieux, Rodolfo and Cavaradossi. Before long, however, he had almost reconciled himself to Caruso's heir-apparent Gigli, whose Rodolfo had charmed the Metropolitan in his first season, despite a manner which some critics thought 'provincial' and his weakness for taking bows in mid-opera. He had also registered superbly in *Tosca* which Puccini saw as an encouraging sign for Jeritza's own début, although fully understanding her nervousness at appearing during the adored Farrar's farewell season. He wrote sympathetically, urging her to ignore the abusive letters from angry gallery girls who threatened to wreck her Tosca, one of their idol's standard rôles.

Farrar would later comment sourly in her memoirs, 'I was

surprised by the questionable flaunting of a well-cushioned and obvious posterior', but Jeritza's Tosca in December 1921, even opposite a bloodless Pertile as Cavaradossi, hit New York like a tidal wave. Next day the critics rated her acting in the Bernhardt class, the veteran Henry E. Krehbiel declaring that in all his years the rôle had never been sung more admirably. She consolidated her triumph in partnership with Gigli and Scotti, although the baritone found her histrionics alarming. On the opening night she stabbed him so vigorously that the stage hunting knife pierced his Empire coat, waistcoat and silk shirt, grazing his skin. He refused to go on again until she had been issued with a leather dagger. But her success was a warning signal to Farrar who resisted hysterical demands to sing Tosca for her valedictory the following April. With the management's approval, she wisely played safe with a vivid performance in Leoncavallo's *Zazà*, a rôle which would have suited Lina Cavalieri to perfection, but she too had retired from the operatic stage to open a beauty salon in Paris.*

By the end of the year the Puccinis had settled into their new villa. Both were charmed by Sybil's many tasteful gifts, including a handsome Dutch carpet for the dining-room. In the studio with its excellent view of the sea, he now had more space for his scores of Verdi, Debussy, Strauss, and of course Wagner. On the Steinway he often played the Prelude, the Grail and the Good Friday music from *Parsifal*. While agonising over his own slow progress on *Turandot* he once cried out, 'Enough of this music! Beside him, we are nothing but mandolinists and dilettantes.'

This note of despair echoed throughout the composition of his last opera. '*Turandot* gives me no peace . . .' he wrote to Adami. This time he was not simply setting a Sardou novel or an anecdote to music but a universal parable glorifying the

* Cavalieri died, together with her fourth husband, in an American air raid near Florence during the Second World War. In 1957 her life story was filmed under the title 'La donna più bella della mondo', with Gina Lollobrigida as the star.

theme of love conquering death. To succeed in convincingly transforming Turandot's ice into fire, he would need more than pretty *chinoiserie*, novelettish tear-jerking and the 'veristic' melodrama of his earlier operas. He had no doubt that his musical invention and dramaturgy would be equal to the challenge of fusing realism with fantasy, but his exhortations to Adami to 'humanise' the libretto betrays an uneasiness at having sacrificed the clear-cut suffering heroines of his earlier operas for a muddled symbolism. Mosco Carner, maintaining his Freudian mother-fixation theory, implies that Puccini was attempting in *Turandot* to resolve his obsessive guilt complex by transforming the 'man-hating Amazon into a loving woman.' He suggests that the composer's frustrations with this opera, notably in making the love duet a satisfactory climax, sprang from his 'psychological inability to feel himself entirely into such a situation . . . His fundamental miscalculation lies in the fact that, having raised all our sympathies for the little slave-girl, he asks us in almost the same breath to transfer them to the Princess whom, up to this point in the drama, he had done his Puccinian best to portray as an inhuman monster.' Against this, however, one suspects that Dr Carner, starting from his interesting hypothesis of Puccini's 'eroto-nihilism' to explain an obsession with flawed heroines, has perhaps gone rather overboard to make *Turandot* fit the original theory.

By early in 1922 Puccini had all but decided against compressing the opera into two acts. He began orchestrating Act One with its delicate choral Invocation to the Moon, which may have been inspired by many duck-shooting vigils among the reeds of Lake Massaciúccoli, and was busily sketching out ideas for the lament of the three mandarins Ping, Pang and Pong. He continued as usual to deplore the tardiness of his writers but his letters to Sybil suggested more cheerfulness.

The re-opening of La Scala, newly-decorated and renovated, provided a quite unexpected bonus. Toscanini had overcome his personal prejudices and decided to stage *Il Trittico* in his first season as artistic director, although stubbornly refusing to conduct. He handed his baton to Ettore Panizza. Although both yearned to end their feud, Puccini and the fiery little Maestro pointedly avoided each other in the theatre, exchanging only curt nods like Diamond Horseshoe dowagers when their paths crossed. Toscanini declared later that he had been tempted to go round to the artists' room 'to kees the Maestro and forget all thees silly quarrel', but the moment passed.

The triptych opened on 29 January 1922 with moderate success but enough to justify a further seven performances which brought over a million lire in box-office receipts. Puccini hurried back to Viareggio where more and more friends called to inspect the villa and goggle at his numerous gadgets. A favoured minority was entrusted with the secret combination of a brass plaque which opened the gate at a touch. They admired his collection of electric clocks and dutifully pressed all his jangling bells, but few escaped being drenched in the garden. The host had installed a watering system through ingeniously camouflaged pipes and could not always resist giving them a playful shower while they strolled under the pines. Apart from the Steinway in his studio he had two other pianos for the musically-minded, but his wireless set was a stronger attraction. He would never forget the excitement of hearing a *Bohème* excerpt from a London studio crackling through his headphones. It almost matched his bliss on receiving a signed portrait from Thomas Alva Edison inscribed, 'Men die and governments change, but the songs of *La Bohème* will live forever.'

Between June 1922, when his librettists delivered the final portion of their text, and his sketching and orchestration almost two years later, he constantly scrapped what he had written. Having declared himself satisfied with the libretto, he would abruptly insist on vital changes, like Liù's death by torture, to give tragic emphasis to the whole opera. Such drastic revisions naturally involved extensive re-correction of music already written, with predictable effects on his temper. His moods oscillated between near-despair, when he threatened to return Casa Ricordi's advance and cancel the whole contract, and dizzy exaltation. After one splenetic outburst he assured Adami, 'Hour by hour and minute by minute I think of *Turandot*, and all the music I have written up to now seems a jest by comparison and pleases me no more. Is it a good sign? I think so.'

This inner uncertainty was reflected in a desperate need for reassurance. He was elated to hear that Gatti-Casazza had opened the Metropolitan's 1922-3 season with *Tosca* sung by Jeritza, Martinelli and Scotti, followed by several performances of *Bohème* with Gigli and Lucrezia Bori heading brilliant companies. *Butterfly* had been embellished with Joseph Urban's exquisite new sets which may have reinforced Puccini's first inclination to stage the opening of his new opera at the Metropolitan. Meanwhile he hoarded lists of performances with squirrel-like determination and once announced to his house-guests that *Tosca* was currently playing in seventy-three different cities around the world. He boasted to Sybil that his royalties for the first six months of 1922 totalled a handsome £16,000, which prompted him, somewhat illogically, to observe, 'I think I might have received some form of recognition from your great country.' She ignored that hint for the best of reasons. Since the passing of King Edward, Tosti and Lady Ripon, she had no influence at Court and would have had small chance of impressing George V, who once declared gruffly that *La Bohème* happened to be his favourite opera, 'only because it's the shortest'.

For the most popular of all living composers, Puccini's craving for recognition became almost pathetic in his last years when the smallest whiff of criticism could throw him off-balance. Extravagant praise for Pizzetti's overrated new opera, coupled with false reports that his own *Turandot* was about to be scrapped after irreconcilable disputes with his librettists, stimulated an appetite for self-publicity which he had always avoided. A fellow-writer had to be persuaded by Adami to prepare a eulogistic profile which was rejected by the editor of the *Corriere della Sera* in the absence of some 'event' to justify the space.

Toscanini's decision to stage and conduct a new production of *Manon Lescaut* soon had reporters pursuing Puccini for interviews. 'There have been six performances and the takings are half a million lire—tell that stupid old Higgins', he wrote excitedly to Sybil. He was even more overwhelmed by the gala performance conducted by Toscanini on 1 February 1923, the opera's thirtieth anniversary. After scenes of riotous enthusiasm he went backstage and tearfully embraced the Maestro, who was clearly moved but masked his feelings. 'Perhaps you wouldn't be so impressed by a decent performance if you didn't run so often to all those terrible productions,' he shrugged. It did not prevent Puccini from writing him a fervent note of gratitude; 'You have given me the greatest satisfaction of my life... Last night I truly felt the greatness of your soul and all your affection for your old friend and companion of those early struggles.' Following their reconciliation, Puccini soon decided to offer the première of *Turandot* to La Scala instead of the Metropolitan.

Five days after the gala performance, which had yielded bumper receipts as prices for all seats had been doubled, he was honoured by a banquet for 500 guests at the Ristorante Cova. He declined to make a speech and sat at a side table with Elvira rather than among the critics and rival composers who had so often sniped at him in the past. In sparkling spirits he resumed work on *Turandot* and bought himself a new 8-cylinder Lancia for 90,000 lire as well as a motor-boat capable of over 25 mph.

With the unexpected loss of his youngest sister Romelde, soon after Iginia's death, he relapsed into mournful introspection. Suddenly he had an overpowering urge to explore his ancestral roots. The last lap of this sentimental pilgrimage to the remote Val di Roggio had to be made on horseback over rough mountain roads, but the villagers of Celle lined the streets to give him almost a regal welcome. A triumphal arch spanned the tiny piazza where his portrait framed in flowers was displayed in every window. He stammered a few words of thanks and burst into tears when the children ran forward with bouquets.

The altitude may have affected his breathing. On his return he went down with a fever and an inflamed throat. Over-smoking was the primary cause, possibly aggravated by a goose-bone splinter which had been removed surgically but may have left an unhealed lesion. It made him apprehensive and increased a morbid preoccupation with his symptoms. He had studied all the latest claims for insulin injections but Romelde's death switched his thoughts to the problems of senescence, and he became avidly interested in Voronoff's monkey-gland experiments in rejuvenation. Meeting a sixty-seven-year-old South American visitor to Viareggio, who boasted that he felt 'like a young man again' after consulting the ex-Kaiser's Austrian doctor, Puccini decided to follow his example but hesitated when Sybil's London physician, Sir Aldo Castellani, warned him of the dangers in his diabetic condition. But he was still pathetically hopeful of recovering his lost youth when an invitation arrived to attend rehearsals in Vienna for another anniversary production of *Manon Lescaut*.

Before driving off in the Lancia with Tonio he had a presentiment of death and decided to make his Will, nominating his son as his sole heir subject to Elvira's beneficial enjoyment of half the estate. His last surviving sister, the widowed Nitteti, was to receive a niggardly 300 lire a month. No provision was made for charitable endowments in Torre or, perhaps more surprisingly Lucca, where he had recently chaired a fund-raising committee to rebuild the neo-classical Teatro del Giglio on the square, later renamed the Piazza Puccini.

In Vienna his neurotic crankiness vanished practically over-night. He neglected to visit the Kaiser's doctor and absorbed himself in rehearsing *Manon* while good-humouredly keeping the peace between Jeritza and the tenor Alfred Piccaver. He was fêted by the Austrians and as always expressed warm appreciation of the orchestra, chorus and stagehands at the State Opera, but though he luxuriated at the Hotel Bristol he grumbled at paying an 'exorbitant' 500,000 crowns a day for his suite. *Manon Lescaut* won its expected ovation and *Tosca* took fifty ecstatic calls, the composer sharing the final curtain with Jeritza.

He was back in Viareggio by June, sketching the last act of *Turandot*. He had completed and inserted the aria 'Nessun dorma', which some months earlier Martinelli had sung to his accompaniment while on a brief visit to the villa. It was then more or less understood that he would interpret Calaf, with Jeritza as the Princess. Meanwhile many revisions had to be made during severe attacks of throat trouble and persistent melancholia. He wrote with wry self-pity to Adami, 'Elvira and I are here, the two *ancêtres*, like two old family portraits frowning from time to time at the cobwebs which tickle us. We sleep, eat, read the *Corriere* and with a note or two the old composer keeps himself alive.' Accompanied by his wife and son, he returned to Vienna at the end of October for a festival of his works, each meticulously produced, although *Tosca* had little appeal for him with Jeritza far away in New York.

On New Year's Day 1924, the Metropolitan staged a benefit performance of *Tosca* to celebrate Scotti's silver jubilee with the opera house. Partnered by Jeritza, he netted $20,000 which helped to pay off a few of his debts. Puccini remembered to wire cordial greetings from himself and Sybil, who had arrived in Viareggio for a short visit. Soon after returning to London, she sent another carpet to replace the first which had not worn too well. She responded to every request, large or small. When one of his friends, a local poet, organised a fund to put up a memorial to Shelley on the shore where his body was found, she generously sent a cheque for £200 and inspired others in London to follow suit.

Throughout that spring and summer Puccini orchestrated so fast that he overtook the librettists and implored them to send their verses for the final love duet. But his feverish progress was interrupted by a severe inflammation of the throat.

Instead of visiting London for the British Empire Exhibition at Wembley as he had planned, he hurried off to Salsomaggiore to see a laryngologist, who minimised the trouble which he thought 'rheumatic' in origin. Heartened by this mistaken diagnosis, he attacked Sybil's latest consignment of Turkish cigarettes with renewed enjoyment and was once again tempted to consult Voronoff.

The monkey-gland plan had to be shelved while he worked on the troublesome love duet and discussed arrangements to mount his opera at La Scala the following April. He now flippantly signed himself 'Sonatore' (Musician) to prove to his friends that he was not preening himself on having recently been created a Senatore 'for exceptional services towards the Fatherland.' Soon after Mussolini's March on Rome he had written to Adami, 'I hope he will prove to be the man we need,' but his one and only meeting with the Duce had been discouraging. Mussolini seemed quite unmoved by his pleas for the establishment of a National Opera House in Rome similar to that in the Austrian capital. He was given no more than a few nervous minutes to stammer out his views which were brusquely rejected on the grounds of economy.

The Royal Family was far more gracious and often asked him to lunch at their summer residence in San Rossore. He played over some of his new melodies for Queen Elena and her dark-eyed daughter Mafalda, a talented musician to whom he planned to dedicate *Turandot*. He had already drafted the graceful phrase, 'My Princess to a Princess'.*

His acceptance of honorary membership of the Fascist Party went unremarked, even by Toscanini, who had openly demonstrated his contempt for the régime by refusing to display Mussolini's portrait in La Scala or to start performances with the martial hymn *Giovinezza*. One can assume that he now considered Puccini a political innocent whose

* Mafalda, who later married Prince Philip of Hesse, became an outspoken opponent of the Nazi alliance. Hitler once called her 'the trickiest bitch in the House of Savoy'. She died in Buchenwald in August 1944 during an Allied bombardment of the camp area.

views did not justify reopening old wounds. He arrived at Viareggio early in September 1924 to hear part of the *Turandot* music which he pronounced 'delightful'. But he was plainly less impressed by the preliminary sketches for the love duet, thereby confirming Puccini's own secret doubts. He now urged Adami to make a supreme effort to ensure 'a great musical peroration'.

He was himself working under the handicap of a severe cough which had sufficiently alarmed Sybil during a brief visit to Viareggio to advise Tonio to seek a specialist's opinion. Puccini however had stubbornly postponed taking further medical advice until plans were finalised for the first performance of his opera. Towards the end of September he went to Milan for a detailed conference on the score. In a small rehearsal room at La Scala he played over the remaining portions for Toscanini, who sadly turned the pages while Puccini, obviously a very sick man, sang excerpts in a husky voice. After the lengthy audition Toscanini slapped his back and declared, 'This is a fine work'. He made no secret of his eagerness to direct the orchestra at the world première arranged for the following April, subject to completion of the love duets and the finale. Galileo Chini still had to complete dozens of sketches but he could be replied on to have the elaborate scenery and costumes ready in time. Casting would be a more serious matter, but the composer seemed supremely confident. With Jeritza and Dalla Rizza long in his mind's eye for Turandot and Liù, he quickly cabled Gigli in Los Angeles, inviting him to sing Prince Calaf, as Martinelli's engagements ruled him out. The tenor accepted joyfully, still unaware that Gatti-Casazza had absolutely no intention of allowing his leading artists to grace any La Scala opening under Toscanini's baton.

Puccini had received his verses for the duet early in October, but his painful throat condition now made further work impossible. After seeing his local doctor he decided to consult a specialist in Florence, who detected a small growth at the base of the larynx. He did not think it malignant but

Tonio became alarmed and demanded a further examination. This time the doctor diagnosed the condition as cancer. The dreaded verdict was kept from Puccini who, to please his son, agreed to undergo a full-scale examination by three specialists, headed by Professor Gradenigo of Naples. Tonio now learned with horror that the growth was too advanced for surgery, but the doctors seemed genuinely hopeful of a course of radium therapy at the Ledoux Clinic in Brussels.

Elvira, herself ill in Milan with acute bronchitis, remained in the dark and Puccini apparently expected a full recovery after six weeks' treatment. Toscanini, one of the few close friends in the secret, saw him off at Viareggio on 4 November 1924 when he boarded the express for Brussels with Tonio and Fosca. As they embraced, Puccini whispered, 'If anything happens to me, Arturo, do not abandon my dear beautiful princess, my Turandot.' In his valise he had carefully packed his reading spectacles, Simoni's verses and over thirty pages of notes for the final scene, including two song fragments with a sketch of the piano accompaniment of twenty or thirty bars, together with a series of harmonic modulations and isolated chords.

On the train he had a bout of coughing which resulted in a severe haemorrhage, but he seemed quite reassured after an encouraging meeting with Dr Ledoux. The early external treatment did not prevent him from taking walks. One night he saw a performance of *Butterfly* and enjoyed a most sympathetic ovation from the audience. He made such satisfactory progress that Fosca went home to nurse her mother. After a fortnight, however, he suffered renewed bleeding and had to have a collar fitted for the internal applications of radium. He could only breathe through a rubber tube but remained surprisingly cheerful and already spoke of taking a shooting trip to the Maremma after the La Scala première. Although he dreaded the final and most crucial stage of the treatment, when the tumour itself would have to be directly treated by radioactive crystal needles, he greeted Carla Toscanini smilingly and assured her and Clausetti, Ricordi's director, that before long he would be resuming work on his notes.

Sybil Seligman braced herself to visit him and fought back the tears as he laid his head gratefully on a specially soft pillow she had brought him. Racked by sciatica, she could not stay long, but sent Fosca a sharpish letter urging her to return to Brussels without delay as her father would need comfort during the agonising next few days. Elvira was in no condition to travel and had to be spoonfed with reassuring lies about her husband's progress.

On Monday 24 November the needles were inserted into the tumour, an operation lasting nearly four hours and performed under local anaesthetic to avoid heart strain. It was planned to remove the needles on the following Sunday. Meantime the patient had to be nasally fed with liquids and could breathe only through the tube above his Adam's apple. As speech was forbidden he scribbled little messages on a pad. Although in considerable pain, he had not lost his sense of mischief. He took a dislike to his nurse, an elderly nun, and complained that her noisily rattled beads disturbed him far more than the 'cruel bayonets' in his throat. Tonio and Fosca exchanged amused looks when he sent a note to the Mother Superior demanding that pretty Sister Maria should take over. She reminded him, he explained, of his Suor Angelica.

On the fourth day he sat up in bed and glanced through the newspapers. Doctor Ledoux cheerfully assured the manager of the Théâtre de la Monnaie, '*Puccini en sortira*', but quite properly advised the Queen of Italy to postpone her proposed visit until the patient's condition had improved. Tonio took turns with his step-sister in maintaining a day-and-night vigil. On Friday morning he had sent his mother a most comforting cable, and at six that evening Fosca was writing in similar terms to Sybil. She had left for a minute or two to look up the Seligmans' London address when Sister Maria ran into her room to announce agitatedly that Puccini had collapsed in his armchair. He was already unconscious from a heart attack when Dr Ledoux hastily removed the needles.

He lingered for the next few hours. Reports of his relapse

brought dozens of callers, but only the Italian Ambassador was briefly admitted to the room, followed by the Papal Nuncio, who administered the Last Rites. As midnight passed he opened his eyes and smiled gently at Tonio and Fosca, who knelt at his bedside. It is said that his fingers moved over the coverlet as if he were playing the piano. At four am he sighed and his lips seemed to flicker. Fosca put her arms about him and heard him whisper, 'My poor Elvira, my poor wife', before he stared sightlessly into eternity.

Tito Ricordi heard the news in Paris and at once travelled to Brussels. In Vienna Mascagni said brokenly, 'We had been friends for forty-three years . . . We have lost in him the creator of the sweetest melodies of modern times which charmed everyone.' The body was embalmed and the coffin, covered with the Italian flag and wreaths from the King and Mussolini, borne in procession to the Church of Ste Marie. Two days later it was put on a train for Milan. At the memorial service in Il Duomo, Toscanini directed the La Scala orchestra and chorus in the Requiem from *Edgar*. Among those who emerged into a driving rainstorm on that day of national mourning were Giordano, Rosina Storchio, the librettists of *Turandot* and a few gnarled old men who had shot or sailed with Puccini in Torre del Lago long before his name was celebrated. Crowds lined a route almost a mile long as the cortège passed on its way to the Cimitero Monumentale where the body would be interred temporarily in the Toscanini family vault.

Orchestras throughout the world played Puccini music in tribute, and on 7 December a vast audience of 4,000 packed the Metropolitan Opera for a huge memorial concert which included the first act duet from *Tosca*, sung by Jeritza and Gigli. In view of the composer's distinctly uncharitable will, it is not perhaps without interest to note Gatti-Casazza's kindlier and more judicious allocation of the proceeds; he sent 100,000 lire to the Verdi Home for Aged Musicians in Milan; 25,000 for the poor of Lucca; and 12,000 towards the erection of a suitable monument. A month later a commemorative plaque was fixed to the wall of Puccini's birthplace in Lucca.

The estate was valued at some £800,000 ($4m.) Family wranglings started almost at once, stimulated perhaps by lawyers who tried to prove that Tonio's illegitimacy disqualified him from legally inheriting. They failed to convince the courts, who relied on a decree by Mussolini legitimising children born out of wedlock to parents who subsequently married.

Toscanini had handed over Puccini's 36 pages of notes and pencilled sketches to Franco Alfano, a Neapolitan composer who had, coincidentally, himself once planned an opera on Gozzi's fable. At best a second-rater and not in the class of Mascagni who it was hopefully rumoured might complete *Turandot*, he could be relied upon not to stray too far from Puccini's footprints. Under Toscanini's critical eye he did a workmanlike job, but it was asking too much of him to echo Puccini's individual style or emulate the fluency and subtle orchestration which the all-important love duet demanded. Pardonably nervous, he played safe and took his time in mapping out the finale. The designers also spent months on the scenery before they could satisfy Toscanini, whose anxiety to do justice to the dead composer caused him to dragoon singers and musicians almost beyond endurance. By the time the première was at last settled for 25 April 1926, a full year after the date originally scheduled, the whole operatic world was in a fever of excitement.

There was intense curiosity about Alfano's tacked-on finale but Toscanini, judging the event too solemn for a ghoulish peepshow, decreed that only Puccini's music should be performed at the opening performance. He was equally emphatic in resisting a blatant attempt to extract political capital from the occasion. As the Duce happened to be in Milan that week for Empire Day celebrations, he had agreed to attend the performance on condition that the *Giovinezza* hymn would be given before the curtain rose. Toscanini snapped back at the La Scala management, 'If you want it played, then get someone else to conduct.' They backed down hurriedly, leaving Mussolini to find a face-saving excuse for his non-appearance.

Toscanini was in a highly emotional state before leaving home for the theatre. He had asked a friend to lunch with him but did not touch his food, staring silently at a portrait of Puccini propped beside his plate. That night, when Liù snatches a dagger to stab herself in the third act, he turned and said huskily, 'At this point the Maestro laid down his pen.' The curtain fell to complete silence, many weeping unashamedly. Toscanini was too moved to return to the pit when the audience stood up and paid its tribute in a storm of applause.*

The principals, supported by a first-class chorus and orchestra, had done well enough in the absence of Jeritza, Gigli and Dalla Rizza, the composer's own nominees. Rosa Raisa who had created Asteria in the world première of Boito's *Nerone* at La Scala, sang Turandot. The Spanish tenor Miguel Fleta had made his Metropolitan début as Cavaradossi and was equal to the less exacting demands of Calaf, while Maria Zamboni sang and acted Liù with finesse.

Next day the *Corriere della Sera* declared fervently that 'a few beats from the firm baton of Toscanini sufficed to bring before the great assembly the living spirit of the sweet singer of Manon, of Mimi and of Butterfly.' Alfano's additions were played at subsequent performances, reminding critics that the last two scenes, while faithful enough to the composer's general style, conspicuously lacked his genius for weaving subtle mood changes into a seamless texture. Moreover, it was sadly evident that the static narrative and over-orchestration in parts of Act Two might have benefited from the final cutting and polishing which Puccini had so often given to his scores at rehearsals or after early productions.

★   ★   ★   ★

* Toscanini broke down in health soon afterwards and left other conductors, including Panizza, to complete the season while he recuperated on the Italian Riviera.

Italian audiences, with a native taste for outdoor performances suited to a 'spectacular' like *Turandot*, were readier to make allowances for its deficiencies than the public in either England or the United States. Outside Italy, there was naturally less sentimental emotion over the composer's posthumous work. Admirers of *Bohème* and *Butterfly* found its harshness distasteful and the elaborate symbolism too confusing, if not downright monotonous. Budget-minded impresarios were also daunted by the sumptuous settings, while stagehands did not welcome interludes like the Trial by Riddle which could necessitate scene-changes of up to an hour. Furthermore, despite the appeal of superb arias like Calaf's 'Nessun dorma' and Liù's 'Signore, ascolta!', singers were nervous of taking unrewarding vocal parts of quite exceptional difficulty. Commenting in his *Memoirs* on the La Scala première, Gigli wrote, 'To tell the truth, I felt very grateful to him (Fleta) for relieving me of the responsibility, for the rôle was completely unsuited to my voice.' He was possibly sincere but may have been influenced by his feuding with Jeritza. At the Metropolitan they had quarrelled violently over billing and curtain calls. During a scene in *Fedora*, when she fell and sprained her wrist, she accused Gigli of having deliberately pushed her. In the end Gatti-Casazza was forced to prohibit them from appearing together.

Puccini did not live to witness Jeritza's Covent Garden début in *Tosca* on 16 June 1925. People had queued all night for the gallery, as much as £10 changing hands for 25-shilling stalls. 'Her voice was beautiful, powerful and delicate in turn and always admirably under control,' declared Ernest Newman. In November of the following year, after acclaimed performances of *Turandot* in Vienna by Lotte Lehmann and Leo Slezak, Jeritza gave the Metropolitan audience unforgettable delight as the Princess, partnered by Lauri-Volpi.

Her New York season had prevented her from attending the ceremony on the second anniversary of Puccini's death when his body was finally brought home to Torre del Lago. It had been planned to bury him in the garden of the villa but the ground was found to be unsuitable. Tonio therefore built a small mausoleum between his father's study and the gunroom. The coffin would lie on the other side of the wall from the Förster upright on which he had composed so much of his music.

The little station at Torre was draped in black as trains arrived with friends and dignitaries from Florence, Rome and Milan to join local mourners in a last tribute. After a solemn Mass in the church where Puccini and Elvira had been married, an orchestra played the Requiem from *Edgar* and Mascagni gave an oration recalling many years of companionship dating back to their days at the Conservatoire. As the cortège moved slowly through the narrow streets, crowded with weeping villagers, including a few survivors from the Club La Bohème, children timidly came forward to place freshly-picked flowers on the coffin.

Tonio, also a victim of cancer at the age of forty-six, lies in the mausoleum beside his parents. Elvira had died in 1934, and Sybil Seligman a few months later. Their last years had united them even more firmly in affection and mutual understanding. Sybil never quite recovered from the shock of Puccini's death. She was already a very sick woman when her son Esmond succumbed mercifully in 1930. She disintegrated rapidly, her mind clouded by grief and an increasing addiction to drugs to which she turned for relief. Among her private papers were hundreds of letters from Puccini, each bundle be-ribboned and meticulously arranged in chronological order, from the first in October 1904 thanking her for an invitation to dinner, to the last almost twenty years later, when he wrote pathetically, 'I've still got so much work to do on *Turandot* . . .' In a locked drawer she kept copies of each of his scores, all but one affectionately signed by the composer. The flyleaf of the unfinished *Turandot* manuscript was inscribed, 'To Sybil, our faithful friend, from Elvira and Tonio.'

Postscript

During the past half-century élitist attempts have often been made to decry Puccini's 'handkerchief operas' as monuments to bad taste, cheap sadism and crude tear-jerking sentimentality. It cannot be denied that his plots are often framed in spun sugar and only held together by remarkable stagecraft and melodies that continue to delight successive generations. Spike Hughes has rightly judged Puccini as 'not a composer of great operas, but a great opera composer'. Even his most besotted devotees would not dare to rank him with giants like Mozart, Wagner and Verdi, but since his death no other composer, with the possible exception of Richard Strauss, has commanded anything approaching the world appeal of *La Bohème*, *Tosca* and *Madama Butterfly*. These three masterpieces, created during a single miraculously fertile decade in early middle-age, have not only survived changing tastes but the silencing of such legendary voices as Caruso, Melba, Farrar, Scotti, Gigli and Jeritza. *Tosca*, dismissed by Joseph Kerman as 'a shabby little shocker', has nevertheless captivated a new generation of operagoers and disc collectors with vivid interpretations by Callas and Tito Gobbi; *Butterfly* still squeezes tears from Milwaukee to Moscow, while few would disagree with the critic who recently affirmed that '*La Bohème*' is no longer an Italian opera but as universally accepted as a Beethoven symphony.'

La Rondine demonstrated Puccini's light hand with pastry but, despite Lucrezia Bori and Gigli, failed to win a place in the Metropolitan repertory. Although La Scala and Philadelphia hopefully fluffed it out, the piece has always crumbled like a stale meringue. It was not played in London until 1965 when Magda waltzed around the humble stage of the Fulham Town Hall. *La Fanciulla del West* has worn far better, but revivals remain sparse. Jeritza gave it a brief impetus in the late 'twenties and in 1961 a Metropolitan audience was appreciative. More surprisingly, perhaps, the new Sydney Opera House decided to include *Il Trittico* among its first season's attractions.

Puccini's premature death possibly robbed the world of his supreme operatic triumph. *Turandot* even in its unfinished and imperfect state, has continued over the years to enthral audiences. It languished after Jeritza's retirement but enjoyed a revival at the Metropolitan in the early sixties under Stokowski's baton, with Birgit Nilsson outstanding in the title-rôle. She repeated her triumph at Covent Garden, following such notable English interpreters as Eva Turner (perhaps the finest of all Turandots) and Amy Shuard, while Lotte Lehmann's interpretation delighted the Viennese.

Almost forty years after the composer's death, Peter Heyworth of *The Observer* came away from a Covent Garden performance to write; '*Turandot* is the summit and synthesis of everything that Puccini achieved. In this great work ... the lyrical sweetness of *Bohème* is married to the sombre expression of *Tabarro*; the delicate exoticism of *Butterfly* is combined with the harsh brutality of *Tosca* ... In the dimensions and range of its idiom *Turandot* towers over all its predecessors.'

But whatever the merits of this posthumous work or Puccini's true place in the pantheon of operatic composers, his melodies have created something of a cult among admirers. Lucca, now more accessible to motorists on the Strada del Mare, is the focus of an all-year-round pilgrimage. Tourists pause dutifully outside the composer's birthplace in Via di Poggio and, if so minded, can promenade on the tree-lined ramparts where he and Elvira snatched moments of intimacy. Revivals of his most popular operas are always a holiday attraction in Lucca. A few years ago, an evening performance in the Teatro del Giglio was devoted to sacred music by members of the entire Puccini dynasty, ranging from his great-great-grandfather's Handelian anthem to his own Agnus Dei from the Mass first performed in 1880. Two of his nieces, daughters of his sister Romelde, were in the audience.

Viareggio, blasted almost to rubble in World War Two, now offers little to the nostalgic-minded. Puccini's villa was plundered but an American soldier salvaged a batch of private papers and handed them to the New York Public Library at Fifth Avenue and Forty-Second Street. It included several hitherto unpublished letters which George Marek used to good effect in his biography of 1950.

The villa at Torre del Lago has become a magnet for international tourists. German and Austrian admirers are usually in force and anxious to round off a strenuous Tuscan itinerary with a little sentimental *gemütlichkeit*. Prince Paul Troubetzkoi's lifelike statue of the composer, the hat tilted and overcoat collar characteristically turned up, stands in the garden looking out over the lake. To the piped music of familiar melodies, a Mississippi-type showboat ('Visit Puccini with Mark Twain') was even put into service by enterprising travel agencies for the delectation of holidaymakers. So far, however, no serious attempt has been made to market either kimonos or replicas of tiny frozen hands.

The star attraction is the composer's studio which has been preserved with taste and meticulous realism. Passing through the gunroom, with several of Puccini's weapons and stuffed birds displayed, visitors can inspect the upright piano with its signed portraits of Jeritza, Caruso, Mahler and other friends. The writing table is spread with his notes and a pair of spectacles lies on the blotting pad, precisely as he left them before leaving for the Brussels clinic. Specimen pages from his scores and other miscellania provide fascinating treasure for music-lovers, but to students of Puccini's career nothing is perhaps more evocative than a facsimile of Maestro Ponchielli's reassuring letter to Donna Albina, dated 8 January 1883: 'Your son is one of the best pupils in my class, and I am well satisfied with him . . .'

The Operas of Puccini

Le Villi. Teatro dal Verme, Milan. 31 May 1884.
Edgar. La Scala, Milan. 21 April 1889.
Manon Lescaut. Teatro Regio, Turin. 1 February 1893.
La Bohème. Teatro Regio, Turin. 1 February 1896.
Tosca. Teatro Costanzi, Rome. 14 January 1900.
Madama Butterfly. La Scala, Milan. 17 February 1904.
La Fanciulla del West. Metropolitan, New York. 10 December 1910.
La Rondine. Casino Theatre, Monte Carlo. 27 March 1917.
Il Trittico:
  (*Il Tabarro,*
  Suor Angelica,
  Gianni Schicchi). Metropolitan, New York. 14 December 1918.
Turandot. La Scala, Milan. 25 April 1926.

Bibliography

Special acknowledgement is due to previous books on Puccini, notably Mosco Carner's *Puccini: A Critical Biography* (Duckworth, London, 1958 and Knopf, New York, 1959); *Letters of Puccini*, tr. Ena Makin (Harrap, London, 1931 and J. B. Lippincott, Philadelphia, 1931); *Puccini* by George Marek (Simon & Schuster, New York, 1951 and Cassell, London, 1952); *Immortal Bohemian* by D. del Fiorentino (Gollancz, London, 1952 and Prentice-Hall, New York, 1952); *Puccini among friends* by Vincent Seligman (Macmillan, London, 1938); *Giacomo Puccini* by Richard Specht (Dent, London, 1933 and ——? New York, 1933); *Giacomo Puccini* by Wakeling Dry (Hirsch, London and New York, 1906); *Puccini: Keeper of the Seal* by Edward Greenfield (Arrow Books, London, 1958); *Puccini Nelle Immagini*, ed. L. Marchetti (Garzanti, Milan, 1949); *La Vita di Giacomo Puccini* by Arnaldo Fraccaroli (Milan, 1925); *Giacomo Puccini Intimo* by Guido Marotti and Ferruccio Pagni (Florence, 1926).

Other sources consulted or quoted:

Alda, Frances, *Men, Women and Tenors* (Houghton Mifflin, Boston, 1937).

Ashbrook, William, *The Operas of Puccini* (Oxford University Press, New York, 1968).

Brockway and Weinstock, *The Opera, 1600–1941* (Simon & Schuster, New York, 1941).

Busoni, F. B., *Letters to My Wife* (Edward Arnold, London, 1938).

Birmingham, Stephen, *Our Crowd*, (Harper, New York, 1967 and Longmans, London, 1968.)

Farrar, Geraldine. *Such Sweet Compulsion* (Greystone Press, New York, 1938).

Gallati, Mario, *Mario of the Caprice* (Hutchinson, London, 1960).

Gatti-Casazza, Giulio, *Memoirs of the Opera*, (Scribners, New York, 1941).

Gigli, Beniamino, *Memoirs*, (Cassell, London, 1957).

Jackson, Stanley, *Caruso* (W. H. Allen, London, 1972, and Stein & Day, New York, 1972).

Jeritza, Maria, *Sunlight and Song* (D. Appleton Century, London and New York, 1924).

Jolly, W. P., *Marconi* (Constable, London, 1972).

Jullian, Philippe, *d'Annunzio* (Pall Mall Press, 1973).

Katz, Robert, *Fall of the House of Savoy* (Macmillan, New York, 1971).

Lara, Isidore de, *Many Tales of Many Cities* (Hutchinson, London, 1928).

Lochner, L. P., *Fritz Kreisler* (Rockliff, London, 1951 and Macmillan, Toronto, 1950).

Melba, Nellie, *Melodies and Memories* (Butterworth, London, 1925).

Nijinsky, Romola, *Nijinsky* (Gollancz, London, 1933).

Reid, Charles, *John Barbirolli* (Hamish Hamilton, London, 1971).

Rosenthal, Harold, *Two Centuries of Opera at Covent Garden* (Putnam, New York 1958).

Sacchi, F., *The Magic Baton* (Putnam, London, 1957).

Schonberg, H. C., *Lives of the Great Composers* (W. W. Norton, New York, 1970 and Davis–Poynter, London, 1971).

Shaw, Bernard, *Music in London 1890-94* (Constable, London, 1950).

Sheean, Vincent, *Oscar Hammerstein* (Simon & Schuster, New York, 1956).

Taubman, Howard, *The Maestro* (Simon & Schuster, New York, 1951 and (under the title *Toscanini*) Odhams, London, 1951).

Teyte, Maggie, *Star on the Door* (Putnam, London, 1958).

Wechsberg, Joseph, *Red Plush and Black Velvet* (Weidenfeld & Nicolson, London, 1962.

Westerman, G. von, tr. Harold Rosenthal, *Opera Guide* (Thames & Hudson, London, 1963).

Winter, William, *The Life of David Belasco* (Moffat, Yard & Co., New York, 1918).

Index